D0780170

How to Enter & Win Fiction Writing Contests

How to Enter & Win Fiction Writing Contests

By
ALAN GADNEY

Managing Editor
CAROLYN PORTER

How to Enter & Win Fiction Writing Contests

Published by Facts On File, Inc.
460 Park Ave. South, New York, N.Y. 10016

In cooperation with Festival Publications

Library of Congress Cataloging in Publication Data

Gadney, Alan.
How to enter and win fiction writing contests.

Includes index.
1. Literature—Competitions. I. Title.
PN171.P75G29 808.'02'079 81-2182
ISBN 0-87196-519-4 AACR2
ISBN 0-87196-552-6 (pbk.)

PRINTED IN THE UNITED STATES OF AMERICA

9 8 7 6 5 4 3 2 1

Computer Programming and Typesetting by Datagraphics Inc.

TO MARY M. GADNEY
whose confidence, love, and hard work
helped to make this series possible.
Thanks Mom.

EDITORIAL STAFF

Associate Editor:	Aida R. Bustos
Assistant Editors:	Christina J. Moose Lois Smith
Editorial Assistants:	Peter Betcher Alice Ober Monica Olofsson Lisa Zemelman Christine Conrad
Research Assistant:	Holly Christos

CONTENTS

INTRODUCTION

WELCOME . . . to How to Enter and Win FICTION WRITING CONTESTS, an all new, completely up-to-date sourcebook for the contest competitor and grant seeker in the fiction writing field (books, articles, short stories, poetry, plays and scripts) . . . one of an ongoing series of contest-grant books covering writing and other related arts fields.

Each book in the series focuses in detail on an individual art or medium (Fiction Writing, Nonfiction Writing & Journalism, Film, Video-Audio-TV/Radio Broadcasting, Photography, Art, Crafts, and so on).

And each book in the series lists complete entrance information for anyone wanting to:

- Enter their work in national and international contests, festivals, competitions, salons, shows, exhibitions, markets, tradefairs, and other award events and sales outlets.
- Apply for grants, loans, scholarships, fellowships, residencies, apprenticeships, internships, training and benefit programs, and free aids and services.

The books also have: ALPHABETICAL INDEXES listing each event, sponsor, and award by its various names. SUBJECT/CATEGORY INDEXES to the entrants' specific areas of interest. Extensive CROSS-REFERENCES and DEFINITIONS throughout. And introductory HELPFUL HINTS on how to analyze and enter the events, and possibly come up a winner!

HOW THE BOOKS BEGAN

This series of contest-grant guides actually began several years ago with the first release print of *West Texas* (a one-hour featurette I made while completing my graduate work at the USC Cinema Department). One week after our first showing, I sent our premiere print off to the first film festival, and the contest entry process started to grow from there . . . with one major problem, however: The festival contact information was almost impossible to find.

After extensive research, all I could come up with were names and addresses (and an occasional brief blurb) of intriguingly titled film events in far-off places, but with no hard facts as to their entry requirements, eligibility restrictions, awards, deadlines, fees, statistics, judging procedures, etc. That sort of vital information was practically nonexistent, unless you took the time and postage to write away to every contest you discovered an address for . . . which I did.

Through several years of continuous address researching, blindly writing off for contest entry information and periodically submitting the film, *West Texas* won 48 international film awards, and a large file of information had been collected on about 180 international festivals—quite a few of which were not even open to *West Texas* for a variety of reasons (wrong gauge, length, category, the event turned out not to be a film festival, etc.).

The need was evident for an accurate, up-to-date, and detailed entry information source to the world's Contests, Festivals and Grants . . . Thus evolved the two editions of my previous book (GADNEY'S GUIDE TO INTERNATIONAL CONTESTS, FESTIVALS & GRANTS). Their first-of-a-kind success ultimately lead to this all new series of contest-grant guides.

ABOUT THE FICTION WRITING BOOK

This book (devoted solely to the field of FICTION WRITING is a single-source reference guide, providing you with vital entry information and statistics about a contest/grant before you even have to send away for the entry forms and shipping regulations (which you must always eventually do, as most require their own entry forms, and some have rather intricate shipping and customs requirements).

The 420 separate events listed in this volume were compiled through 3 years of active research on my earlier book, an additional year of research on this book, and thousands of questionnaires sent to worldwide writing events (many requiring repeated mailings to obtain complete and up-to-date entry information). During this process, we have totally updated, revised, and expanded the scope of the original fiction writing listings, added new competitions, and deleted a few which were too restricted or no longer in existence. (Nonfiction Writing and Print Journalism sections of writing events have been included in a companion volume covering Nonfiction/Journalism contests and grants.)

The individual events have been further grouped into 35 special-interest subcategories (an increase in the number of subject categories over the earlier book, particularly in the areas of creative writing scholarships, fellowships, and grants). These subcategories are further divided and cross-referenced in the SUBJECT/-CATEGORY INDEX at the back of the book.

We have included two general types of events:

- Those AWARD EVENTS and SALES OUTLETS to which entrants may submit their works in order to receive SOMETHING OF VALUE in return, such as contests, festivals, competitions, salons, shows, exhibitions, markets, tradefairs, and various other award and sales programs primarily for new and unknown works.
- And BENEFIT PROGRAMS to which individuals or organizations may apply for some type of AID or SERVICE, such as grants, money and equipment loans, scholarships, fellowships, residencies, apprenticeships, internships, training programs, and so on.

Due to page length restrictions we have given condensed listings to those events that (1) are restricted to members of a specific organization, or limited to residents of a small city or geographical area (usually of less than state size), or (2) are not open to general entry but whose participants are nominated or invited by the sponsors or national selecting organizations. Workshops, seminars, conferences, schools, service programs, and the like, have only been listed if they are free, have free benefits attached, or encompass a contest, festival, grant, scholarship, fellowship, residency, etc.

We have listed as much detailed information about each separate event as possible (that is, as much as could be culled from the materials provided us by the event—usually including current addresses, dates, deadlines, complete entry requirements, eligibility and fee information, awards available, judging aspects, catch clauses, purpose, theme, sponsors, average statistics, where held, and various historical aspects). All information was transcribed from the questionnaires and entry materials provided us and edited to fit the format of the book. (See HOW TO USE THE BOOK for description of format.)

The information listed is the most current we could obtain, and will normally be revised and updated every two or three years in this continuing reference series.

We have also included older events when there was no direct confirmation that the events had gone out of existence. Many events come and go in an on-again, off-again manner, depending on their finances, administration changes, and other factors . . . again, good reason to ALWAYS WRITE TO AN EVENT BEFORE ENTERING YOUR WORK. Most events require entry forms, which they provide. Many have special shipping regulations. And, as we have condensed and edited their rules and regulations, it is best to write for the complete versions (especially important in interpreting the meanings of occasional tricky "catch clauses" about the use and ownership of winning entries). Also remember to send along a self-addressed, stamped return envelope (SASE), particularly to smaller events operating on tight postage budgets.

It would be almost impossible to give an exact figure for the total amount of money offered through this book. Some events give cash, others give equipment (of varying value depending on how badly you need the equipment or how much you can sell it for), and others give trophies, cups, plaques, medals, certificates, etc. (all of great value to the winner, but of little real monetary worth). Grant sources, on the other hand, may offer millions of dollars in direct financial aid. Probably the safest thing to say about the total amount of money offered through this book is that it is well into the millions.

HOW TO USE THIS BOOK

In the TABLE OF CONTENTS you will find that this volume has been divided into a series of "special-interest" SUBCATEGORIES. Each contains all those events whose primary emphasis is within that particular subcategory. The listing is usually alphabetical—first those in the United States, followed by other countries in alphabetical order.

At the start of each subcategory is an italicized INTRODUCTORY SECTION giving (1) specific contents of that subcategory, (2) definitions, and (3) "also see" CROSS-REFERENCES to similar events in other subcategories in the book.

To find additional events accepting entries in your specific interest area (but which may be listed in other subcategories because their primary emphasis is stronger in those areas), use the SUBJECT/CATEGORY INDEX at the back of the book. This lists subjects of special interest by an identifying code number for each event. The code number is located in the box above each event.

To find a specific event, sponsor, or award by name, use the ALPHABETICAL EVENT/SPONSOR/AWARD INDEX at the back of the book (again listing entries by identifying code number). In this index, sponsors and events are usually listed by full names, abbreviations, and unique titles.

EACH EVENT consists of (1) a current address and telephone number; (2) month/season held; (3) introductory paragraph, including entry restrictions, date of establishment, former names, purpose, theme, motto, sponsors, average statistics, historical information, facilities and other aspects; (4) technical entry regulations and categories; (5) eligibility requirements; (6) awards; (7) judging aspects and catch clauses; (8) sales terms; (9) entry fees; (10) deadlines. All have a similar format designed for easy use, with the five most important aspects of each event noted in bold type:

1. Identifying Code Number (in box)
2. Name of event
3. Month/Season of event
4. Entrant restrictions
5. Type of event and subject-category

With these five main points in mind, a potential entrant can quickly skim through a series of events to find those of particular interest.

HOW TO ANALYZE AN EVENT

We have usually provided enough information about each event to help you in making various determinations before you send away for entry forms, shipping regulations, and additional instructions. These are some of the points you should consider in your analysis.

- **When is the event held?** The month/season held is designated by bold type immediately following the address.

- **When is the entry deadline?** Months of entry are found in the DEADLINES section at the end of each event listing, and are usually well in advance of the month held. The event should be contacted about the specific entry date for the year you are applying.

- **Do I qualify?** Entrant restrictions are listed in bold type in the first sentence, and may be further clarified in the ELIGIBILITY section.

- **Does my work qualify?** The type of event and specific subject categories are listed in bold type at the beginning of the second and subsequent paragraphs. Various technical entry requirements follow each.

- **How much does it cost?** Costs and hidden costs are found in the ENTRY FEE section.

- **What are the prizes?** Found in the AWARDS section are prizes varying from trophies, cups, plaques, and medallions (of personal value), to cash, trips, equipment, and services (of a more material value—meaning you may be able to resell them at a later date if you already have better equipment, cannot take the trip, or do not want the services). Exhibition, distribution, broadcast, sale, and publication may also be offered, but should always be analyzed in terms of their financial and legal implications (what you get for what you have to give in return, and how valuable your entry may become in the future).

- **What are the catch clauses?** A few events have tricky qualifying clauses, condensed in the JUDGING section. These may involve claims to use and ownership (sometimes of all entries, and on an extensive basis), or responsibility in the event of loss, damage, nonreturn, etc.

Occasionally the actual entry forms and regulations may be rather vague as to whether the sponsors just keep a copy of your winning entry or whether they receive full ownership of the work (and for what use). Possibly, in these instances, you should write to the sponsors for further clarification.

• **How is my work judged?** The number of judges, judging procedures, and criteria are listed in the JUDGING section. It is important to understand that during preliminary judging (sometimes performed by the event's staff and aides), many entries may be immediately disqualified because of failure to adhere to the various contest regulations, or eliminated because of technical flaws or oversights (good reason always to send away for, and to read carefully, the latest rules). This is especially true of large contests that thousands enter. Sponsors have to narrow the competition as rapidly and efficiently as possible, and the first to go are the rule breakers and sloppy entries.

A program of the event or listing of past winners may give you an overall feel for the event (if it is conservative or liberal, oriented in certain directions, etc.). There is the possibility of talking to past entrants and winners in order to get an idea of specific likes and dislikes of the event and its judges. Or if you know who the judges will be, you may be able to make an educated guess as to what they will choose. However, I have found that it is almost impossible to predict how judges will act on anything other than the widest of generalities. Judges change from year to year, the philosophy of the event may alter, and single-judge contests put you at the mercy of that particular year's judge. So, you can never really outguess the judges.

• **How old is the event?** Usually included in the first sentence is the founding date, the inference being that the older the event, the more stable and reputable it is.

• **How large is the event?** Average attendance, distribution, and sales figures can often be found in the first paragraph, indicating the potential promotional and sales values of participating in the event.

• **What is the duration of an event, and how long will it tie up my entry materials?** The number of days the event is usually held is found in the first paragraph; the entry and return-of-material dates are in the DEADLINES section.

• **What is the competition?** Average statistics on number of entries, entrants, countries competing, acceptances into final competition, and winners can be found in the first paragraph, giving some idea of possible competition in future events.

• **How legitimate is the event?** This can be determined to some extent by the names of familiar sponsors, cosponsors, financial supporters, and those organizations that officially recognize the event—again, all found in the opening paragraph, and giving some idea of reputability. Also important may be the purpose, theme, and motto.

These are just a few of the aspects to examine before writing away for further information, entry forms, the most current regulations . . . and before sending away your work.

YEARLY PLANNING GUIDE

This book can also serve as a planning guide for your contest entries throughout the year. By using the SUBJECT/CATEGORY INDEX, you can get an overall picture of the various world events accepting entries in your areas of interest. We would then suggest setting up a calendar, listing those events you wish to enter by (1) the date you should write away for entry forms and current rules (several months before the actual entry month), (2) the entry dates, and (3) the dates the event is held, which will give you some indication of when the sponsor will be announcing the winners and returning your materials.

HELPFUL HINTS ON HOW TO WIN

Here are a few recommendations to enhance your chances of winning:

• ANALYZE THE STATISTICS—Look at the average statistics (found in the first paragraph of an event listing) to determine the size of your competition. Remember, you should always calculate the number of awards/honors given against the number of entrants, and not just analyze on total entrants alone. Larger events with a greater number of entrants and more awards may in reality have a higher winner-ratio than smaller events with only one award. You may also stand a better chance of winning in newer events which have not yet built up their patronage.

• ANALYZE THE TYPE OF EVENT—Based on past winner/award listings, is the event consistently conservative or liberal in its selections (or does it change moods from one year to the next)? If a contest says it leans toward contemporary or experimental works, you should take this into account before entering. You may also wish to try and analyze how the judges will vote, again based on past records and who the current judges are. (See HOW TO ANALYZE AN EVENT for additional information.)

• PATRONIZE THE SPECIALIZED EVENTS—If you have a specialized entry, while it will normally qualify for more generalized contests, you might begin by concentrating on those events which have a special interest in, or specific subject categories for your particular entry. Because of their highly specialized nature, these contests may get fewer entries, and if your work fits their interests, you should stand a better chance of winning. You might also consider patronizing those events that have changing annual themes by designing your entry to fit that particular year's needs.

• FOLLOW THE RULES—The contest rules (obtained directly from the event) should be studied carefully, first to find hidden clauses, and second to ensure you will not be inadvertently excluded because you entered the wrong category, sent an incorrect entry fee or no return postage, entered with improper technical aspects, or not enough supplementary information, etc. So read the rules and follow them, and fill out the entry forms completely. Rule breakers usually are disqualified, sometimes even before the preliminary judging. Then, to further cut down the number of competitors, most judges go strictly by the regulations, automatically discarding those entries that in any way deviate from the rules.

• KEEP IT CLEAN—Keep it technically perfect. Again, judges will usually reject sloppy entries (sometimes these don't even reach the judges, but are weeded out by the contest staff). So send only clean entries in good condition. No dirty covers, messy type, ultra-thinpaper, smudges, spots, or ripped pages. All of these reflect badly on your entry's artistic content. And if the sponsors tell you they want an entry mounted in a special cover or written in a specific format, you had better follow their instructions. Also, it is best to send a duplicate rather than your original work (unless they request the original, in which case you should study their rules carefully to see if you will ever get your original back).

• SEND IT AHEAD OF TIME—Send your materials well in advance of the entry deadlines. Last-minute entries may get abbreviated handling by judges who have already looked over the earlier entries and have made up their minds. They may not get listed in the contest programs, which have already gone to the printers—and if they are shown, they may be scheduled during the least desirable exhibition times. And of course, *late* entries are usually sent back unopened.

• SEND PUBLICITY AND INFORMATION MATERIALS—Send supporting materials unless positively prohibited. (Definitely send them when they are requested.) Every little bit helps: biographical, technical, and project background information; publicity and press materials; still photos, production philosophy, synopsis, translation, transcription (and advertising materials if appropriate). The judges may occasionally use some of these in making their final decisions, and the events may use the publicity in their programs, flyers, and press rooms. Remember to send along any special technical instructions or return shipping requests you feel are needed.

• USE PROPER SHIPPING—First a word about the U.S. and international mail systems (as opposed to international Air Freight; some foreign contests even prohibit the use of air freight, as the entries may become held up in customs). Provided your entries are properly packaged, sealed, marked, stamped, and insured, and have correctly filled-out customs stickers (information about all of this is available through the U.S. Post Office), they should be able to travel almost anywhere in the world with relative safety. (This is based on personal experience. *West Texas* was mailed to a large number of film festivals all over the world, and I never lost a print or received one back damaged in transit.)

Remember always to ship by air to overseas competitions (as boat mail may take as long as three months from the U.S. to Australia, for example). On domestic U.S. shipments, you can mail at various rates lower than First Class, if you take into account the time for possible delays. (Again, contact the post office for information about mailing costs and times.)

Of course, if you have a heavy international shipment (A large box of books for example), you may be over the postal weight limitations, and have to ship by Air Freight. In this case, it may be best to contact a customs house broker/international freight forwarder about services and charges.

Short overseas messages will travel very rapidly by international telegram. And always remember to enclose sufficient return postage and a correctly sized self-addressed stamped return envelope (SASE) when requested. Finally, if your entry arrives with "Postage Due," it could be a negative factor in the contest staff preselection process.

A WORD ABOUT GRANTS

It would take an entire volume to discuss all the "ins" and "outs" of grant solicitation. However, we can touch on a few of the more important aspects.

• FIND OUT AS MUCH AS POSSIBLE about a potential grant source before investing the time in sending a proposal. Write to the granting organization for more information—and once you have this information, analyze it and focus your energies on the most likely prospects.

• WRITE AN INQUIRY LETTER—a brief letter of introduction, to see if they are interested in your project. Include a short description of the project and its unique aspects, background information about yourself and your sponsoring organization, the proposal budget, and ask them if they would be interested in further information. Keep your introductory letter brief, to the point, well written, easy to understand, and not exaggerated. If the foundation is interested, it will request what it needs, which may run anywhere from an expanded summary to a full-scale proposal and budget.

• GET AN ORGANIZATION TO SPONSOR YOU—Many foundations restrict their granting to only nonprofit, tax-exempt organizations, institutions, etc. However, this does not necessarily prohibit you from securing a grant from them. Simply get a nonprofit organization to sponsor you and your project, and have the organization apply for the grant in their name. Many organizations offer grant solicitations as one of their services, and this can have benefits for the sponsoring organizations: You give them credit and publicity through your finished project. They have a track-record as a successful fund raiser, which may help them in obtaining future grants. And they can even be paid through your budget for handling certain administrative and bookkeeping duties.

• GET SOME NAMES ON YOUR SIDE—well-known persons in the roles of advisors, technical consultants, etc. can help greatly toward building an impressive project package.

• TRY SPECIAL INTEREST GROUPS—If you have designed a project involving a special interest (a Medical Book, for example), rather than only approaching sources that grant your medium (Books), you might consider going to those grant sources that fund the special interest instead (i.e., Medical Grants). Or you may find similar money sources through special-interest organizations, associations, institutions, and businesses. The public library is a good place to start your search.

WHY ENTER CONTESTS

Finally, a word about the positive benefits of entering your work in contests, festivals, and competitions.

To start with, it is an extremely good way to test (and prove) the artistic and commercial value of your work before professional judges, critics, and the public. There is also the challenge of the competition—the excitement and glamour of knowing that your work is being seen in contests, festivals, salons, exhibitions, and publications around the world. Your entry competes with those of your peers —and if it reaches the finals and wins, there is the great personal satisfaction and certification of acceptance.

If you do win, you can win substantial cash prizes, trips, art items, equipment, services, exhibition, distribution, broadcast, publication, sales, trophies, and other awards. There can be useful free publicity for both you and your work, through (1) press information and literature released by the event, (2) the writings and reviews of others about your work, and (3) your own promotional materials designed around your winnings.

All of this can bring valuable international exposure through the print and broadcast media, and the resulting recognition and prestige can certainly help to sell both your award-winning work and yourself as an award-winning writer.

The end benefits can be sales, valuable contacts, jobs, contracts, increased fees, and the financing of other projects.

How does this translate into real terms . . . The 48 international film awards won by *West Texas* resulted directly in: (1) a large number of valuable art objects, trophies, and awards; (2) enough cash winnings to cover all the film festival entry fees, shipping, promotion, and other costs; (3) an enormous amount of free personal publicity; (4) the eventual sale and distribution of the film; (5) the writing and directing of a subsequent feature-length theatrical, *Moonchild;* (6) several paid speaking engagements; (7) a TV script assignment; (8) a stint as a film magazine contributing editor; and (9) eventually to writing this series of books on contests and grants . . . So, the entering of contests and the winning of awards in many ways can be quite profitable.

THE CHANGING NATURE OF CREATIVE WRITING CONTESTS

In the three years since my previous book was published, several changes have taken place in the number and types of creative writing contests and grants offered throughout the world. Two interesting aspects should be noted:

First, there has been a distinct increase in the overall number of poetry, poetry book, and playwriting contests currently available (many of which have definite commercial ramifications—the acquiring of high-quality poetry for special "awards" issues of literary magazines and book anthologies, and new play productions for regional theaters). All of this can be of great benefit to the poet or playwright; they not only win a cash prize, but may also have their work published or performed as well.

The second and possibly more important increase has come in the number of creative writing grants, scholarships, fellowships, residence and emergency assistance grants currently available (aided in part by the leadership in government grant funding over the past few years). Let us hope that these grant outlets can continue through aid from private sources.

A FEW CLOSING THOUGHTS — While I have found the vast majority of events to be highly reputable and continually striving to improve their quality, there are still a few bad exceptions (lost entries, withheld awards, judging problems, etc.).

However, the interesting thing is that just as numbers and types of events change from year to year, so do most of these questionable conditions. Just when you hear someone complain about an unfair judging process, the next year the judges change, and that same person may come out a winner. Or the rules and administration change, and what was once a suspect practice disappears.

With this in mind, there has been no attempt on our part to editorialize about the occasional bad occurrences we hear of. This is strictly a reference guide (not a critical work). We list all those events which qualify, from the largest to the smallest, the oldest to the youngest, the well-known and the not so well-known. And we have tried to print enough information about each event to give you a firm basis upon which to decide whether or not to write for further information. (See HOW TO ANALYZE AN EVENT.)

It should also be stated that we do not endorse (or accept any responsibility for the conduct of) the events listed in this book.

Finally, no book of this type can ever be all-inclusive. That would be virtually impossible. Each year hundreds of new events start up, old ones lapse or go out of business, only to be replaced by similar events in a new form. As I have mentioned, there is constant growth and progression based on general changes in the art and media fields. However, considering the many individual events we have listed, each as thoroughly as possible within the edited format, and each updated and verified to the best of our knowledge based on entry materials and questionnaires provided us, we feel that we have brought you quite a comprehensive reference guide.

A special thank you to the American Library Association (the Reference and Adult Services Division, Reference Committee) for awarding the previous contest book an "OUTSTANDING REFERENCE SOURCE OF THE YEAR" . . . and to the many readers and reviewers of that book for their favorable response. These honors have been extremely gratifying.

And an additional thanks and grateful appreciation to the many events, sponsors, contributors, and correspondents who have so graciously provided us with the information included in this directory.

As a final reminder, please remember that to ensure you have the latest information, complete regulations, and proper entry forms, ALWAYS WRITE TO AN EVENT BEFORE ENTERING YOUR WORK

And please advise us of any new Contests and Grants you may know of, so that we may include them in our future editions.

Alan Gadney
Festival Publications
P.O. Box 10180
Glendale, California 91209 U.S.A.

ABBREVIATIONS

AAP	Academy of American Poets Association of American Publishers
AJL	Association of Jewish Libraries
ALA	American Library Association
ALS	Australian Literature Society
ASPS	Arizona State Poetry Society
AWG	Australian Writers Guild
AWP	Associated Writing Programs
BPANZ	Book Publishers Association of New Zealand
BTA	Black Theater Alliance
BSFSA	British Science Fiction Association
CAA	Canadian Authors Association
CCL	Conference on Christianity and Literature
CCLM	Coordinating Council of Literary Magazines
CLA	Catholic Library Association
COSMEP	Committee of Small Magazine Editors & Publishers
CPB	Corporation for Public Broadcasting
CSP	Canadian Society of Poets
CSPS	California State Poetry Society
FAW	Fellowship of Australian Writers
IBBY	International Board of Books for Young People
IPA	Iowa Poetry Association
IRA	International Reading Association
JWB	Jewish Book Council
KSPS	Kentucky State Poetry Society
LSPS	Lousiana State Poetry Society
NCTE	National Council of Teachers of English
NEA	National Endowment of the Arts
NEH	National Endowment for the Humanities
NFSPS	National Federation of State Poetry Societies
NLAPW	National League of American Pen Women
NMSPS	New Mexico State Poetry Society
NYSCA	New York State Council on the Arts
OSPA	Oregon State Poetry Association
PEN	Poets, Playwrights, Essayists, Editors, Novelists
PSA	Poetry Society of America
SCBW	Society of Children's Book Writers
SDSPS	South Dakota State Poetry Society
TCG	Theatre Communications Group
WGA	Writers Guild of America
WWA	Western Writers of America

How to Enter & Win Fiction Writing Contests

FICTION WRITING

BOOK (for Children, Youth)

Book, Poetry, including GRAPHICS, ILLUSTRATED, PICTURE STORY BOOK, PEACE-SOCIAL JUSTICE-WORLD COMMUNITY, SCIENCE FICTION. (Also see other BOOK CATEGORIES.)

1

American Library Association (ALA) Awards and Citations Program (Children's)
Children's Services Division
50 East Huron Street
Chicago, Illinois 60611 U.S.A.
Tel: (312) 944-6780

Winter

National; **entry restricted to U.S. (nomination by ALA);** annual. Mildred L. Batchelder Citation to publisher for **Foreign Children's Book** published in U.S. Randolph Caldecott Medal to U.S. citizen-resident illustrator for **Children's American Picture Book.** John Newberry Medal to U.S. citizen-resident for **American Children's Literature.** Laura Ingalls Wilder Medal to author-illustrator for **U.S. Children's Literature** contributions over period of time (triennial). Sponsored by Children's Services Division of American Library Association (ALA). Also sponsor Awards and Citations for Librarianship, Reference Works. Awards, Winter.

2

Boston Globe-Horn Book Awards
The Boston Globe
Stephanie Loer, Children's Book Editor
Boston, Massachusetts 02170 U.S.A.
Tel: (617) 359-8542

September

National; **entry restricted to U.S. publishers;** annual; established 1967. Purpose: to honor children's books of excellence. Sponsored by *The Boston Globe,* Horn Book, Inc. Held at fall conference of New England Library Association.

BOOK CONTEST: **Children's,** published in U.S. in year prior to award; 3 maximum per publisher, each category. Submit 5 copies each book. No textbooks, new or revised editions. Categories: Original Fiction, Illustration.

AWARDS: $200 and Pewter Bowl, each category. Pewter Plate to Runners-Up, each category. 3 Honor Books, each category. Winners featured at Boston Globe Book Festival, John B. Hynes Auditorium, Boston.

JUDGING: By 3 judges appointed by editor of *Horn Book Magazine.*

ENTRY FEE: None.

DEADLINES: Entry, March. Awards, Fall.

California Young Reader Medal Awards
California Reading Association
Ellis Vance, Publicity Chair
5545 East Herndon Avenue
Clovis, California 93612 U.S.A.
Tel: (209) 298-8011, ext. 46

November

International; **entry restricted to English-speaking countries (nomination by school children);** annual; established 1974. California Young Reader Medal to **Children-Youth Books** (original, in English, by living author, published in previous 5 years). Purpose: to encourage California children to become acquainted with good literature. Sponsored and supported by California Reading Association, California Library Association, California Association of Teachers of English. Held at annual conference. Candidates chosen by California young readers; final judging of top 5 books by state children during May-March. Awards, November.

Charlie May Simon Children's Book Award
James A. Hester, Chair
10213 Sylvan Hills Road
North Little Rock, Arkansas 72116
U.S.A.

September

National; **entry restricted to U.S. (selection by members);** annual; established 1971. Medallion to **Author of Children's Literature** published in previous 2 years. Named after Charlie May Simon, Arkansas author of more than 25 books. Purpose: to promote children's reading of literature. Sponsored by Arkansas Department of Education, state colleges, universities, civic organizations. Average statistics: 18-24 entries, 1 award. Held at annual banquet. Sponsoring agencies select 18-24 books for Arkansas school children Master Reading List. Children grades 4-6 vote in March. Second contact: Elementary School Council, Arkansas Department of Education, Little Rock, Arkansas 72201. Award, September.

5

Children's Reading Round Table (CRRT) Award
Children's Reading Round Table of Chicago
Caroline Rubin, Bulletin Editor
1321 East 56th Street
Chicago, Illinois 60637 U.S.A.

May

Regional; **entry restricted (nomination by CRRT members);** annual; established 1953. $100 and Plaque to individual for **Continuing Contribution to Children's Books** (usually in Chicago-Midwest area). Formerly called MIDWEST AWARD. Purpose: to honor authors, illustrators, editors, librarians, teachers working in children's books field. Sponsored and supported by 600-member CRRT, established 1931. Also sponsor CRRT literature conference (even years), summer seminars for children's book writers and illustrators (odd years). Second Contact: Ellen Schweri, President, 5735 North Washtenaw, Chicago, Illinois 60659. Event, May.

Dorothy Canfield Fisher Children's Book Award
Vermont Department of Libraries
Carol Chatfield, Chair
138 Main Street

Montpelier, Vermont 05602 U.S.A.

June

National; **entry restricted to U.S. publishers;** annual; established 1956. Purpose: to encourage Vermont school children to read more and better books; honor memory of Dorothy Canfield Fisher, Vermont literary figure. Sponsored by Vermont Congress of Parents and Teachers, Vermont Department of Libraries. Also sponsor Nonfiction Book Contest.

BOOK CONTEST: Children's Fiction, published during preceding copyright year for grades 4-8, by living American authors.

AWARDS: Illuminated Scroll to author.

JUDGING: 30-book Master List chosen by 8-member committee; Vermont school children (grades 4-8) vote for favorite.

ENTRY FEE: None.

DEADLINES: Entry, February. Master List selection, March. Children vote, April. Award, June.

7

Ethical Culture School Book Award
Cathleen Szabo, Librarian
33 Central Park West, Room 305
New York, New York 10023 U.S.A.
Tel: (212) 874-5200, ext. 345

May

National; **entry restricted to U.S. publishers;** annual; established 1976. Purpose: to give children a voice in critical judgement of children's literature. Theme: Science Fiction (to change after 1985). Sponsored and supported by Ethical Culture School. Recognized by Children's Book Council. Average statistics: 50 entries, 3 semifinalists, 1 award. Held at Ethical Culture School.

BOOK CONTEST: Children's Science Fiction, published in previous calendar year; in English; grades 5-7 reading level; 3 entries maximum.

AWARDS: Parchment Certificate to author.

JUDGING: Title list prepared by committee. Judging by minimum 100 Ethical Culture School students, grades 4-6. Based on literary quality, excellence of design. Materials returned on request.

ENTRY FEE: None.

DEADLINES: Entry, December. Award, May.

8

George G. Stone Recognition of Merit
George G. Stone Center for Children's Books
Harper Hall
Claremont University Center
Claremont, California 91711 U.S.A.

February

Regional; **entry restricted (nomination by Southern California school children, teachers);** annual; established 1965. Scroll to **Children's Book or Author** for increasing awareness of world. Sponsored by George G. Stone Center for Children's Books. Held at annual Claremont Reading Conference for Young People. Final selection by school librarians. Awards, February.

Golden Archer and Little Archer Award Program
University of Wisconsin-Oshkosh
Dr. Shirley Wilbert, Dr. Norma Jones
Department of Library Science

Oshkosh, Wisconsin 54901 U.S.A.
Tel: (414) 424-2313

Fall

National; **entry restricted to U.S. (nomination by school students);** annual; established 1974 (Golden Archer), 1976 (Little Archer). Golden Archer Award Medal and Certificate to **Children's Book** (grades 4-8), Little Archer Award Medal, Certificate to **Children's Picture Story Book** (grades K-3); published in previous 5 years by living American Author. Named after Marion Fuller Archer. Purpose: to honor juvenile books by living American authors. Sponsored by Department of Library Science, University of Wisconsin-Oshkosh. Held during Fall Conference at UW-Oshkosh. Judging: Preliminary by Wisconsin elementary and middle school students; final by 6-member committee. Event, Fall.

10

Golden Kite Award
Society of Children's Book Writers (SCBW)
Stephen Mooser, President
P.O. Box 296, Mar Vista Station
Los Angeles, California 90066 U.S.A.
Tel: (213) 347-2849

March

National; **entry restricted to SCBW members;** annual; established 1973. Golden Kite Statuette, Honor Book Certificate to **Children's Book Writers.** Sponsored by 400-member Society of Children's Book Writers. Have annual national children's book writers' conference. Publish *Bulletin* (bimonthly). Also sponsor $750 **Work-in-Progress Grant to Children's Book Writer** (SCBW member). Second contact: Sue Alexander, SCBW, 6846 McLaren, Canoga Park, California 91307. Awards, March.

11

Hans Christian Andersen Awards for Books for Children
International Board on Books for Young People (IBBY), United States National Section
John Donovan, Executive Director
Children's Book Council
67 Irving Place
New York, New York 10003 U.S.A.

April

International; **entry restricted (nomination by IBBY National Sections);** biennial; established 1956. Medals and Diplomas (2) to living **Children's Book Author and Illustrator.** Sponsored by IBBY, founded 1951 for international understanding through children's literature. Publish international honor list of children's books. Second contact: Leena Maissen, Secretary, IBBY, Leonhardsgraben 38A, CH-4051 Basel, Switzerland. Awards, April.

12

International Reading Association (IRA) Children's Book Award
Drew Cassidy, Public Information Officer
800 Barksdale Road
P.O. Box 8139
Newark, Delaware 19711 U.S.A.
Tel: (302) 731-1600

Spring

International; **entry restricted to publishers;** annual; established 1975. Purpose: to recognize promising, unestablished authors in children's book field. Sponsored by IRA, 65,000-member, nonprofit educational association with members in over 85 countries, dedicated to reading instruction improvement, reading habit development. Supported by Institute for Reading Research. Held at IRA Convention awards banquet. Also sponsor Print Media Awards (outstanding reporting in newspapers, magazines, wire services); Broadcast Media Awards for Radio and Television (dealing with reading, literacy); Outstanding Dissertation of the Year Award. Second contact: Zena Sutherland, 1418 East 57th Street, Chicago, Illinois 60637.

BOOK CONTEST: **Children's,** published, copyrighted in calendar year prior to award, any language. Publisher submits 7 copies. Must be first or second book author.

AWARDS: $1000 stipend, Medal. "Honor Book" awards to other outstanding entries.

JUDGING: By IRA committee. No entries returned. Not responsible for loss or damage.

ENTRY FEE: None.

DEADLINES: Entry, November. Awards, Spring.

13

Irma Simonton Black Award
Bank Street College of Education
Publications-Communications Division
610 West 112th Street
New York, New York 10025 U.S.A.

Spring

International; entry open to all; annual; established 1973. Named for Irma Simonton Black, educator-author-editor. Sponsored by Bank Street College of Education.

BOOK CONTEST: **Young Children,** published during previous year.

AWARDS: Irma Simonton Black Award Scrolls, to author and illustrator of outstanding book for young children. Award Seal for cover.

JUDGING: By Publications-Communications Division of Bank Street College (children participate in judging). Based on storyline, language, illustration.

ENTRY FEE: None.

DEADLINES: Entry, January. Awards, Spring.

14

Jane Addams Children's Book Award
Women's International League for Peace and Freedom
1213 Race Street
Philadelphia, Pennsylvania 19107
U.S.A.

September

International; **entry restricted to publishers;** annual; established 1953. Purpose: to award book promoting peace, social justice, world community; combining literary merit with world community-social justice themes. Theme: Children's Books That Build for Peace. Sponsored by Jane Addams Peace Association, founded 1948 to foster understanding between world peoples; Women's International League for Peace and Freedom, founded 1915 with Jane Addams as first president. Second contact: Annette C. Blank, 5477 Cedonia Avenue, Baltimore, Maryland 21206.

BOOK CONTEST: **Peace-Social Justice-World Community for Children,** published previous year, in English or English translation; for preschool to high school age.

AWARDS: Jane Addams Scroll and Silver Seals for book jacket. Honor Scrolls.

JUDGING: By national librarian committee.

ENTRY FEE: None.

DEADLINES: Awards, September 6 (Jane Addams' birthdate).

15

Kerlan Collection Award
Children's Literature Research Collections (CLRC)
Dr. Karen N. Hoyle, Curator
109 Walter Library
University of Minnesota
Minneapolis, Minnesota 55455
U.S.A. Tel: (612) 373-9731

Spring

International; **entry restricted (nomination by member-staff);** annual; established 1975. Kerlan Collection Award (Plaque) to **Creator of Children's Literature.** Purpose: to recognize creation of children's literature; donation to Kerlan Collection for study of children's literature. Sponsored and supported by CLRC, University of Minnesota Libraries. Held at University of Minnesota for 1 day. Also sponsor exhibitions, conferences. Event, Spring.

16

Mark Twain Award
Missouri Library Association (MLA)
Marilyn Lake, Executive Secretary
402 South Fifth Street
Columbia, Missouri 65201 U.S.A.

May

National; **entry restricted to U.S. (nomination by members);** annual; established 1972. Mark Twain Award Bronze Bust, travel expenses to conference to U.S. author for **Children's Book** (published 2 years previous). Sponsored by MLA and Missouri Association of School Librarians (MASL). Held at MASL Conference. Have workshops. Also sponsor Literary Awards to Missouri author who has written a **Book on Missouri Life;** Meritorious Achievement Award for contribution to Missouri library cause. Judging by Missouri school children (grades 3-8). Second contact: Jane Benson, Frank Hughes Memorial Library, 210 East Franklin, Liberty, Missouri 64068. Entry, May.

17

Nene Awards
Hawaii Association of School Librarians
Mrs. Sally Morgan
Wahiawa Community Library
820 California Avenue
Wahiawa, Hawaii 96786 U.S.A.
Tel: (808) 623-1331

Fall, Spring

International; **entry open to living authors;** annual; established 1964. Named after Hawaiian state bird. Purpose: to acquaint Hawaiian children with contemporary children's fiction writers; make them aware of good fiction. Sponsored and supported by Hawaii Association of School Librarians, Children's Section of Hawaii Library Association.

BOOK CONTEST: Children's Fiction, published, grades 4-6; copyrighted in previous 6 years, in hardback. No winners from previous 5 years.

AWARDS: Letter, Plaque. Winner kept at Hawaii Library.

JUDGING: By Children of Hawaii.

ENTRY FEE: None.

DEADLINES: Judging, Fall-Spring.

18

Regina Medal Award
Catholic Library Association (CLA)
Matthew R. Wilt, Executive Director
461 West Lancaster Avenue

Haverford, Pennsylvania 19041
U.S.A. Tel: (215) 649-5250

April

International; **entry restricted (nomination by CLA);** annual; established 1959. Silver Medal to individual for **Children's Literature.** Purpose: to recognize continued distinguished contribution to children's literature. Sponsored by CLA, professional association promoting Catholic principles through library resources, services, publications, education. Held at annual CLA Convention. Also sponsor $1500 Reverend Andrew L. Bouwhuis (graduate) Scholarship in library science (open to college seniors, graduates); $1000 member-only World Book-Childcraft Award Scholarships in school, children's librarianship. Award, April.

19

Southern California Council on Literature for Children and Young People Book Awards

Fullerton Public Library
Carolyn Johnson
353 West Commonwealth Avenue
Fullerton, California 92632 U.S.A.
Tel: (714) 738-6339

Annual

Regional; **entry restricted to Southern California residents (selection by members);** annual; established 1961. Plaques to **Southern California Authors, Illustrators of Children's Book.** Purpose: to promote interest in literature; establish excellence standards. Sponsored by 450-member Southern California Council on Literature for Children and Young People. Publish *The Sampler* (quarterly newsletter). Also sponsor annual Spring workshop. Second contact: Joan Blumenstein, Orange Public Library, 101 North Center Street, Orange, California 92666; tel: (714) 532-0379.

20

University of Southern Mississippi Medallion

Jeannine Laughlin, Director
Children's Book Festival
School of Library Service
Southern Station, Box 5146
Hattiesburg, Mississippi 39401
U.S.A. Tel: (601) 266-7167

March

International; entry open to all (nomination by general public); annual; established 1969. Purpose: to recognize outstanding achievement in children's literature. Sponsored by School of Library Service, University of Southern Mississippi. Held during annual Children's Book Festival at University of Southern Mississippi for 2 days.

BOOK CONTEST: Children's Literature.

AWARDS: Silver Medallion to Best author-illustrator.

JUDGING: Nomination by general public; winners by national committee.

ENTRY FEE: None.

DEADLINES: Awards, March.

21

William Allen White Children's Book Award

Emporia State University
George V. Hodowanec, Executive Director
William Allen White Library
1200 Commercial
Emporia, Kansas 66801 U.S.A.
Tel: (316) 343-1200, ext. 205

April

International; **entry open to authors residing in U.S., Canada, Mexico (by nomination);** annual; established 1952. Award program extended to include Braille, large print, recorded books for handicapped children, 1974. Purpose: to encourage Kansas children to read and enjoy good books. Sponsored by Emporia State University, William Allen White Library. Supported by William Allen White Library Endowment Fund, established 1969. Also sponsor May Massee Workshop.

BOOK CONTEST: **Children's Fiction, Poetry,** published in previous calendar year. No translations, anthologies, textbooks. No nominations by publishers, authors.

AWARDS: William Allen White Medal, invitation to speak at Library Colloquium.

JUDGING: Master List selected by Book Selection Committee and Kansas citizens. Kansas school children (grades 4-8) vote for favorite. Final by Book Selection Executive Committee. Based on originality, vitality, clarity, factual accuracy (where applicable), sincerity, respect for reader.

ENTRY FEE: None.

DEADLINES: Selection, January-October. Children's vote, March. Winner announced, April. Award, Fall.

22

Children's Book of the Year Award

Children's Book Council of Australia (CBCA), Queensland Branch
Robyn Collins, Judges' Secretary
G.P.O. Box 1319
Brisbane, Queensland 4000,
AUSTRALIA Tel: 07-2218400, ext. 227

July

National; **entry restricted to Australia;** annual; established 1946. $2500 (Aust.) and Medal to **Australian Children's Book, Children's Picture Story Book.** Purpose: to promote, encourage writing of children's books in Australia. Sponsored by CBCA (formerly called Sydney International Children's Book Week Committee to 1958). Supported by CBCA, state government. Average statistics: 80 entries. Publish *Reading Time* (reviewing journal). Also sponsor seminars, workshops. Awards, July.

23

Alvine-Belisle Prize

Association for the Advancement of the Sciences and Documentation Techniques (ASTED)
Marthe Laforest, Librarian
360, rue Le Moyne
Montreal, Quebec H2Y 1Y3
CANADA Tel: (514) 844-8023

October

National; **entry open to Canada;** annual; established 1974. Purpose: to encourage editors, authors of French literature for young readers. Sponsored by Comite de Litterature de Jeunesse, ASTED. Supported by ASTED. Average statistics: 50-60 entries. Held during ASTED Congress.

BOOK CONTEST: **For Youth in French,** first published in Canada during previous year, in French. Publishers submit 2 copies per entry.

AWARDS: $500 Alvine-Belisle Prize.

JUDGING: By 5 ASTED-member librarians. No entries returned. Not responsible for loss or damage.

ENTRY FEE: None.

DEADLINES: Judging, September. Award, October.

24

Marie-Claire Daveluy Prize
Association for the Advancement of the Sciences and Documentation Techniques (ASTED)
360 rue Le Moyne
Montreal, Quebec H2Y 1Y3
CANADA

Open

National; **entry restricted to French-Canadian residents aged 15-21;** annual; established 1969 (formerly MAXINE PRIZE). Purpose: to encourage youth to write Canadian works for youth. Sponsored by ASTED.

BOOK CONTEST: For Youth in French, original interesting to youth age 12-15 (prose, poetry, drama, science-fiction, romance, story, narrative, etc.). Submit manuscript in French, 75 pages minimum, typed.

AWARDS: $700 Marie-Claire Daveluy Prize. $300 Second Prize. Possible publication of winners.

ENTRY FEE: None.

DEADLINES: Open.

25

Vicky Metcalf Award
Canadian Authors Association (CAA)
24 Ryerson Avenue
Toronto, Ontario M5T 2P3 CANADA
Tel: (416) 868-6916

Spring

National; **entry open to Canada;** annual; established 1963. Purpose: to stimulate writing for Children. Sponsored by CAA, Mrs. Vicky Metcalf. Held at CAA Awards Dinner. Also Sponsor CAA Poetry, Play-Script, Fiction, Nonfiction Book Contests.

BOOK CONTEST: Children's, fiction or picture book of interest to young people. Submit nominating letter in triplicate listing nominee's published works.

AWARDS: $1000 Vicky Metcalf Award.

JUDGING: By 3 judges.

ENTRY FEE: None.

DEADLINES: Entry, March. Awards, Spring.

26

Children's Book Circle (CBC) Eleanor Farjeon Award
The Bodley Head
Rona Selby, Secretary
9 Bow Street
Convent Garden, London WC2E 7AL, ENGLAND Tel: 01-836-9081, ext. 222

May

International; **entry restricted (nomination by members);** annual; established 1965. Eleanor Farjeon Award of 500 pounds for **Distinguished Serivce to Children's Book.** Sponsored by CBC (founded 1962). Held in London; 200-300 attendance. Award, May

27

Library Association Medals
Miss A.E.L. Hobart, Development Secretary
7 Ridgmount Street
London WC1E 7AE, ENGLAND
Tel: 01-636-7543

National; **entry restricted (nomination by members);** annual; established 1936 (Carnegie), 1955 (Greenaway). Carnegie Medal to **Children's Book.** Kate Greenaway Medal for **Children's Book Illustrations** to artists. For books in English (fiction-nonfiction), first published in United Kingdom during preceding year. Sponsored by the Library Association, established 1877. Judged by Youth Libraries Group.

28

Other Award
Children's Book Bulletin
4 Aldebert Terrace
London SW8 1BH, ENGLAND

July

National; **entry restricted to Great Britain;** annual; established 1975. Commendations to **British Published Children's Books.** Purpose: to show new writing, illustration for children; widen literary experience for young people. Sponsored by *Children's Book Bulletin.* Event, July.

29

Times Educational Supplement Information Book Awards
Times Newspapers Limited
Michael Church, Literary Editor
P.O. Box 7, New Printing House Square
Gray's Inn Road
London WC1X 8EZ, ENGLAND
Tel: 01 837 1234

October

International; **entry restricted to Great Britain-Commonwealth book Publishers;** annual; established 1972. Purpose: to induce improvement in quality of children's books. Sponsored by *Times Educational Supplement,* Times Newspapers.

BOOK CONTEST: Children's, originated in Great Britain-Commonwealth September previous to August current year. Submit 3 copies. Categories: Junior (to age 9), Senior (10-16).

AWARDS: Junior Award, Senior Award, to authors, 150 pounds each. 150 pounds to winners' illustrators at judges' discretion.

JUDGING: By 3 judges each category, together with Editor. Entrants retain all rights. Not responsible for loss or damage.

ENTRY FEE: None.

DEADLINES: Entry, August. Awards, October.

30

Bologna Children's Book Fair Prizes
Ente Autonomo per le Fiere di Bologna
Dr. G. C. Alberghini, Secretary General
Piazza Costituzione 6
40128 Bologna, ITALY Tel: (051) 503050

April

International; **entry restricted to Book Fair exhibitor publishers;** annual; established 1964. Purpose: to recognize remarkable illustration-graphic value from international high-quality children's books. Sponsored by and held at Bologna Children's Book Fair. Average statistics: (Graphic Prize) 134 entrants, 500 entries, 20 countries; (Erba Prize) 142 entrants, 500 entries, 20 countries. Have Illustrators' Exhibition. Tickets: free.

BOOK CONTEST: Children-Youth Graphics *(Graphic Prize),* published, 1 or more entries, 5 copies. Categories: For Children, For Youth.

Children's Illustrated *(Erba Prize),* published, 1 or more entries, 3 copies.

ELIGIBILITY: Published for first time January of second year previous to January of current year. Publishers must confirm participation by December of previous year. Also open to nonfiction entries.

AWARDS: Critici in Erba Prize, Gold Plate to publisher of Best Illustrated Book. Graphic Prize for Children, Graphic Prize for Youth, Gold Plates, Winners displayed at Fair.

JUDGING: Erba Prize by 9-child committee (ages 6-9) from 50 Bologna schools. Graphic Prizes by committee from Study Centre "G.B. Bodoni" in Parma, based on graphic, artistic, technical criteria. Not responsible for loss or damage. No entries returned.

ENTRY FEE: None. Entrant pays postage, delivery charges, customs duties.

DEADLINES: Entry, January. Judging, February. Awards, April.

31

Kathleen Fidler Award
National Book League (NBL)
15a Lynedock Street
Glasgow G36 6EF, SCOTLAND

February

National; **entry restricted to young Scottish writers;** established 1980. Kathleen Fidler Award of 100 pounds, Silver Trophy to **Unpublished Children's Novel** by Scottish-born or resident author (age 30 maximum; for readers ages 8-12). Named after Kathleen Fidler, author of over 80 children's books. Sponsored by Blackie and Son, Ltd. First and final selection by adult panel; shortlisted manuscripts submitted to children. Award, February.

32

Swiss Children's Book Prize
Swiss Teachers' Association
Heinrich Weiss, Assistant Secretary
P.O. Box 189
CH-8057 Zurich, SWITZERLAND
Tel: 1-311-83-03

Summer

National; **entry restricted to Swiss-German area;** established 1943. 3000 Swiss francs to Best **Swiss Children's Book** (published in Switzerland). Purpose: to promote good literature for young people. Sponsored and supported by Swiss Teachers' Association, Swiss Female Teachers' Association. Average statistics: 50 entries, 1 award. Award, Summer.

BOOK (fiction)

Book, Short Story and Book Design, including FOR CHILDREN, SCIENCE FICTION. (Also see other BOOK CATEGORIES.)

33

Editors' Book Award
Pushcart Press
P.O. Box 380
Wainscott, New York 11975 U.S.A.

Fall

International; **entry restricted (nomination by U.S., Canadian editors);** annual. Purpose: to encourage writing distinguished books of uncertain financial value; support editors' enthusiasm for literary merit. Sponsored by Pushcart Press. Also sponsor Nonfiction Book Contest.

BOOK CONTEST: Fiction, unpublished. Submit 1 copy (photocopy OK), nomination letter from editor. Only book-length manuscripts making rounds of commercial publishers without acceptance will be considered.

AWARDS: $1000, publication on standard royalty contract, and national advertising-promotion (including nonfiction entries).

JUDGING: By panel of editors. Not responsible for loss or damage.

ENTRY FEE: Not specified. Entrant pays postage (include SASE).

DEADLINES: Entry, May-August. Award, Fall.

34

Houghton Mifflin Literary Fellowship

Houghton Mifflin Company
2 Park Street
Boston, Massachusetts 02107 U.S.A.

Continuous

National; **entry open to U.S.;** continuous; established 1935. Considered oldest publisher-sponsored award of its kind. Purpose: to help American authors complete projects of outstanding literary merit. Sponsored by Houghton Mifflin Company (book publishers). Also sponsor semiannual Houghton Mifflin New Poetry Series Poetry Competition.

BOOK CONTEST: Fiction, unpublished book author for finished manuscript or work in progress; typed double-spaced; in English. Require 50 pages minimum, theme-intention description, biography. Authors published by private press, regional publisher, or university press are considered.

AWARDS: Houghton Mifflin Fellowships, $2500 cash and $7500 advance against publication royalties (10% of retail price on first 5000 copies, 12 1/2% on 5000-10,000, 15% on over 10,000; 90% of net proceeds of first serial, dramatic, motion picture, radio, television rights sale; 80% of net proceeds of British rights; 75% of net proceeds of translations; 50% of net proceeds of second serial rights, selections or abridgements, reprint publisher, book club, similar organization sale).

JUDGING: Sponsor may publish any book written under fellowship; has publishing option on winner's next book. Non-award winners also considered for publication. May withhold award.

ENTRY FEE: None. Entrant pays postage (include SASE).

DEADLINES: Open throughout year.

35

Author's Awards for Mass Market Writing

Periodical Distributors of Canada
Sheryll Reid, Coordinator
322 King Street West, 4th Floor
Toronto, Ontario M5J 1J2 CANADA
Tel: (416) 977-9977

October

National; **entry open to Canadians;** annual; established 1977. Purpose: to recognize outstanding Canadian writers, artists. Sponsored by Foundation for the Advancement of Canadian Letters, Periodical Distributors of Canada.

BOOK CONTEST: Mass Market Paperback, published. Categories: Fiction, Cover Design.

MAGAZINE SHORT STORY CONTEST: Mass Market. No book excerpts. Categories: Fiction, Cover Design.

ELIGIBILITY: Canadian citizens or landed immigrants, published in mass market form and distributed in Canada July previous to June current year. Hardcover reprints acceptable if original published not prior to second calendar year previous. Submit 1 category only; 4 copies each. No weekend newspaper supplements, free distribution publications. Request entrant photograph. Publisher submits nominations (with reasons) for Author of the Year, maximum 2 titles for Book of the Year.

AWARDS: $600 First, $300 Second Place, Best Fiction Paperback; $400, $200, Best Short Story. $300 each First Place, Book and Magazine Cover Designs (including nonfiction entries). Book of the Year Award to author with greatest impact on Canadian paperback publishing industry. Author of the Year Award to Outstanding Canadian Paperback author of past year.

JUDGING: By 3 independent judges. Based on literary merit (fiction), artistic skill, aesthetics, effectiveness (Cover Design). Judging by wholesalers' panel for Book of the Year. No materials returned.

ENTRY FEE: Not specified.

DEADLINES: Entry, July. Awards, October.

36

Books in Canada Award for First Novels
Canadian Review of Books Ltd
Douglas Marshall, Editor
366 Adelaide Street East
Toronto, Ontario M5A 1N4 CANADA
Tel: (416) 363-5426

National; **entry open to Canada;** annual. Sponsored by Canadian Review of Books Ltd.

BOOK CONTEST: Canadian First Novel, in English, published in previous calendar year.

AWARDS: $1000 First Prize.

ENTRY FEE: Not specified.

DEADLINES: Not specified.

37

Seal Books First Novel Competition
60 St. Clair Avenue East, #601
Toronto, Ontario M4T 1N5 CANADA

April

National; **entry open to Canada;** annual. Sponsored by Seal Books (mass-market imprint of McClelland & Stewart Ltd-Bantam Books of Canada Ltd); E.P. Dutton Ltd; Bantam Books (U.S.); Andre Deutsch (U.K.); Corgi Books (U.K.).

BOOK CONTEST: First Novel, unpublished; 60,000 words minimum, in English; double-spaced on white paper, by Canadian citizens-landed immigrants who have not previously published a novel. No employees, families of sponsoring publishers.

AWARDS: Seal Books Novel Award, $10,000 cash and $40,000 nonreturnable advance against publishing earnings. Winner published in hardbound-paperback in Canada, U.S., U.K.

JUDGING: By Canadian panel. May withhold award.

ENTRY FEE: None. Entrant pays postage (include SASE).

DEADLINES: Entry, December. Winner announced, April.

38

John W. Cambell Award for Best Science Fiction Novel of the Year
Prof. T. A. Shippey
School of English, Leeds University
Leeds LS2 9JT, ENGLAND
Tel: 0532-31571

July

International; entry open to all; annual; established 1970. Named after J.W. Cambell, former editor of *Astounding Science Fiction.* Purpose: to recognize merit of, promote excellence in science fiction writing. Average statistics: 50 entries, 6-8 countries, 3 winners. Held during 3-day conference in conjunction with science fiction events in various countries.

BOOK CONTEST: Science Fiction Novel, first published during calendar year preceding award; first translations into English from obscure languages and suppressed books occasionally accepted.

AWARDS: Bronze sculptures, cash prizes, invitations to attend award ceremony, air fare.

JUDGING: By 6-7 writers, critics. Entrant retains all rights. Not responsible for loss or damage.

ENTRY FEE: None.

DEADLINES: Entry, April. Judging, June. Event, awards, July.

39

Whitbread Literary Awards

Booksellers Association of Great Britain & Ireland
Andrea Livingstone, Administrator
154 Buckingham Palace Road
London SW1W 9TZ, ENGLAND
Tel: (01) 730-8214 (5) (6)

November-December

National; **entry restricted to United Kingdom and Ireland publishers of U.K.-Irish authors;** annual; established 1971. Purpose: to acknowledge literary merits, readability of books. Sponsored and supported by Whitbread Brewery; administered by The Booksellers Association of Great Britain & Ireland. Average statistics: 200 entries (including Nonfiction), 3 awards. Held during 1-day awards luncheon in London. Have Conference and Trade Exhibition in Spring. Also sponsor Nonfiction Children's Book and Biography-Autobiography contests.

BOOK CONTEST: Novel, published, 4 book or proof copies.

Children's published, 4 book or proof copies. Should be primarily literary rather than pictorial.

ELIGIBILITY: First published in U.K.-Ireland October previous year to November current year; by authors domiciled in U.K.-Ireland for preceding 5 years. Submission only by publishers who have books in stock. Page proofs acceptable with prior permission. No galley proofs.

AWARDS: 2500 pounds each to Best Novel, Best Children's Book (including Nonfiction), Whitbread Book of the Year (chosen from all entries). Award bands supplied to winners' publishers. Sponsor may provide liaison between publishers and Booksellers Association.

JUDGING: By panel of 3 judges appointed by Whitbread in consultation with Booksellers Association. May vary, withdraw categories or conditions, consider unsubmitted books. No entries returned.

ENTRY FEE: None.

DEADLINES: Entry, July (published before July), September (published July-November). Awards, November-December.

40

Yorkshire Post Book of the Year

Yorkshire Post
Richard Douro
P.O. Box 168
Leeds LS1 1RF, ENGLAND

April

National; **entry restricted to U.K. publishers;** annual; established 1964 (Book of the Year), 1965 (First Work), 1972 (Art-Music). Held at Literary Luncheon in Leeds. Sponsored by Yorkshire Post Newspapers Ltd. Also sponsor Nonfiction Book Contest and Literary Luncheons for Yorkshire writers.

BOOK CONTEST: Fiction (Book of the Year).
First Fiction (First Work), by new author.
Art-Music (Art-Music).

ELIGIBILITY: Published (or due for publication) by publisher based in United Kingdom during previous-current year. 3 entries maximum per publisher. Submit review cuttings. No translations, reissues.

AWARDS: Yorkshire Post Book of the Year, 400 pounds First, 250 pounds Second Prize (one to be Nonfiction). Best First Work, 350 pounds First, 150 pounds Runner-up Prize. Music, 350 pounds. Art, 350 pounds.

JUDGING: By panel.

ENTRY FEE: None.

DEADLINES: Entry, November (Book of the Year), January (First Work, Art-Music). Winners announced, April.

41

Wattie Book of the Year Award

Book Publishers Association of New Zealand (BPANZ)
Gerard E. Reid, Director
P.O. Box 78-071
Grey Lynn, Auckland 2, NEW ZEALAND Tel: 09-767-251

September

National; **entry restricted to New Zealand BPANZ members;** annual; established 1968. Wattie Book of the Year Award of $4000 First, $2500 Second, $1000 Third to **New Zealand Fiction-Nonfiction Book** authors; scrolls to publishers. Named after Sir James Wattie, prominent industrialist, philanthropist, founder of Wattie Industries. Purpose: to recognize, award authorship and production of quality New Zealand books. Sponsored and supported by Wattie Industries and BPANZ. Recognized by New Zealand Book Publishers Association, Booksellers Association, Book Trade Organization. Average statistics: 65 entries, 10 semifinalists, 3 awards, 200 attendance. Held in Auckland, Wellington, Christchurch, or Hastings (by rotation). Tickets: $20. Awards, September.

42

James Tait Black Memorial Prizes

University of Edinburgh
Department of English Literature
David Hume Tower, George Square
Edinburgh EH8 9JX, SCOTLAND
Tel: 031-667-1011, ext. 6259

January

International; **entry restricted to British publications;** annual; established 1918. Named for James Tait Black of A & C Black Ltd., book publishers. Sponsored by University of Edinburgh. Supported by estate of

James Tait Black, Scottish Arts Council.

BOOK CONTEST: **Novel,** published by British publisher in award year, in English. May be published simultaneously or slightly earlier in another country. Submit 2 copies.

AWARDS: 1000 Pounds.

JUDGING: By Regious Professor of Rhetoric, English Literature at University of Edinburgh and assistants. Judging not limited to entries. Not responsible for loss or damage.

ENTRY FEE: None.

DEADLINES: Entry, Open. Judging, Continuous. Winners announced, February.

BOOK (Fiction, Short Story Collection)

Book, Novella, Short Story, including EXPERIMENTAL, JEWISH, SCIENCE FICTION, SOCIAL CONCERN. (Also see other BOOK CATEGORIES.)

43

Hugo Science Fiction Achievement Awards
Howard DeVore
4705 Weddel Street
Dearborn, Michigan 48125 U.S.A.

Annual

International; **entry restricted (selection by SF fans);** annual; established 1953. Hugo Awards to **Science Fiction Novel, Novelette, Short Story, Novella, Professional Editor, Fan Writer, Fanzine.** Voted by Science Fiction fans prior to annual convention in September.

44

Iowa School of Letters Award for Short Fiction
University of Iowa
Department of English
English-Philosophy Building
Iowa City, 52242

Winter

International; entry open to all; annual; established 1969. Purpose: to encourage writing in typically American literary genre. Sponsored by University of Iowa School of Letters. Supported by Iowa Arts Council, Iowa Writers' Workshop, University of Iowa Press. Average statistics: 250 entries, 20 semifinalists, 5 finalists, 1 award. Publish *Iowa Short Fiction Award Series, Iowa Translation Series.* Also sponsor Iowa Writers' Workshop.

BOOK CONTEST: **Short Story Collection,** unpublished, 150 typewritten pages minimum. Accept photocopies; previously submitted, newly revised manuscripts; stories published in periodicals; entrants with published poetry volume.

AWARDS: $1000 Cash Award and publication by University of Iowa Press.

JUDGING: Preliminary by Writers' Workshop. Final by prominent writer or critic. Not responsible for loss.

ENTRY FEE: None. entrant pays postage (include SASE).

DEADLINES: Entry, September. Winner announced, Winter.

45

Janet Heidinger Kafka Prize
University of Rochester
Dean Robert G. Koch
University College
Wilson Blvd.

Rochester, New York 14627 U.S.A.
Tel: (716) 275-2340

Fall

National; **entry restricted to U.S. women;** annual; established 1976. Named in memory of Janet Heidinger Kafka. Purpose: to honor literary, personal ideals of Kafka. Sponsored by Writers Workshop and English Department of University of Rochester. Average statistics: 40 entries. Have 1-week Writers Workshop (July). Second contact: L.J. Davis, 138A Dean Street, Brooklyn, New York 11217.

BOOK CONTEST: **Prose Fiction,** published in previous calendar year, full-length (novel, short stories, experimental writing); 5 copies. Collections of short stories must be assembled for first time (one-third of material previously unpublished). No children's, vanity press.

AWARDS: 1 prize (value variable). Recorded in University of Rochester Archives.

JUDGING: All entries read in entirety by 5 judges. No entries returned.

ENTRY FEE: None.

DEADLINES: Entry, December. Judging, Spring. Award, Fall.

46

Pan-American International Literary Awards

Pan-American Publishing Company
Rose Calles, Editor
P.O. Box 1505
Las Vegas, New Mexico 87701
U.S.A. Tel: (505) 454-0132

March

International; entry open to all; annual; established 1978. Purpose: to enable unpublished writers to have their works published and awarded. Sponsored and supported by Pan-American Publishing Company. Average statistics: 100 entries, 3 awards. Also sponsor Essay Collection Contest.

BOOK CONTEST: **Novel,** original, unpublished, in English; 1 copy, typed double-spaced (carbon or photocopy acceptable).

Short Story Collection. Requirements same as for Novel.

Experimental. Requirements same as for Novel.

AWARDS: $250 First, $100 Second, $50 Third Prize (including Essay Contest). First Prize winner offered standard publishing contract, minimum 10% royalties, publication by sponsor. All entries considered for publication.

JUDGING: By panel of judges. All entries read in entirety. Not responsible for loss or damage.

ENTRY FEE: $25. Entrant pays postage (include SASE).

DEADLINES: Entry, December. Awards, March. Material returned, April.

47

PEN Literature Awards

PEN American Center
Karen Kennerly, Executive Secretary
47 Fifth Avenue
New York, New York 10003 U.S.A.
Tel: (212) 255-1977

Spring

National; **entry open to U.S.;** annual. Hemingway Award one of largest literary prizes in country. Purpose: to provide encouragement, financial support for American writers. Sponsored by the 1800-member PEN American Center (founded 1922) of the 10,000-member, 80-country International PEN (Poets-Playwrights-Essayists-Editors-Novelists), founded 1921 as independent, nonprofit world association of writers. Supported by Hemingway Foundation, Book-of-the-Month Club. Also sponsor PEN Writing Award for Prisoners, PEN Translation Awards, PEN Fund for Writers; Lucille J. Mednick Memorial Award ($500, annual) for distinguished service to the literary community and commitment to serve the young, unrecognized and unpopular (candidates by nomination only).

BOOK CONTEST: **First Fiction Novel or Short Story Collection** *(Hemingway Award),* published in previous calendar year by established publishing house, first-published fiction by American author, in English, 1 copy. No mysteries, children's, westerns.

Fiction *(Faulkner Award)* book-length work, published in previous calendar year by American author; in English, 2 copies (or 1 copy and 1 set of bound galleys). No children's books.

AWARDS: $6000 Ernest Hemingway Foundation Award. $2000 Faulkner Award for Fiction.

JUDGING: By panel.

ENTRY FEE: None.

DEADLINES: Entry, December. Awards, Spring.

48

St. Lawrence Award for Fiction

Fiction International Magazine
Joe David Bellamy
Department of English
St. Lawrence University
Canton, New York 13617 U.S.A.
Tel: (315) 379-5961, 386-2866

Spring

International; **entry restricted to U.S. published books;** annual. Sponsored by *Fiction International Magazine,* St. Lawrence University. Also sponsor St. Lawrence-Fiction International Writers' Conference on Saranac Lake in Adirondacks, New York.

BOOK CONTEST: **First Short Fiction,** first short story collection published by U.S. publisher during previous year.

AWARDS: $1000 St. Lawrence Award for Fiction. Winner announced in *Fiction International Magazine.*

JUDGING: Not responsible for loss or damage.

ENTRY FEE: None. Entrant pays postage (include SASE).

DEADLINES: Entry, January. Award, Spring.

49

British Science Fiction Award

British Science Fiction Association (BSFA)
Alan Dorey, Chairman
64 Hartford Avenue
Kenton, Harrow, Middlesex HA3 8SY, ENGLAND Tel: 01-902-8876, ext. 211

Easter

National; **entry restricted to U.K. (nomination by BSFA members);** annual; established 1973. BSFA Award to **Science Fiction Novel, Short Story,** artist, media presentation. Formerly called CARNELL AWARD after John Carnell, late British science fiction editor; changed to BSFA Award, 1978. Purpose: to promote science fiction writing, publishing in United Kingdom. Sponsored and supported by BSFA, Ltd. Held at Easter Science Fiction Conference. Have films, panels, discussions.

50

National Book League Literary Prizes

B. A. Buckley, Publicity Officer
Book House, 45 East Hill
London SW18 2QZ, ENGLAND
Tel: 01-870-9055

October-January

International; **entry restricted to U.K. publishers of British Commonwealth, Eire, Pakistan, South African citizen authors;** annual; established 1942 (Rhys), 1969 (Booker McConnell), 1976 (Jewish Chronicle). Sponsored by National Book League and Booker McConnell Ltd (founded 1969). Also sponsor Nonfiction Book Contests. Second contact (Jewish Chronicle): G. D. Paul, 25 Furnival Street, London EZ4A 1JT England.

BOOK CONTEST: Novel *(Booker McConnell Prize),* published or to be published January to November current year; in English; by British Commonwealth, Eire, Pakistan, South African citizen; 6 copies each; 4 books maximum per entrant. Publishers may submit additional list of 4 titles. No short stories, translations, novellas. No books returned.

First Novel-Short Story Collection *(David Higham Prize),* published or to be published during current year; in English; by unpublished adult author, British Commonwealth, Eire, Pakistan, South African citizen; 4 copies. No Preference to quality fiction showing promise. No translations.

Young Author Fiction *(John Llewelyn Prize),* published during previous calendar year; by British Commonwealth author under 30; 5 copies.

Jewish Theme Fiction *(Jewish Chronicle-Harold H. Wingate Prize),* published before March current year; in English; by author living in British Commonwealth, Eire, South Africa, Israel.

Irish-European Theme *(Christopher Ewart-Biggs Prize).* Requirements, restrictions not specified.

Social Concern Fiction *(Manchester Oddfellows Prize),* first published in English August previous to July current year; by British Commonwealth, Eire, Pakistan, South African citizen. Book pamphlet of 10,000 words minimum.

AWARDS: In English pounds: Booker McConnell, 10,000. Higham, 500. Rhys, 500. Jewish Chronicle-Wingate, 1500. Ewart-Biggs, 1500. 2 Oddfellows, 500 each.

JUDGING: By 3-5, each award. For Booker McConnell, publisher agrees to spend 750 pounds minimum on direct, paid-for media advertising of winner and 150 pounds for publicity if entry reaches 3-6-book final short-list in October.

ENTRY FEE: None.

DEADLINES: Entry, March (Jewish Chronicle-Wingate), June (Rhys), July (Booker McConnell), August (Higham), others not specified. Awards, October (Oddfellows), November (Booker McConnell, Higham), December-January (Jewish Chronicle-Wingate).

51

Leonilde Castellani Settembrini Award for Fiction

Silvana Di Marcantonio
Via Carducci 38
30171 Mestre (Venice), ITALY
Tel: 41-972020, 41-55327

October

International; entry open to all; annual; established 1959. Named after sponsor's late wife. Sponsored and supported by Arnaldo Settembrini. Average statistics: 20 entries, 5 finalists, 1 winner. Presented during public ceremony in Mestre (Venice).

BOOK CONTEST: Short Stories in Italian, published prior to June current year; in Italian; 8 copies.

AWARDS: 2,000,000 lire First Prize.

JUDGING: By 8 judges. Entrant retains all rights. All entries read in entirety.

ENTRY FEE: Not specified.

DEADLINES: Entry, July. Judging, September. Award, October.

BOOK (Fiction, Short Story, Poetry, Play Collection)

Book, Play, Poetry, Short Story Collections including Book Design, Translation, and BLACK-MINORITY, FOR CHILDREN, JUVENILE, SMALL PRESS. (Also see other BOOK CATEGORIES.)

52

American Book Awards
Association of American Publishers (AAP)
Joan Cunliffe, Director
One Park Avenue, 20th Floor
New York, New York 10016 U.S.A.
Tel: (212) 689-8920

Spring

National; **entry open to U.S. citizens (by publishers' submission);** annual; established 1979. Formerly called NATIONAL BOOK AWARD to 1979, TABA (The American Book Award) to 1980. Purpose: to recognize books of distinction, exemplary achievement, literary merit; select, honor, promote these books; generate public awareness. Motto: "Books make a difference." Sponsored by AAP. Supported by AAP, other book-related organizations. Average statistics: 1300 entries, 85 finalists, 18 awards. Held at Carnegie Hall, New York, for 1 day. Tickets: $50. Also sponsor National Medal for Literature ($15,000 and Bronze Medal for distinguished, continuing contribution to American Letters). Second contact: Laura Brown, Ingram Book Company, 347 Reedwood Drive, Nashville, Tennessee 37217.

BOOK CONTEST: United States Fiction, Poetry, written or translated by U.S. citizens; published during previous calendar year by U.S. publisher; 1 category maximum per entry, either hardback or paperback, 12 copies; 6 copies of translations. No reprints, newly edited or revised books previously published in same format, anthologies, compendiums. Categories: Fiction, Children's Fiction (Hardcover, Paperback); First Novel, Poetry, Translation (Hardcover or Paperback).
United States Book Graphics, by U.S. citizen, manufactured and published in U.S. during previous calendar year with minimum 1000-copy printing. Separate entry fee each category; 1 copy book, 2 covers, 2 jackets per entry. Categories: Book Design (Typographical, Pictorial), Illustration (Original, Adapted-Collected), Jacket Design (Hardcover), Cover Design (Paperback).

AWARDS: $1000 and Louise Nevelson Wall Sculpture to Best First Novel, Best Poetry, Best Translation (either hardcover or paperback); Best Hardcover, Best Paperback (Fiction, Children's Fiction). Nevelson Wall Sculpture to Best Book Design or Illustration, Best Jacket, Best Cover. Recognition Certificates. Promotion materials for winners distributed to 10,000 bookstores, libraries.

JUDGING: Panel of 11 authors, critics, librarians, booksellers, editors, publishers choose 5 nominees and winner each category. For Translations and Graphics, separate 5-member panels choose nominees, winner each category. All jurors selected by Awards Administration Council. Graphics based on originality, aesthetic value, manufacturing. Not responsible for loss or damage.

ENTRY FEE: $25 per entry per category.

DEADLINES: Entry, November (Books), February (Graphics). Awards, Spring.

53

Commonwealth Club of California Literature Medal Award

Michael J. Brassington, Executive Director
681 Market Street
San Francisco, California 94105
U.S.A. Tel: (415) 362-4903

Spring

State; **entry open to California residents;** annual; established 1931. Purpose: to honor books with experimental literary merit. Sponsored by Commonwealth Club of California, founded 1903 as public-spirited organization offering educational perspective on important regional, national, international affairs (14,000 members). Have Newsmaker luncheons, study sections.

BOOK CONTEST: Fiction, Poetry, original, published during previous year, authored by California resident at date manuscript delivered to, accepted by publisher. Submit 3 copies per entry. Categories: Fiction, First Fiction, Poetry, Children's Fiction, California-Related Fiction, Any Classification.

AWARDS: Gold Medal, Best Fiction. Silver Medals, 2 Next-Best entries, Best First Fiction, Best Poetry, Best Fiction for Children Under Age 16, Best California-Related Fiction.

JUDGING: By Jury. No entries returned.

ENTRY FEE: None.

DEADLINES: Entry, January. Awards, Spring.

54

English-Speaking Union Book Award

English-Speaking Union of the United States
John I. B. McCulloch, President
16 East 69th Street
New York, New York 10021 U.S.A.
Tel: (212) TR9-6800

Annual

International; **entry restricted to African, Asian, Third World nonnative speakers of English (selection by Union);** annual; established 1974. $2000 (and travel expenses to award presentation) English-Speaking Union Book Award to **Best Book (Fiction, Poetry, Drama) in English by nonnative writer from Asia, Africa, Third World.** Purpose: to foster among English-speaking peoples understanding, mutual trust, friendship. Sponsored by 32,000-member English-Speaking Union of the United States. Also sponsor Biography Book Award; Books-Across-the-Sea (international book exchange-aid to foreign American studies programs); loan program of Commonwealth books to U.S. libraries; Traveling Librarian Program; grants for British study-travel; scholarships; fellowships.

55

Great Lakes Colleges Association (GLCA) New Writers Awards

Wabash College
Donald W. Baker, Director
Department of English
Crawfordsville, Indiana 47933 U.S.A.
Tel: (317) 362-1400

May

International; **entry restricted to publishers in U.S., possessions, Canada;** annual; established 1968. Purpose: to recognize, promote good fiction, poetry. Sponsored and supported by GLCA (12 midwestern member colleges). Second contact: Jon W. Fuller, President, GLCA, 220 Collingwood, Suite 240, Ann Arbor, Michigan 48103.

BOOK CONTEST: **First Fiction Novel-Short Story,** author's first book in genre, published previous calendar year; 1 entry maximum. Publishers submit 4 copies (galleys, printed book).

First Poetry. Requirements same as for Book.

AWARDS: Winners invited to participate in discussions, lectures, colloquia, readings, interviews, at GLCA colleges. Each college guarantees $100 honorarium, room, board, entertainment expenses, transportation between colleges.

JUDGING: By literature professors, writers-in-residence at colleges. Based on literary excellence. May withhold awards.

ENTRY FEE: None.

DEADLINES: Entry, February. Winners announced, May.

56

International Black Writers Conference Awards

Alice C. Browning, Founder-Director
4019 South Vincennes Avenue
Chicago, Illinois 60653 U.S.A.
Tel: (312) 624-3184

June-July

International; **entry restricted (selection by conference);** annual; established 1970. Award to **Black-Minority Writers for Novels, Poetry and Drama.** Sponsored by International Black Writers Conference. Average statistics: 300-500 attendance. Publish *Black Writers News.* Second contact: Barbara L. Cordell, 7357 Euclid, Chicago, Illinois; tel: (312) 463-4308. Awards, June-July.

57

Joseph Henry Jackson and James D. Phelan Awards

San Francisco Foundation
Martin A. Paley, Director
425 California Street, Suite 1602
San Francisco, California 94104
U.S.A. Tel: (415) 392-0600

June

Regional; **entry restricted to residents of Northern California, Nevada age 20-35 (Jackson); age 20-35 born in California (Phelan);** annual; established 1957 (Jackson), 1936 (Phelan). Named for Joseph Henry Jackson, reviewer-critic-author-editor, and James Duval Phelan, banker-San Francisco mayor-U.S. Senator, who contributed to promoting, aiding the arts. Purpose: to encourage types of writing Jackson was most interested in (Jackson); develop California talent (Phelan). Sponsored and supported by San Francisco Foundation. Also sponsor James D. Phelan Award in Art. Second contact: San

Francisco Foundation, 1100 Larkspur Landing Circle, Suite 250, Larkspur, California 94939; tel: (415) 499-1555.

BOOK CONTEST: Fiction Prose, Short Story, Poetry *(Jackson Award),* unpublished, partly completed; by Northern California, Nevada resident for 3 consecutive years immediately prior to entry date; typed on 8 1/2x11-inch paper. Require proof of age, residence.

WRITING CONTEST: Fiction Prose, Short Story, Poetry, Drama *(Phelan Award),* unpublished, incomplete, by authors born in California. Other requirements same as for Book.

ELIGIBILITY: Entrants may enter both contests but are eligible for one award.

AWARDS: $2000, each award. Honorable Mentions.

JUDGING: By 3 judges. May withhold awards. Manuscripts become property of sponsor after July. Not responsible for loss or damage.

ENTRY FEE: None. Entrant pays postage (include SASE).

DEADLINES: Entry, January. Winners announced, June.

58

North Carolina Literary and Historical Association Literary Competition

109 East Jones Street
Raleigh, North Carolina 27611
U.S.A. Tel: (919) 829-7442

November

State; **entry open to North Carolina;** annual. Purpose: to stimulate interest in North Carolina literature. Sponsored by North Carolina Literary and Historical Association, founded 1900 to foster, encourage literary activity in literature, history of North Carolina. Supported by Society of Mayflower Descendants in North Carolina (Mayflower Cup), Historical Book Club of North Carolina (Raleigh Award; Margaret Hites, President, 1008 Bradbury Drive, Greensboro, North Carolina 27410), Roanoke-Chowan Group (Roanoke-Chowan Award), North Carolina Division of American Association of University Women (AAUW Award). Also sponsor annual Culture Week, Christopher Crittenden Memorial Award (for preservation of North Carolina history), Tar Heel Junior Historian Contest (for local history projects), R. D. W. Conner Award (for article in *North Carolina Historical Review*), Undergraduate Student Award (for research paper on North Carolina history). Publish *Carolina Comments* and *North Carolina Historical Review* (quarterly).

BOOK CONTEST: Fiction *(Raleigh Award),* published June previous to July current year, original, 3 copies. No technical, scientific works.

Poetry *(Roanoke-Chowan Award).* Requirements same as for Book.

Juvenile *(AAUW Award).* Requirements same as for Book.

ELIGIBILITY: Authors maintaining North Carolina legal, physical residence for 3 years preceding entry date.

AWARDS: Sir Walter Raleigh Award for Fiction, Roanoke-Chowan Award for Poetry, AAUW Award in Juvenile Literature.

JUDGING: Based on creative, imaginative quality, style excellence, universality, relevance to North Carolina.

ENTRY FEE: None.

DEADLINES: Entry, July. Awards, November.

59

San Francisco Arts and Letters Foundation Award
Bay Area Small Press Bookfair
Todd S. J. Lawson, Director
P.O. Box 99394
San Francisco, California 94109
U.S.A. Tel: (415) 771-3431,
771-6711

Summer

International; entry open to all; annual; established 1971. Purpose: to bring together small presses with poets, writers, journalists; display wares and provide forum. Theme: International Arts for All. Sponsored and supported by San Francisco Arts and Letters Foundation (formerly called Peace and Pieces Foundation; non-profit grass-roots arts agency), California Arts Council, NEA, COSMEP, City of San Francisco. Average statistics: 2000 entries, 20 countries, 50,000 attendance. Bookfair held at Fort Mason Center (Building D, San Francisco) for 2 days. Have room for 300 displays, 3 stages. Tickets: $.50-$3; free to handicapped, deaf, elderly, exhibitors. Also sponsor Video Prose and Poetry for Hearing and Deaf, photo displays.

BOOK AWARD: **Small Press Any Subject,** published material only. Categories: Poetry, Prose, Journalism, Mixed Media, Magazines.

AWARDS: Plaques and $250 First, $100 Second, $50 Third Place Best Small Press. 20 Honorary Award Plaques. TV promotion as part of book fair coverage.

JUDGING: By 3 judges from Arts and Letters Foundation board; 3 selected by attending presses; 1 city or state official involved in mixed-media arts. Not responsible for loss or damage.

ENTRY FEE: $25 all exhibitors. (Display space $100 per table; or $20 per book in combined exhibit.) Entrant pays all shipping.

DEADLINES: Entry, December. Acceptance, February. Materials, March. Event, award, June.

60

Central News Agency (CNA) Literary Award
M. Jennings, Secretary
P.O. Box 9380
Johannesburg, REPUBLIC OF SOUTH AFRICA Tel: 838-8161

April

National; **entry restricted to South African citizens, residents (nomination by publishers)**; annual; established 1961. R3500 award each to **English and Afrikaans Books,** including Novels, Short Story Collections, Poetry, Drama published during calendar year. Publishers submit 4 copies each entry, brief biography. Purpose: to foster creative writing by South African authors. Sponsored by CNA. Average statsitics: 60 entries. Awards, April.

BOOK (Historical Fiction)

Book, Play, Script, including COLONIAL, ENGLISH, LINCOLN THEME, SOUTHERN. (Also see other BOOK CATEGORIES.)

61

Civil War Round Table of New York Awards
George M. Craig, Chairman
83-12 St. James Street

Elmhurst, New York 11373 U.S.A.
Tel: (212) NE9-1172

February

International; entry open to all; annual; established 1960. Purpose: greater appreciation of life, works of Abraham Lincoln. Sponsored and supported by Civil War Round Table of New York. Held at Round Table dinner meeting. Also sponsor Fletcher Pratt Award (to best book dealing with Civil War); awards for Lincoln-theme musical works, paintings, radio-television programs. Second contact: Arnold Gates, 168 Weyford Terrace, Garden City, New York 11530.

BOOK CONTEST: **Lincoln Theme.**

PLAY CONTEST: **Lincoln Theme.**

AWARDS: $100, copy of Lincoln Bust, Plaque.

JUDGING: By committee. Not responsible for loss or damage.

ENTRY FEE: None.

DEADLINES: Entry, December. Awards, February.

62

Jules F. Landry Award

Catherine Silvia, Promotion Manager
Louisiana State University Press
Baton Rouge, Louisiana 70803
U.S.A. Tel: (504) 388-2210

Continuous

International; entry open to all; annual. Sponsored by Louisiana State University (LSU) Press. Also sponsor Biography Contest.

BOOK CONTEST: **Southern History, Literature,** unpublished manuscript.

AWARDS: $1000 Landry Award and publication by LSU Press (includes Biography Contest).

ENTRY FEE: None.

DEADLINES: Open.

63

Society of Colonial Wars Awards

Joan Sumner, Executive Secretary
122 East 58th Street
New York, New York 10022 U.S.A.

Various

International; entry open to all; annual; established 1951. Purpose: to promote wider knowledge, encourage material on life and times of early America. Sponsored by Society of Colonial Wars. Also sponsor awards for music, art, photography.

BOOK CONTEST: **Colonial Period Literature,** bound volumes or pamphlets.

SCRIPT CONTEST: **Colonial Period Drama** (film, television, theater).

WRITING CONTEST: **Colonial Period.**

ELIGIBILITY: At least 75% of content must be in Colonial Period (1607-1775).

AWARDS: Parchment Citations of Honor and Bronze Medallions to winners. Honorable Mention Citations. Sponsor may withhold awards.

ENTRY FEE: None.

DEADLINES: Open.

64

Historical Novel Prize

Bodley Head Ltd
Jill Black, Director
9 Bow Street

London WC2E 7AL, ENGLAND
Tel: London 836 9081 (BH)

May

International; entry open to all; annual; established 1978. Sponsored and supported by Bodley Head Ltd and Corgi Books Ltd. Average statistics: 200 entrants. Second contact: Diane Pearson, Corgi Books, Century House, Uxbridge Road, London W5 5SA; 579-2652 (CB).

BOOK CONTEST: Historical Novel, unpublished, full-length, in English; typed double-spaced. No translations.

AWARDS: 2000 pounds, publication in hardback (by Bodley Head), paperback (by Corgi). Runners-up may be offered publication. Terms negotiated by authors.

JUDGING: Each entry read in entirety by 5 judges. Submission to contest automatically entails submission for publication in British market. May withhold awards. Not responsible for loss or damage.

ENTRY FEE: None. Entrant pays postage (include SASE).

DEADLINES: Entry, August. Winners announced, October. Award, May. Publication (hardback), Spring.

65

Rose Mary Crawshay Prizes for English Literature
The British Academy
Burlington House
Piccadilly
London W1V 0NS, ENGLAND
Tel: 01-734-0457

Various

International; **entry restricted to women;** annual; established 1914. Sponsored by the British Academy. Supported by Byron, Shelley, Keats in Memoriam Yearly Prize Fund, founded 1888 by Mrs. Rose Mary Crawshay.

BOOK CONTEST: English Literature Historical-Critical, written or published in previous 3 years; any subject; preference to work regarding poets Byron, Shelley, Keats.

AWARDS: 2 Rose Mary Crawshay Prizes.

ENTRY FEE: None.

DEADLINES: Open.

66

Alexandre Dumas Prize
Societe des Amis d'Alexandre Dumas
Mme. D. S. Neave
1 bis, rue Champflour
78160 Marly-le-Roi, FRANCE
Tel: 33-9584898

May

International; entry open to all; annual; established 1970. Named after 19th-century French author Alexandre Dumas. Purpose: to promote writing historical romances in Dumas's tradition. Sponsored and supported by Societe des Amis d'Alexandre Dumas. Average statistics: 30 entries, 3 semifinalists, 1 winner. Held in Paris for 1 day.

BOOK CONTEST: Historical Fiction in French, published; 12 copies submitted by publishers.

AWARDS: Medal to Best Entry.

JUDGING: By 12 judges.

ENTRY FEE: None.

DEADLINES: Entry, March. Award, May.

BOOK (Humanitarian, Religious, Culture)

Book, Play, Poetry, Short Story, including HUMAN VALUE, HUMANITARIAN, SOCIAL EQUALITY, CHRISTIAN, RELIGIOUS, FRENCH CULTURE-MINORITY, JEWISH. (Also see other BOOK CATEGORIES.)

67

Association of Jewish Libraries (AJL) Book Awards

Hazel B. Karp, Chair, Book Award Committee
880 Somerset Drive N.W.
Atlanta, Georgia 30327 U.S.A.
Tel: (404) 237-5882, 634-7388

June

National; **entry open to U.S.;** annual; established 1968. Purpose: to honor, encourage books with Jewish themes, backgrounds for young readers. Sponsored by AJL. Average statistics: 50 entries, 100-200 attendance. Held at AJL National convention for 3 days. Have workshops, convention, exhibits. Also sponsor Library Science Scholarship to student in Judaic field. Second contact: Barbara Leff, AJL National President, Stephen S. Wise Temple, 15500 Stephen S. Wise Drive, Los Angeles, California 90025.

BOOK CONTEST: **Jewish Interest Juvenile,** original, published previous calendar year, in English.

AWARDS: AJL Book Award, Plaque or Scroll to author, award and publicity-promotion for winning book. Sydney Taylor Body of Work Award.

JUDGING: By 5 Judaic librarians. May withhold awards. All entries read, reviewed in writing.

ENTRY FEE: None.

DEADLINES: Entry, open. Judging, continuous. Winners announced, Spring. Award, June.

68

Blue Ridge Christian Writers Conference Award for Excellence in Literature

Yvonne Lehman, Director
Walker Cove Road
P.O. Box 188
Black Mountain, North Carolina
28711 U.S.A. Tel: (704) 669-8421

August

International; **entry restricted to former Conference students;** annual; established 1975. Plaque, free conference tuition for **Christian Book, Short Story, or Poem.** Formerly called NORTH CAROLINA CHRISTIAN WRITERS CONFERENCE to 1977. Purpose: to bring writers together with editors, publishers; encourage, instruct writers; realize all talents are from God. Sponsored by Blue Ridge Christian Writers Conference. Average statistics: 70-80 entrants, 3-4 countries, 1-5 winners. Held at YMCA Blue Ridge Assembly, Black Mountain for 5 days. Have workshops, group sessions, lodging, meals, classrooms, chapel, bookstore. Tuition: $80. Awards, August.

69

Christopher Awards

The Christophers
Peggy Flanagan, Coordinator
12 East 48th Street
New York, New York 10017 U.S.A.
Tel: (212) 759-4050

January

International; entry open to all; annual; established 1949. Purpose: to recognize individuals producing works promoting sound values, with realistic, hopeful view of man and world; replace fault-finding with positive action. Motto: "Better to light one candle than to curse the darkness." Sponsored by The Christophers, founded 1945 as nonprofit mass media organization based on Judeo-Christian concept of service to God and humanity. Average statistics: 8 adult, 5 juvenile awards. Held in New York City. Sponsor publications, nationally syndicated TV-radio series, daily and weekly newspaper columns.

BOOK CONTEST: **Human Value Adult, Juvenile,** published in previous year; original; 2 copies.

AWARDS: Bronze Medallions.

JUDGING: By 2-level panel of "grass-roots" judges and experts. Based on affirmation of human spirit, artistic or technical proficiency, public acceptance. All entries reviewed in entirety. Not responsible for loss or damage.

ENTRY FEE: None.

DEADLINES: Entry, open. Awards, January.

Edward Lewis Wallant Book Award

Dr. and Mrs. Irving Waltman
3 Brighton Road
West Hartford, Connecticut 06117
U.S.A. Tel: (203) 236-3372

Spring

National; **entry open to U.S.;** annual; established 1963. Sponsored by Dr. and Mrs. Irving Waltman, Hartford Jewish Community Center. Second contact: Hartford Jewish Community Center, 335 Bloomfield Avenue, West Hartford, Connecticut 06117.

BOOK CONTEST: **American-Jewish Fiction Novel, Short Story Collection,** published during previous year, with significance for American Jew.

AWARDS: $250 Edward Lewis Wallant Memorial Book Award and Scroll.

JUDGING: By 3 judges. Preference to writers who have not achieved literary prominence.

ENTRY FEE: None.

DEADLINES: Award, Spring.

71

National Jewish Book Awards

Jewish Welfare Board (JWB) Jewish Book Council
15 East 26th Street
New York, New York 10010 U.S.A.
Tel: (212) 523-4949

Spring

International; **entry restricted to U.S., Canadian authors-translators (nomination by Council members);** annual. Frank and Ethel S. Cohen Award ($500) for **Jewish Thought Book.** William and Janice Epstein Award ($500) for **Jewish Fiction Book** (novel or short story collection). JWB Jewish Book Council Award ($500) for **Jewish Poetry Book** published during previous 2 years. William Frank Memorial Award ($500) for **Jewish Children's Book.** Workmen's Circle Award ($500) for **Yiddish Literature Book in Yiddish** (fiction, poetry). Citations to publishers of winning books. All books in English, published during previous calendar year unless otherwise specified. No anthologies, reprints, new editions. Purpose: to promote greater awareness of American-Canadian-Jewish literary creativity. Sponsored by JWB Jewish Book Council. Event, Spring.

72

National Religious Book Awards

Religious Book Review
Charles A. Roth, Publisher
P.O. Box 1331
Roslyn Heights, New York 11577
U.S.A. Tel: (516) 621-7242

March

National; **entry open to U.S.;** annual. Formerly called RELIGIOUS BOOK AWARDS. Purpose: to acknowledge contribution religious book publishing makes to American society. Sponsored by Religious Book Review, Omni Communications.

BOOK CONTEST: **Religious,** published during previous year, original; 3 copies. Categories: Inspirational, Community Life (Social Awareness), Children-Youth.

AWARDS: Omni Trophy to author, publisher (translator, illustrator if applicable), each category. Seals for book covers. NRBA Plaques to Runners-Up.

JUDGING: By 3-4 reviewer, educator, editor, author judges, each category.

ENTRY FEE: $15 each.

DEADLINES: Entry, December. Finalists announced, February. Awards, March.

73

Robert F. Kennedy Book Awards

Coates Redmon, Executive Director
4014 49th Street N.W.
Washington, District of Columbia
20016 U.S.A. Tel: (202) 362-2410

May

National; **entry open to U.S.;** annual; established 1981. Purpose: to honor author whose work faithfully and forcefully reflects Robert Kennedy's purposes. Sponsored by RFK Journalism Awards Committee. Supported by Arthur Schlesinger, Jr., endowment from his *Robert Kennedy and His Times.* Also sponsor Robert F. Kennedy Journalism Awards.

BOOK CONTEST: **Social Equality,** published in U.S. previous year. Require 3 copies, description letter.

AWARDS: $2500 First Prize.

JUDGING: By 5 authorities in social affairs.

ENTRY FEE: None.

DEADLINES: Entry, February. Event, May.

74

Champlain Prize

Le Conseil de la Vie Francaise en Amerique (CVFA)
Pauline Dumais, Chef du secretariat
59 rue d'Auteuil
Quebec G1R 4C3, CANADA
Tel: (418) 692-1150

July

International; **entry restricted to French-speaking minorities in Canada, U.S.;** biennial (alternates yearly between fiction, nonfiction); established 1957. Named after founder of Quebec. Purpose: to encourage literary production among French-speaking minorities living outside Quebec; create in Quebec interest in these French-speaking minorities. Sponsored and supported by CVFA. Held at CVFA annual meeting.

BOOK CONTEST: **French Minority Experience Novel, Short Story, Poetry, Play in French;** published in previous 3 years or under contract at time of submission. Submit 4 copies of work, curriculum vitae.

ELIGIBILITY: By French-speaking authors born or raised in minority situation in U.S. or Canada, or Quebec-born authors who at time of publication have lived at least 3 years in minority situation.

AWARDS: $1000 Champlain Prize and Certificate, travel and expenses to awards ceremony. Honorable Mention.

JUDGING: By 3-member jury. May withhold awards.

ENTRY FEE: None.

DEADLINES: Entry, December. Awards, July.

75

La Presse Prize for Literature
Antoine Des Roches, Public Relations Director
7 rue Saint-Jacques
Montreal, Quebec H2Y 1K9
CANADA

November

National; **entry restricted;** annual; established 1975. $7500 to **Quebec French Culture Literature** (novel, historic novel, poetry, critical-philosophical-artistic essay) by French Canadians, legal immigrants. Award, November.

Thomas-Mann Award
Lubeck Office of Culture
Rathaushof
2400 Lubeck 1, WEST GERMANY (FRG) Tel: 0451-1224102

Triennial

International; **entry restricted (nomination by judges);** triennial; established 1975. 10,000 DM to Author for **Humanitarian Literary Works.** Sponsored by Hansestadt Lubeck.

BOOK (Humor, Satire)

Book, Short Story, including FOR YOUNG PEOPLE.

77

Hitar Petar (Artful Peter) Prize for Humor and Satire in Literature
House of Humor and Satire (HHS)
Stefan Furtounov, Director
P.O. Box 104
5300 Gabrovo, BULGARIA Tel: (066) 2-72-29, 2-93-00

May

International; entry open to all; biennial; established 1977. Named after Hitar Petar (Artful Peter), famous Bulgarian folkloric figure. Purpose: to stimulate humorous, satirical artistic work serving humanism, progress, moral perfection. Sponsored and supported by HHS, Committee for Arts and Culture, Bulgarian Writers' Union. Average statistics: 60 entries, 22 countries. Announced during National Festival of Humor and Satire in Gabrovo. Tickets: 40 stotinki. Also sponsor Bulgarian International Festival of Comedy and Satirical Films.

BOOK CONTEST: Humor, Satire, published during previous 2 years; 3 copies in published language; 1 copy of translation in Bulgarian, Russian, English, French, German, or Spanish; and 3 copies of evaluation by literary critic.

AWARDS: Hitar Petar Prize, 2000 Lev for Best Literary Work. Winner published in *Humor of the Nations* series.

JUDGING: By commission appointed by Bulgarian Writers' Union. Entries retained for HHS Humor of the Nations Fund. Not responsible for loss or damage.

ENTRY FEE: None.

DEADLINES: Entry, January. Award, May.

78

Stephen Leacock Medal For Humor

Stephen Leacock Associates
Jean Bradley, Chair, Awards Committee
P.O. Box 854
Orillia, Ontario L3V 3K8 CANADA
Tel: (705) 325-6546

June

National; **entry open to Canadians;** annual; established 1946. Named after Stephen Leacock, Canadian humorist and founder of Canadian Authors' Association. Purpose: to serve as memorial to Leacock; encourage writing-publishing of Canadian humor. Sponsored by Stephen Leacock Associates, Hudson's Bay Company. Average statistics: 20 entries. Held at Awards dinner in Orillia, Ontario. Tickets: $28 (nonmembers). Publish *Newspacket* (quarterly newsletter). Also sponsor Student Award for Humor for essays by Simcoe County high school students.

BOOK CONTEST: **Humor,** any form; published in previous calendar year; 6 copies.

AWARDS: Stephen Leacock Memorial Silver Medal and $2000 Hudson's Bay Company Prize (including Fiction-Nonfiction entries).

JUDGING: By Canadian judges. May withhold awards. Sponsor keeps entries.

ENTRY FEE: None.

DEADLINES: Entry, February. Winners announced, May. Awards, June.

79

Bordighera International Prizes for Humor

International Salon of Humor
Gigia Perfetto, President
Corso Italia, 46
18012 Bordighera (IM), ITALY
Tel: 0184-261727

July-August

International; entry open to all; annual; established 1952 (Humorous Book); 1954 (Short Story); 1962 (For Young People). Purpose: to discover humorous books for development and wider renown of humor everywhere. Sponsored by Tourist Organization of Bordighera and Council of Europe. Average statistics: 6000 entrants, 12,000 entries, 51 countries. Held during annual Salon of Humor, Bordighera. Have exhibition of drawings, pictures. Tickets: 1000 lire. Also sponsor Humorous Drawing, Illustrated Literature, Publicity categories; Rama Di Palma d'Oro Prize (established 1968) for journalists, radio-TV editors, entertainment people contributing to diffusion of optimistic humor; Photography Contest.

BOOK CONTEST: **Humorous,** published in Italy after January of previous year; 12 copies. Require photo, biography.

Humor for Young People. Requirements, restrictions same as for Humorous Book.

SHORT STORY CONTEST: **Humorous,** unpublished; in Italian; 2-4 typed pages, 3 copies. Require photo, biography.

AWARDS: Humorous Book: First Prize Golden Palm Trophy, Second Prize Golden Date, Third Prize Silver

Date. Humor for Young People: Silver Palm Trophy. Short Story: First Prize Silver Palm Trophy, Second and Third Prize Silver Date.

JUDGING: By international jury. Not responsible for loss or damage.

ENTRY FEE: None. Sponsor pays return postage.

DEADLINES: Entry, July. Event, Awards, July-August. Materials returned, December.

BOOK (Language, Translation)

Book, Play, Poetry, Short Story Translation or In Foreign Language, including FRENCH, GERMAN, ITALIAN, JAPANESE, POLISH, PORTUGUESE, SCANDINAVIAN, SPANISH, CASTILIAN. (Also see other BOOK CATEGORIES.)

80

American-Scandinavian Foundation (ASF) PEN Translation Prizes

Kathleen Madden
127 East 73rd Street
New York, New York 10021 U.S.A.
Tel: (212) 879-9779

May

International; entry open to all; annual; established 1980. Purpose: to promote contemporary Scandinavian literature in English translation. Sponsored by ASF and PEN. Supported by ASF, founded 1910 for advancement of U.S.-Scandinavian cultural relations. Held at PEN American Center, New York City for 1 evening. Publish *Scandinavian Review* (quarterly). Also sponsor Alice and Corrin Strong Fund for Creative-Performing Arts, Literature; Graduate Fellowships to U.S. and Scandinavian exchange students; scholarships for study in Scandinavian countries.

BOOK CONTEST: **Scandinavian Fiction Translation**, 30-35 pages.
Scandinavian Poetry Translation, 15-20 pages.

ELIGIBILITY: English translation of Danish, Finnish, Icelandic, Norwegian, or Swedish authors born after 1880. Entry should be by one author, conceived as part of book. Submit 1 photocopy of original language work with source-publication data, 4 double-spaced copies of translation, table of contents.

AWARDS: $500 and publication, each contest.

ENTRY FEE: Not specified. Entrant pays postage (include SASE).

DEADLINES: Entry, February. Awards, May. Materials returned, July.

81

Friendship Fund Prize for Japanese Literary Translation

Japan-United States Friendship Commission (JUSFC)
Francis B. Tenny, Executive Director
1875 Connecticut Avenue N.W.
Suite 709
Washington, District of Columbia 20009 U.S.A. Tel: (202) 673-5295

Summer

National; **entry open to U.S.;** annual; established 1979. Purpose: to encourage literary translation from Japanese to English; increase Japanese literature available in English. Sponsored by JUSFC, Japan Society, Inc. Recognized by Association of Asian

Studies. Average statistics: 15 entries. Also sponsor Japan Exchange Fellowship Program. Second contact: Peter Grilli, Japan Society, Inc., 333 East 47th Street, New York, New York 10017; tel: (212) 832-1155.

BOOK CONTEST: Japanese Literature to English Translation (fiction, drama, poetry), unpublished or newly published in previous 2 years; any period; book-length; 5 photocopies (if unpublished), 5 copies (if published). Translations in process considered if over half complete. No shorter works.

ELIGIBILITY: U.S. translators with no book-length translation published or widely sold in U.S. more than 2 years previous.

AWARDS: $1000 Friendship Fund Prize for Best Translation (including nonfiction), assistance in finding publisher.

JUDGING: By editors, writers, established translators. Based on (in order of importance) literary merit of English, accuracy reflecting spirit of Japanese original, literary merit of Japanese original. All entries read in entirety. May withhold award.

ENTRY FEE: None. Entrant pays postage (include SASE).

DEADLINES: Entry, February. Judging, Spring. Winner announced, June. Award, Summer.

82

PEN Translation Prizes

PEN American Center
Karen Kennerly, Executive Secretary
47 Fifth Avenue
New York, New York 10003 U.S.A.
Tel: (212) 255-1977

Spring

International; entry open to all; annual (PEN Translation, Goethe, Poggioli), biennial (Gulbenkian). Purpose: to recognize translations for English-speaking public. Sponsored by 1800-member PEN American Center (founded 1922) of the 10,000-member, 80-country International PEN (Poets-Playwrights-Essayists-Editors-Novelists), founded 1921 as independent, nonprofit world association of writers. Also sponsor PEN Writing Award for Prisoners, PEN Literature Awards, PEN Fund for Writers; Lucille J. Mednick Memorial Award ($500, annual) for distinguished service to the literary community and commitment to serve the young, unrecognized, unpopular (candidates by nomination only).

BOOK CONTEST: Into English Translation *(PEN Translation Prize),* published in U.S. during previous calendar year by established publishing house, translated from any language, 2 copies. No technical, scientific, reference books.

German to English Translation *(Goethe House Prize),* published during previous calendar year by established publishing house, 2 copies.

Portuguese to English Translation (Calouste Gulbenkian Prize), published during previous 2 calendar years by established publishing house, 2 copies.

Italian to English Translation *(Renato Poggioli Award),* published during previous calendar year by established publishing house. Require curriculum vitae, translation sample, original text.

AWARDS: $1000 PEN Translation Prize. $500 Goethe House Prize. $500 Calouste Gulbenkian Prize. $3000 Renato Poggioli Award.

JUDGING: By panel.

ENTRY FEE: None.

DEADLINES: Entry, December (for

Poggioli Award, January). Awards, Spring.

83

Austrian State Prize for European Literature

Austrian Federal Ministry of Education and Arts (AFMEA)
Freyung 1
1010 Vienna, AUSTRIA

Fall

International; **entry restricted to European countries;** annual; established 1965. 150 Austrian schillings and Certificate for **European Literature** to poet, novelist, dramatist whose major works have been translated into German. Purpose: to promote cultural relations between Austria and European countries; encourage new young authors to further writing careers. Sponsored by AFMEA. Second contact: Minoritenplatz 5, Postfach 65, 1014 Vienna, Austria. Award, Fall.

84

French Studies Review Prize

Pierre Filion
University of Montreal Press
Case Postale 6128
Montreal, Quebec H3C 3J7 CANADA
Tel: (514) 343-6931

Fall

International; **entry restricted to French-speaking country or territory residents;** annual; established 1968. Purpose: to encourage literary works in French (representative of cultural spheres other than France). Sponsored and supported by University of Montreal Press, Therien Freres (printers).

BOOK CONTEST: **Fiction in French,** (Poetry, Play, Novel, Short Story, Narrative), unpublished, original; written in French; about cultural domains outside France; 100 pages minimum; typed double-spaced.

ELIGIBILITY: 7-consecutive-year resident of French-speaking country, territory (having lived outside of France half of life or more).

AWARDS: $2000 (Canadian) French Studies Review Prize and publication by University of Montreal Press.

JUDGING: By jury selected by University of Montreal Press. Sponsor has exclusive publishing rights for 2 years. Nonwinners returned.

ENTRY FEE: None.

DEADLINES: Entry, May. Awards, Fall.

85

Translators Association Prizes

84 Drayton Gardens
London SW10 9SD, ENGLAND
Tel: 01-373-6642

Spring

International; **entry open to British publishers;** annual. Sponsored by The Translators Association. Supported by Arts Council of Great Britain, British publishers, Italian Institute, and British Italian Society (Florio), French Government (Moncrieff Prize), West German Government (Tieck Prize). Recognized by Society of Authors.

BOOK CONTEST: **Italian to English Translation** *(Florio Prize), 3 proof and 3 original copies.*

French to English Translation *(Moncrieff Prize),* 3 proof and 3 original copies.

German to English Translation *(Tieck Prize),* 3 proof and 3 original copies.

ELIGIBILITY: Translations of twentieth-century works of literary merit-

general interest published in United Kingdom during current year by British publisher.

AWARDS: 500 pound John Florio Prize. 1000 pound Scott Moncrieff Prize. 1600 pound Schlegel-Tieck Prize.

JUDGING: By 3 judges, each award. May withhold, divide awards.

ENTRY FEE: None.

DEADLINES: Entry, December. Awards, Spring.

86

Delegation General of Quebec Prizes Association
France-Quebec Association
54 Avenue de Saxe
75015 Paris, FRANCE Tel: 783-31-34

November

National; **entry restricted (selection by sponsors);** annual; established 1961 (France-Canada), 1965 (Jean-Hamelin). France-Canada Prize of 2000 francs to **Book Published in France-Canada by Quebec-French Canadian Author** (sponsored by France-Canada Association). Jean-Hamelin France-Quebec Prize of 4000 francs to **Book Published in Quebec-France by Quebec Author** (sponsored by French Language Writers Association). Supported by Quebec Government, City of Paris. Awards, November.

87

Medicis Prizes for Fiction
Francine Mallet, Secretary General
25 rue Dombasle
75015 Paris, FRANCE

November

International; entry open to all; annual. Considered foremost French literary award.

BOOK CONTEST: French Language Novel, published since December previous year.
Into French Translation, Novel, published since December previous year.

AWARDS: 4500 French francs First Prize, each category.

ENTRY FEE: Not specified.

DEADLINES: Entry, not specified. Awards, November.

88

German Academy of Language and Literature Prizes
Dr. Gerhard Dette, General Secretary
Alexandraweg 23
6100 Darmstadt, WEST GERMANY (FRG) Tel: 06151-44823

Fall

International; **entry restricted (nomination by Academy members);** annual. 20,000 DM Georg-Buchner Prize for **Literature** (established 1923); 10,000 DM Johann-Heinrich-Voss Prize for **Literature Translation into German** (established 1958). Sponsored by German Academy of Language and Literature. Also sponsor nonfiction awards. Awards, Fall.

89

German Critics Prizes
Society of German Critics
Heinz Ohff, Chairman
Jenaer Stasse 17
D-1000 Berlin 31, WEST GERMANY (FRG) Tel: 030-8543352

Spring

National; **entry restricted to German-speaking countries** (selection by members); annual; established 1950. Critics Prizes to **German-speak-**

ing Fiction Writers. Purpose: to show critics choice of year's artistic production. Event, Spring.

90

Hermann-Hesse Prize
Forderungsgemeinschaft der Deutschen Kunst
E. Hoenselaers
Kantstrasse 6
7500 Karlsruhe 1, WEST GERMANY (FRG) Tel: 721-385751

June

International; entry open to all; triennial; established 1956. Named after Hermann Hesse 1946 winner of Nobel Prize for Literature. Purpose: to promote writers. Sponsored by Forderungsgemeinschaft der Deutchen Kunst, city of Karlsruhe. Average statistics: 100 entries, 6 countries, 10 semifinalists, 3 awards. Held in Karlsruhe, West Germany. Also sponsor Nonfiction Book, Essay, Monograph-Paper Contests.

BOOK CONTEST: In German Language, published or unpublished, 1 entry, 3 copies.

SHORT STORY CONTEST: In German Language. Requirements same as for Book.

AWARDS: (Including nonfiction contests) DM 10,000 Hermann-Hesse Prize, 2 DM 5000 Promotion Awards.

JUDGING: By 5 German writers-literature critics. May withhold awards. All entries reviewed in entirety. Entrants retain all rights. Not responsible for loss or damage.

ENTRY FEE: None. Sponsor pays return postage.

DEADLINES: Entry, July. Winners announced, May. Awards, June. Materials returned, July.

91

Campiello Literary Award
Associazione Degli Industriali
Ca' Mocenigo Gambara
Accademia 1056
30123 Venice, ITALY Tel: 85116

September

International; entry open to all; annual; established 1963. Sponsored by Association of Industrialists.

BOOK CONTEST: In Italian, first published May previous to May current year, Italian language narrative work, 19 copies. No scientific works.

AWARDS: Campiello Literary Award, Gold License Plate, other prizes.

JUDGING: Preliminary writer-critic jury selects 5 works. Final by 300-member foreign and domestic jury.

ENTRY FEE: None.

DEADLINES: Preliminary judging, May. Final judging and award, September.

92

Polish PEN Club Literary Prize
Juliusz Zulawski, President
Palac Kultury i Nauki
00-901 Warsaw, POLAND
Tel: 26-39-48

International; entry open to all; annual; established 1929. Purpose: to award excellent literary translations from Polish language. Sponsored by Polish PEN Club. Recognized by PEN International. Held in Warsaw. Also sponsor prizes for Polish translators, poets, fiction writers, editors.

BOOK CONTEST: Polish Literature Translation.

AWARDS: Not specified.

ENTRY FEE: Not specified.

DEADLINES: Not specified.

93

La Sonrisa Vertical Prize
Tusquets Editores
Mercedes Casanovas
Iradier, 24
Barcelona 17, SPAIN
Tel: 93-2474170

January

International; entry open to all. Sponsored by Tusquets Editores.

BOOK CONTEST: Spanish Language Erotic Novel. Requirements, restrictions not specified.

AWARDS: 500,000 pesetas and publication for Best Erotic Novel.

JUDGING: By 6 known writers, poets, film directors.

ENTRY FEE: Not specified.

DEADLINES: Entry, October. Award, January.

94

Royal Spanish Academy Prizes
Real Academia Espanola
Felipe IV, 4
Madrid, SPAIN Tel: 239-46-05

Various

International; entry open to various; annual (Cartagena, Rivadeneira Prizes), biennial (Pidal Prize), every 9 years (Alba Prize), established 1905 (Alba), 1929 (Cartagena), 1940 (Rivadeneira), 1958 (Pidal), 1973 (Lopez). Sponsored by Royal Academy of Spain, founded 1713. Publish world-famous dictionaries, literary works, scholarly journals. Also sponsor Fastenrath Prize (annual, founded 1909) of 70,000 pesetas for Poetry, Novel-Short Story Collection, Drama by Spaniards in Castilian; Manuel Espinosa y Cortina Prize (every 5 years, founded 1891) of 25,000 pts. for Drama by Spaniards; Manuel Llorente Prize (every 5 years, founded 1925) of 100,000 pts. for Spanish Patriotic Poem-Song in prose or verse; Alvarez Quintero Prize (biennial, founded 1949) of 87,500 pts. for Drama, Novel-Short Story Collection; XVII Marques de Cerralbo Prize (every 4 years, founded 1922) of 5800 pts. for Spanish Language-Literature; Maria Eulalia Asenjo Prize (every 10 years, founded 1934) of 25,000 pts. for Drama-Comedy Works; and San Gaspar Aid to Writers (annual, founded 1895) grants to writers, widows-families of writers.

BOOK CONTEST: Theme in Castilian *(Alba, Cartagena Prizes),* original; unpublished, in Spanish Castilian language *(Alba);* unpublished, by Spaniards or Spanish-Americans in Castilian language *(Cartagena),* various yearly themes.

Spanish Literature in Castilian *(Rivadeneira Prize),* unpublished.

Spanish Literature *(Pidal Prize),* in language of Spanish region-district studied.

Spanish Language *(Lopez Prize),* open to Spaniards, Spanish-Americans.

AWARDS: Duke of Alba Prize, 12,-000 pesetas. 2 Count of Cartagena Prizes, 60,000 pts. each. Rivadeneira Prizes, 2 at 20,000 pts. each. Ramon Menendez Pidal Prize, 30,000 pts. Nieto Lopez Prize, 150,000 pts.

ENTRY FEE: None.

DEADLINES: Various.

BOOK (Poetry)

Includes CONTEMPORARY, POETIC PLAY, SPANISH, TRANSLATION. (Also see other BOOK CATEGORIES.)

95

Academy of American Poets (AAP) Awards

177 East 87th Street
New York, New York 10028 U.S.A.
Tel: (212) 427-5665

Spring, Fall

National; **open to U.S. individuals** (Whiteman Award), **publishers** (Lamont Selection); annual; established 1954 (Lamont), 1975 (Whitman). Sponsored by AAP, nonprofit corporation founded 1934 to encourage, stimulate, foster American poetry. Have poetry readings, workshops, classes, Poets-in-the-Schools program. Publish *Poetry Pilot* (monthly newsletter). Also sponsor by-nomination-only $10,000 Fellowship for distinguished poetic achievement (founded 1946) and $1000 Harold Morton Landon Translation Award for published poetry translation into English (founded 1976). Cosponsor $100 College Poetry Prizes administered by 87 U.S. college-universities (founded 1954).

BOOK CONTEST: **Unpublished Poetry** *(Whitman Award),* original, any type, in book-length manuscript (50-100 pages). Open to U.S. citizen who has not published poetry book. **Second Volume Poetry** *(Lamont Selection)* unpublished, original, in English, 40-75 pages. Publisher submits maximum 2 manuscripts in triplicate, and agrees to publish selected manuscript within 8 months of award announcement. Open to living U.S. citizen with one published poetry book over 40 pages and 500 copies (may have published additional smaller-scale works).

AWARDS: $1000 Walt Whitman Award and publication by major publisher (1000 copies distributed by Academy). Lamont Poetry Selection, publication (1000 copies purchased by Academy for $3000).

JUDGING: By poet (Whitman), 3 poets (Lamont). Not responsible for loss or damage.

ENTRY FEE: None. Entrant pays postage.

DEADLINES: Entry, November (Whitman), May (Lamont). Awards, Spring, Fall.

96

American Poetry Series Poetry Award

Annex 21: American Poetry Series
College of Fine Arts
University of Nebraska at Omaha
Omaha, Nebraska 68182 U.S.A.

December

National; **entry open to U.S.;** annual. Sponsored by Annex 21: American Poetry Series. Publish 3 book-length poetry manuscripts in one volume annually.

BOOK CONTEST: **Poetry,** original; in English; typed single- or double-spaced on 8 1/2x11-inch paper, 35-40-page limit. 1 copy each entry. Require proof of sole ownership, 1-page biography.

ELIGIBILITY: U.S. citizens or residents. No authors of published poetry books over 40 pages in over 500-copy edition.

AWARDS: 3 winners ($500 each),

publication within 1 year, 5 copies to each winner.

JUDGING: May withhold awards, publication. Not responsible for loss or damage.

ENTRY FEE: $3 each. Entrant pays postage (include SASE).

DEADLINES: Entry, December-June. Nonwinners returned, October. Awards, December.

97

Anne Sexton Poetry Contest

Florida International University
Jim Hall, Department of English
Tamiami Campus
Miami, Florida 33199 U.S.A.
Tel: (305) 552-2874

Fall

International; entry open to all; annual. Sponsored by Florida International University and Carnegie Mellon University Press.

BOOK CONTEST: Poetry, original; any type, subject; 50-70 pages. Prior magazine publication encouraged. Not previously in chapbook or limited edition.

AWARDS: $500 and publication in hardback and paperback by Carnegie Mellon University Press. All entrants receive copy of winning book.

ENTRY FEE: $7. Entrant pays postage (include 2 SASEs).

DEADLINES: Entry, October only. Award, Fall. Publication, Winter. Entries returned, March.

98

Associated Writing Programs (AWP) Award Series in Poetry, Short Fiction Novels

Larry Moffi
Old Dominion University
Norfolk, Virginia 23508 U.S.A.
Tel: (804) 440-3839, 440-3840

Summer

National; **entry open to U.S. citizens;** annual; established 1974 (Poetry), 1977 (Short Fiction), 1979 (Novel). Poetry award formerly called AWP SERIES FOR CONTEMPORARY POETRY. Purpose: to encourage publication of fiction-poetry, especially by university presses. Sponsored by AWP, University Presses. Supported by AWP, NEA. Average statstics: 800 entries (500 in poetry), 12-30 finalists, 3 awards. Publish *INTRO* (annual anthology), *AWP Newsletter* (monthly). Second contacts: Stephen Dunn, Director, AWP Award Series in Poetry, English Department, Stockton State College, Pomona, New Jersey 08240; Charles Johnson, Director, AWP Award Series in Short Fiction, English Department, University of Washington, Seattle, Washington 98195; Stephen Goodwin, Director, AWP Award Series in the Novel, English Department, George Mason University, Fairfax, Virginia 22030.

BOOK CONTEST: Poetry, any style, subject. Submit 2 copies, standard format; brief bibliography, vita.

Short Fiction, any style, subject. Submit 2 copies, standard format, double-spaced; brief bibliography, vita.

Novel, any style, subject. Submit 1 copy, standard format, double-spaced; brief bibliography, vita.

ELIGIBILITY: Previously published poems or stories acceptable, but none published in an author's earlier collection. Double submissions permitted; photocopies acceptable.

AWARDS: Publication, invitation to read at AWP Meeting ($500 honorarium plus travel support), Best in each series. Sponsor attempts to place all finalists' manuscripts with participating presses.

JUDGING: Panel of professional readers selects 5-10 finalists, each series. Final judge selects winner, each series.

ENTRY FEE: $5 each, Novel. $3 each, Poetry and Short Fiction. Entrant pays postage (include SASE).

DEADLINES: Entry, October-December. Winners announced, Summer.

99

Devins Award for Poetry (Breakthrough Series)

University of Missouri Press
200 Lewis Hall
Columbia, Missouri 65211 U.S.A.

February-March

International; **entry restricted to published authors;** biennial (odd years). Purpose: to recognize exceptional works of poetry published through Breakthrough Series. Sponsored by University of Missouri Press.

BOOK CONTEST: Poetry, original; 64-104 pages; typed, double-spaced on 8 1/2x11-inch white bond, one side only, no tear sheets. Require contents page, biographical sketch, one-paragraph description, publishing credits.

ELIGIBILITY: Published authors not published in book form. Manuscript accepted for publication in Breakthrough Series (including short fiction, drama) eligible for Devins Award.

AWARDS: $500 Devins Award and invitation to read at University of Missouri-Kansas City. One collection chosen for publication in American Poetry Series.

JUDGING: By editorial committee based on acceptance for Breakthrough Series publication, exceptional quality.

ENTRY FEE: $7.50. Entrant pays postage.

DEADLINES: Entry, February-March. Publication following year.

100

Houghton Mifflin New Poetry Series

Houghton Mifflin Company
666 Third Avenue
New York, New York 10017 U.S.A.
Tel: (212) 599-5280

Periodic

International; entry open to all; periodic. Purpose: to present significant, original work that merits major attention. Sponsored by Houghton Mifflin (book publishers).

BOOK CONTEST: Poetry, unpublished; require 5-poem sample. Poets considered promising invited to submit manuscripts.

AWARDS: Cash advance and publication.

ENTRY FEE: None. Entrant pays postage.

DEADLINES: Entry throughout year. Competition periodically.

101

Juniper Prize Poetry Award Selection

University of Massachusetts Press
P.O. Box 429
Amherst, Massachusetts 01004
U.S.A.

April, May

International; entry open to all; annual. Sponsored by University of Massachusetts Press.

BOOK CONTEST: Poetry, unpublished; original, approximately 64 pages (about 50-60 poems); limit 1 per entrant. Poems published in journals, small chapbooks, anthologies acceptable. No translations, multiple authors, poems by employees or students of University of Massachusetts.

AWARDS: $1000 Juniper Prize (or 2 awards, $500 each) in lieu of first printing royalties.

JUDGING: Preliminary and final. May withhold award. Not responsible for loss or damage.

ENTRY FEE: $5.

DEADLINES: Entry, October. Awards, April-May. Publication, Fall-Winter.

102

National Poetry Series Open Competition

Charlotte Holmes, Coordinator
284 Fifth Avenue
New York, New York 10001 U.S.A.
Tel: (212) 736-2599

April

National; **entry open to U.S. citizens;** annual; established 1978. Purpose: to publish 5 books of poetry annually through 5 trade publishers; establish competition to guarantee selection of at least 2 books (invitation-only for other 3 books). Supported by Doubleday; E.P. Dutton; Harper & Row; Holt, Reinhart & Winston; Random House; Ford Foundation; Witter Bynner Foundation. Average statistics: 1300 entries, 100 finalists, 2 winners.

BOOK CONTEST: Poetry, unpublished as book; limit one manuscript per author; 48-64 pages; typed. No translations.

AWARDS: Publication by major publisher (2 books).

JUDGING: By 5-member National Poetry Series panel. Final by 2. Not responsible for loss or damage.

ENTRY FEE: $5. Entrant pays postage (include SASE).

DEADLINES: Entry, January. Materials, February. Judging, January-March. Winners announced, April. Publication, April of following year.

103

Poetry Book Award

Realities Library
Richard A. Soos, Jr., President
1976 Waverly Avenue
San Jose, California 95122 U.S.A.
Tel: (408) 251-9562

Summer

International; **entry restricted to English-language poets;** annual; established 1975. Sponsored by Realities Library, nonprofit corporation. Recognized by CCLA. Average statistics: 250 entries, 25 winners. Publish bimonthly *Occasional Review.*

BOOK CONTEST: Poetry, original, in English, any subject, style; 1 manuscript maximum per entrant; 20 pages, 1 poem per page, typewritten or printed. Pen and ink drawings by author acceptable. Require biographical material.

AWARDS: First Prize, $100 plus 50 copies of published chapbook with winning poems. Second and Third Prizes. Honorable Mentions. All entrants receive chapbook.

JUDGING: 6 judges read all entries in entirety.

ENTRY FEE: $5. Entrant pays postage.

DEADLINES: Entry, January. Manuscripts acknowledged, March. Awards, Summer.

104

Princeton University Press Poetry Series
Princeton University Press
Marjorie Sherwood, Literature Editor
Princeton, New Jersey 08540 U.S.A.
Tel: (609) 452-4900

Various

International; entry open to all; semiannual. Sponsored by Princeton University Press.

BOOK CONTEST: **Contemporary Poetry** *(Princeton),* unpublished; 60 pages minimum, double-spaced on 8 1/2x11-inch paper. Accept authors who have had some work previously published, but expect major portion of manuscript unpublished. Require listing of previous poetry publications. **Poetry Translated into English** *(Lockert),* unpublished, any length, classic or modern works. Require original language copy, introductory material.

AWARDS: Publication by Princeton University Press as Princeton Series of Contemporary Poetry, Lockert Library of Poetry in Translation.

JUDGING: Lockert judged on ability to stand as poetry in English, fidelity to tone and spirit of original (rather than literal accuracy), importance of translated poet.

ENTRY FEE: None.

DEADLINES: Manuscripts reviewed, February, August (Lockert); June, December (Princeton). Final Selection, April, October (Lockert); August, March (Princeton).

105

Quarterly Review of Literature Poetry Book Series
Quarterly Review of Literature
Renee Weiss, Editor
26 Haslet Avenue
Princeton, New Jersey 08540 U.S.A.

Semi-Annual

International; entry open to all; semi-annual; established 1979. Sponsored by *Quarterly Review of Literature* (QRL).

BOOK CONTEST: **Poetry, Poetic Play,** 40-70 pages; may be single long poem (20 or more pages), group of connected poems, selection of miscellaneous poems, poetic play, or poetry translations.

AWARDS: $500 each to 4-5 manuscripts selected for publication.

JUDGING: By QRL editors.

ENTRY FEE: Subscription to series (paperback, $15; hardback, $20). Entrant pays return postage.

DEADLINES: Entry December, May.

106

Wings Press Chapbook Competition
Wings Press
Arnold Perrin, Editor
RFD 2 Box 325
Belfast, Maine 04915 U.S.A.
Tel: (207) 338-2005

Quarterly

International; entry open to all; quarterly; established 1981. Purpose: to publish readable, understandable poetry that falls between the extremes of sentamentality and obscurantism. Sponsored by Wings Press, established 1976. Recognized by Maine

Writers & Publishers Alliance, AAP. Average statistics: 200 entrants, 3 countries, 3 finalists, 1 award. Publish *Wings Press Chapbook* (200 copies).

BOOK CONTEST: Poetry, published poems acceptable if author holds rights; 20 pages minimum, 1 per page (except Haiku), unlimited entry. Require previous publication information, permission to reprint if poems previously published.

AWARDS: Winner: $50, publication, 5 copies, 10% royalties, right to purchase copies at 40% discount. Finalists: 10% royalties.

JUDGING: By editor. Winning entries copyrighted in author's name. Not responsible for loss or damage.

ENTRY FEE: $3 each. Entrant pays postage (SASE).

DEADLINES: Entry, March, June, September, December. Awards, April, July, October, January.

107

Yale Series of Younger Poets Competition

Yale University Press
Mary Alice Galligan, Editorial Assistant
92A Yale Station
New Haven, Connecticut 06520
U.S.A.

February

National; **entry restricted to U.S. under age 40;** annual; established 1905. Sponsored by Yale University Press.

BOOK CONTEST: First Poetry, 48-64 pages, original, any type or subject; 1 manuscript per entrant; typewritten, 1 per page. Require table of contents, biographical data.

ELIGIBILITY: American writers under age 40 (at time of manuscript submission) who have not published poetry volume (300-copy maximum private limited editions and newspaper-magazine published excepted). No illustrations or translations.

AWARDS: Winner published by Yale University Press with royalties. May withhold award.

JUDGING: No individual criticism. Not responsible for loss or damage.

ENTRY FEE: $5. Entrant pays postage.

DEADLINES: Entry, February. Manuscripts acknowledged, April. Winner announced in public media.

108

Commonwealth Poetry Prize

Commonwealth Institute
Librarian (Poetry Prize)
Kensington High Street
London W8 6NQ, ENGLAND
Tel: 01-602-3252

Summer

International; **entry restricted to published authors from Commonwealth countries;** annual; established 1972. Purpose: to promote poetry in English by authors from Commonwealth countries other than Britain. Sponsored by Commonwealth Institute, National Book League. Average statistics: 40 entries, 20 countries. Have winner reception.

BOOK CONTEST: First Poetry, published between July previous, July contest year; in English. Submit 7 copies each book, no manuscripts. Include short author biography.

ELIGIBILITY: Publishers submit first published book by author from Commonwealth country other than Britain (nationals from other countries living in Britain are eligible).

AWARDS: 500 pounds, Best First Published Poetry Book.

JUDGING: All entries read by seven judges. Not responsible for loss or damage.

ENTRY FEE: None. Entrant pays postage.

DEADLINES: Entry, June. Judging, July. Awards, August-September.

109

"Lovers of Teruel" International Poetry Contests
Excmo. Ayuntamiento de Teruel
Teruel, SPAIN

Summer

International; entry open to all; annual; established 1961. Purpose: to honor lovers of Teruel. Sponsored by Spanish cities of Zaragoza, Aragon, Rioja.

BOOK CONTEST: **Spanish Poetry,** unpublished, in Spanish; typed, 3 copies.

POETRY CONTEST: **Spanish Poetry Various Categories.** Requirements same as for Book. Categories: Love Poem (any form, style; may also be entered as part of Book Contest); Sonnet (love theme); By Native Teruel Poet (any theme, style).

AWARDS: 50,000 pesetas "Lovers of Teruel" Award and publication (Book). 25,000 pts. Natural Flower Award (Love Poem). 15,000 pts. (Sonnet). 10,000 pts. Young Poetry Award (By Native Teruel Poet). Winners must be present to recieve awards; sponsor pays travel, lodging expenses.

JUDGING: By expert panel. May withhold awards. Sponsor may publish with author's permission.

ENTRY FEE: Not specified. Entrant pays postage (include SASE).

DEADLINES: Entry, May. Event, Summer. Materials returned, October.

BOOK (Regional)

About or from a region. Book, Play, Poetry, Short Story, Script, including APPALACHIA, LOUISIANA, NEW JERSEY, NEW ENGLAND, OHIO, TEXAS, WESTERN, MIDWESTERN, ALBERTA, MONTREAL, AUSTRALIA, SCOTLAND, (Also see other BOOK CATEGORIES.)

110

Friends of American Writers Awards
Mrs. Gene F. Lederer, Chair
755 North Merrill
Park Ridge, Illinois 60068 U.S.A.
Tel: (312) 823-5433

April

Regional; **entry restricted to publishers of Midwestern authors, books;** annual; established 1928. Purpose: to recognize beginning authors in adult and juvenile writing. Sponsored and supported by Friends of American Writers (Chicago, Illinois), founded 1922 to study American literature; encourage, promote high standards among new authors. Held at awards luncheon in Chicago. Second contact: Mrs. William Wiener, 2650 Lakeview Avenue, Chicago, Illinois 60614; tel: (312) 871-5143.

BOOK CONTEST: **Midwestern Adult, Juvenile,** published during previous year; 2 copies.

ELIGIBILITY: By author of not over

6 books (who has not received monetary award of $1000 or more), and is native, current resident, or previous 5-year resident of Arkansas, Illinois, Indiana, Iowa, Kansas, Kentucky, Michigan, Minnesota, Missouri, North Dakota, Nebraska, Ohio, Oklahoma, South Dakota, Tennessee, Wisconsin; or author of book whose locale is Midwestern.

AWARDS: Adult: $1000 First, $600 Second Place (may divide) to authors. Juvenile: $500 First, 2 $250 Second Places to authors. 2 $250 or more Distinguished Recognition Award Certificates to publishers.

JUDGING: By 16 judges.

ENTRY FEE: Not specified.

DEADLINES: Entry, December. Awards, April.

111

Golden Spur Awards

Western Writers of America (WWA)
Rex Bundy, Secretary-Treasurer
Route 1, Box 35-H
Victor, Montana 59875 U.S.A.
Tel: (406) 961-3612

June

International; entry open to all; annual; established 1954. Purpose: to encourage high achievement in Western writing. Sponsored and supported by WWA (founded 1951). Held 3-4 days in June at annual WWA Convention, location varies. Publish *The Round-Up* (monthly) about Western writing.

BOOK CONTEST: **Western,** published in English in previous calendar year; 40,000 words minimum. Accept books of short stories or poems all by same author, printed for first time in previous year, with no previous publication. No anthologies, photograph collections, or drawings, maps, diagrams with limited text. Categories: Traditional Western Novel (Old West, 1860-1900 period), For Young People.

SHORT SUBJECT CONTEST: **Western,** poem, article, or short story of 20,000 words maximum, published in English in previous calendar year. Individual items from book-magazine acceptable. No complete magazines.

SCRIPT CONTEST: **Western Motion Picture, Television,** first released for public viewing during current calendar year.

ELIGIBILITY: Living authors. Enter one category only, 3 copies each. No subsidized vanity publications.

AWARDS: Golden Spur Award, outstanding each category. Scrolls to 3 finalists, each category. Duplicate awards, if tie.

JUDGING: By 3 judges, each category; based on written text only. No award if less than 10 entries in category. No entries returned.

ENTRY FEE: None.

DEADLINES: Entry, December. Judging, March. Awards, June.

112

Louisiana Literary Award

Louisiana Library Association (LLA)
Chris Thomas, Executive Director
P.O. Box 131
Baton Rouge, Louisiana 70821
U.S.A.

Periodic

International; **entry restricted (selection by LLA);** periodic. Medallion to **Book about Louisiana.** Sponsored by LLA.

113

New Jersey Authors Awards
New Jersey Institute of Technology
Dr. Herman A. Estrin, Director
315 Henry Street
Scotch Plains, New Jersey 07076
U.S.A. Tel: (201) 889-7633

April

Regional; **entry restricted to New Jersey, New York, Pennsylvania authors (nominated by New Jersey Publishers);** annual; established 1967. Purpose: to award New Jersey authors for their published work. Sponsored by New Jersey Institute of Technology, Division of Continuing Education and Department of Humanities. Average statistics: 100 entrants, 100 awards, 400 attendance. Held at annual New Jersey Authors Luncheon. Tickets: $10-$15. Also sponsor New Jersey Writers Conference, Annual Poetry Contest, and Technical Communications Skills Workshop.

BOOK AWARD: New Jersey Author, published.

ELIGIBILITY: Publishers complete nomination for each New Jersey author.

AWARDS: Citation. Winners serve as consultants during New Jersey Writers Conference.

JUDGING: By publishers and director of New Jersey Writers Conference.

ENTRY FEE: None.

DEADLINES: Entry, June. Judging, September-March. Awards, April.

114

Ohioana Book Awards
Martha Kinney Cooper Ohioana
Library Association
James P. Barry, Director
Room 1105 Ohio Department
Building
65 South Front Street
Columbus, Ohio 42315 U.S.A.
Tel: (614) 466-3831

Fall

International; **entry restricted to Ohioan authors-subjects;** annual; established 1929. Purpose: to honor books by Ohio authors or about Ohio-Ohioans (Fiction, Technology, Ohio Scene). Sponsored by 1400-member Martha Kinney Cooper Ohioana Library Association, established 1929 to preserve-promote Ohio literary, musical, cultural heritage. Also sponsor Pegasus Award to Ohioan in Cultural Fields (periodic, established 1964), Distinguished Service Citations, Career Medals for Ohio authors, artists, composers. Publish *Ohioana Quarterly* magazine. Held during annual Ohioana Day Luncheon in Fall. Also sponsor Nonfiction Book Contest.

BOOK CONTEST: Ohio Fiction, Poetry, published by Ohioan (born or lived 5 years in Ohio) on any subject, or by non-Ohioan about Ohio-Ohioans; 2 copies.

AWARDS: Ohioana Book Awards. Florence Roberts Head Memorial Book Award. Awards are certificates and medals.

JUDGING: By committee of 4-5.

ENTRY FEE: None.

DEADLINES: Judging, Spring. Awards, Fall.

115

Sarah Josepha Hale Award
Richards Library
Jean Michie, Librarian
58 North Main Street
Newport, New Hampshire 03773
U.S.A. Tel: (603) 863-3430

August

Regional; **entry restricted to New England (nomination by Library);** annual; established 1956. Bronze Medal to Individual for **Literature-Letters associated with New England.** Named after Sarah Josepha Hale, native of Newport and editor. Sponsored and supported by Friends of Richards Library (founded 1888). Award, August.

116

Texas Institute of Letters Literary Awards

Marshall Terry, Secretary-Treasurer
SMU Box 3143
Dallas, Texas 75275 U.S.A.

March-April

International; **entry restricted to Texas authors-subjects;** annual; established 1945 (Voertman), 1960 (Jones). Sponsored by Texas Institute of Letters, founded 1936. Also sponsor Nonfiction Book and Newspaper-Magazine Contests.

BOOK CONTEST: Texas Various; 3 copies. Categories: Fiction, For Children, Book Design, Poetry.

SHORT STORY CONTEST: Texas Any Subject, published in book or periodical, 3 copies.

ELIGIBILITY: Published during previous year, by Texas author (born, present resident, or spent formative years in Texas) or on Texas subject.

AWARDS: $1000 Jesse H. Jones Award, Fiction. $200 Steck-Vaughn Award, Book for Children (including nonfiction entries, formerly known as Cokesbury Book Store Award). $250 Short Story Award. $250 Collectors' Institute Award, Book Design (including nonfiction entries). $200 Voertman's Poetry Award, Poetry Book.

JUDGING: By 3 judges each category. Preference to books on Texas or Southwest.

ENTRY FEE: None.

DEADLINES: Entry, January. Awards, March-April.

117

W. D. Weatherford Award Competition

Berea College
Thomas Parrish, Chairman
Appalachian Center
College P.O. Box 2336
Berea, Kentucky 40404 U.S.A.
Tel: (606) 986-9341, ext. 513, 453

April

National; **entry open to U.S.;** annual; established 1970. Named for Dr. W. D. Weatherford, Appalachian author. Sponsored by Appalachian Center, Hutchins Library of Berea College. Also sponsor Appalachian Studies Fellowships.

BOOK CONTEST: Appalachia, published during previous year; single or series, any length; 1 copy.

WRITING CONTEST: Appalachia, published during previous year (article, story); any length; 1 copy.

ELIGIBILITY: Writing of any kind, tone, point of view.

AWARDS: $500 to book, shorter piece illustrating problems, personalitites, unique qualities of Appalachian South. $200 Special Award to work or ongoing works making special contribution to region.

JUDGING: By 7 judges.

ENTRY FEE: None.

DEADLINES: Entry, December. Awards, April.

118

Western Heritage Awards
National Cowboy Hall of Fame and Western Heritage Center
1700 Northeast 63rd Street
Oklahoma City, Oklahoma 73111
U.S.A. Tel: (405) 478-2250

April

International; entry open to all; annual; established 1961. Purpose: to honor drama and heritage of Old West. Sponsored by and held at National Cowboy Hall of Fame and Western Heritage Center (world's largest Western lore exhibit), founded 1965 to perpetuate Western traditions in authentic, artistic exhibits. Also sponsor music category, Western Performer's Hall of Fame Awards (to 1 living, 1 deceased Western contributor).

BOOK CONTEST: **Western Fiction,** published in previous 2 years, 6 copies. One category per entry. Categories: Novel, Juvenile, Art Book.

SHORT STORY CONTEST: **Western.** Requirements same as for Book.

POETRY CONTEST: **Western.** Requirements same as for Book.

AWARDS: Wrangler Trophies (replica of Charles Russell sculpture) for Excellence in Western Achievement, each category.

JUDGING: By panel, based on artistic merit, integrity, achievement in portraying spirit of Western pioneers. May change categories, withhold awards. Sponsor retains all winners for permanent collection.

ENTRY FEE: None. Entrant pays postage.

DEADLINES: Entry, February. Event, April.

119

Miles Franklin Literary Award
Permanent Trustee Company
Box 4270, G.P.O.
Sydney, New South Wales 2001, AUSTRALIA Tel: 232-4400, ext. 250

Spring

International; entry open to all; annual; established 1957. Named after Miles Franklin, author. Purpose: to advance, improve Australian literature; give incentive, monetary aid to authors. Sponsored and supported by Permanent Trustee Company (23-25 O'Connell Street, Sydney, New South Wales 2000, Australia).

BOOK CONTEST: **Australian Life,** published; unlimited entry. Submit 6 copies.

PLAY CONTEST: **Australian Life,** produced; unlimited entry. Submit 6 copies. No farces, musical comedy.

SCRIPT CONTEST: **Australian Life Radio, Television.** Requirements, restrictions same as for Play.

ELIGIBILITY: By 1 or more authors, published-produced during previous calendar year, presenting Australian life in any of its phases. Sponsor must be notified of entry titles within 28 days following publication-production, receive copies within 2 months after publication-production (by January 31 for entries published-produced in December). Novels given preference over plays, scripts.

AWARDS: $2500 Australian, Best Entry.

JUDGING: By 5 judges. Based on literary merit in presentation of Australian life. May divide, withhold award.

ENTRY FEE: None.

DEADLINES: Entry, January. Award, Spring.

120

"The Age" Book of the Year Award

Stuart Sayers, Literary Editor
250 Spencer Street
P.O. Box 257C G.P.O.
Melbourne 3001, AUSTRALIA
Tel: (03) 600421, ext. 2232

November

National; **entry restricted to Australian Citizens;** annual; established 1974. Award to **Australian Identity-Concerns Book,** including Novel, Short Story Collection, Poetry, published November-October award year. No children's books, plays, anthologies. Submit 4 copies each entry, 4 maximum per publisher. Purpose: to encourage, promote Australian writing of literary merit. Sponsored by *The Age.* Awards, November.

121

Alberta Culture Literary Awards

Alberta Culture, Film and Literary Arts
John Patrick Gillese, Director
12th Floor, CN Tower
1004-104 Avenue
Edmonton, Alberta T5J 0K5
CANADA Tel: (403) 427-2554

Spring

Regional; **entry restricted to Alberta residents;** biennial (First Novel), annual (For Young People); established 1972 (Novel), 1980 (For Young People). Purpose: to find, launch outstanding Alberta authors. Sponsored and supported by Alberta Culture, General Publishing, Clarke Irwin Publishing (For Young People), Macmillan Publishing Company (First Novel). Average statistics: 50 entries (First Novel). Have writers' workshops, correspondence courses, consultative and financial services to Alberta authors-publishers. Publish *Alberta Authors Bulletin* (bimonthly newsletter). Also sponsor Play, Nonfiction, and Regional History Book Contests, Literary Grants.

BOOK CONTEST: **Alberta First Novel for Adults,** unpublished, no publication pending; by unpublished novelist; any theme-subject-setting; preference to Canadian background novels; 60-100,000 words; typed double-spaced on 8 1/2x11-inch paper; 1 maximum per entrant.

Alberta for Young People, unpublished, any subject, 1 entry; illustrations unnecessary. No entries by children. Categories: For Young Adults (to age 16; 40,000 words average); For Younger Readers (age 8-12; 12-20,000 words).

ELIGIBILITY: Canadian citizens or landed immigrants, living minimum 24 months in Alberta in 3 years prior to entry date.

AWARDS: $2500 Best First Novel (Search for a New Alberta Novelist) Award and $1500 advance against royalties from Macmillan Company of Canada if publishable; $1000 and $500 advance, each finalist. $2500 Writing for Young People Award (including fiction-nonfiction). Other For Young People entries accepted for publication receive $500 award, $500 advance.

JUDGING: By 3 judges. May withhold awards. Nonwinning entries returned. Not responsible for loss or damage.

ENTRY FEE: None. Sponsor pays return postage (registered mail).

DEADLINES: Entry, December. Awards, Spring.

122

Grand Prize for Literature of the City of Montreal
Greater Montreal Council of Arts
Ferdinand F. Biondi, Secretary General
2, Complexe Desjardins
C.P. 129
Montreal, Quebec H5B 1E6 CANADA
Tel: (514) 872-2074, 866-4114

April

International; **entry restricted to Montreal published authors;** annual; established 1965. Sponsored by Greater Montreal Council of Arts, established 1956 to subsidize nonprofit artistic groups in Montreal (communication-film, literature, theater, music, visual-plastic art, ballet). Held during Montreal International Book Fair at Centre Pierre Charbonneau in the Olympic Complex. Also sponsor Nonfiction Book Contest.

BOOK CONTEST: Montreal Published, first published during previous year in Montreal, 5 copies. No educational texts, books containing advertising or previously published contents. Categories: Fiction, Novels, Short Stories; Theater, Poetry; English Language.

AWARDS: $3000 Grand Prize for Literature (includes nonfiction).

JUDGING: Preliminary by 3 judges, each category; final by 7 judges. Judges keep entries.

ENTRY FEE: Not specified.

DEADLINES: Entry, January. Award, April.

123

Frederick Niven Award
International PEN Scottish Centre
Mary Baxter, Secretary
18 Crown Terrace
Glasgow G12 9ES, SCOTLAND
Tel: 041-357-0327

Triennial

National; **entry restricted to Scottish writers;** triennial; established 1956. Frederick Niven Award of 500 pounds to **Novel by Scottish-Born, Resident Author (published, full-length novel; entry by publisher). Sponsored by Scottish Arts Council.**

124

Scottish Arts Council Literature Awards
Tim Mason, Director
19 Charlotte Square
Edinburgh EH2 4DF, SCOTLAND
Tel: 031-226-6051

January

International; **entry open to publishers;** annual. Sponsored by Scottish Arts Council. Also sponsor biennial Neil Gunn International Fellowship (established 1973) to international fiction writers (not open to entry, selection by Council); 4000 pound one-year Writers Fellowships at Dundee, Glasgow Universities.

BOOK CONTEST: Scottish-Scotland, published November of previous to October of current year; of Scottish interest or by Scottish citizen, resident author; 1 copy. Require biography. Categories: By Established Author, First By New Author.

AWARDS: Scottish Arts Council Book Awards, 500 pounds each.

JUDGING: By writer-critic reading panel. Based on literary merit.

ENTRY FEE: None.

DEADLINES: Awards, January.

BOOK (Other)

Book, Play, Poetry, including AMERICANISM, DOG, GEOGRAPHY, HEART DISEASE, LEGAL-JUDICIAL, LITERATURE-IDEAS.

125

Banta Award

Wisconsin Library Association (WLA)
Literary Awards Chairman
1922 University Avenue
Madison, Wisconsin 53705 U.S.A.

Open

State; **entry restricted to Wisconsin authors;** annual; established 1974. Named after George Banta Company. Purpose: to recognize literary achievement by Wisconsin author. Sponsored by WLA. Supported by George Banta Company, Menasha, Wisconsin. Held at WLA annual conference.

BOOK CONTEST: **Literature-Ideas,** published in previous calendar year by current or previous resident of Wisconsin; 50 pages minimum, copyrighted, contributing to world of literature-ideas. No texts, specialized or technical works.

AWARDS: Banta Award Medal for outstanding literary achievement by Wisconsin author.

JUDGING: By WLA.

ENTRY FEE: None.

DEADLINES: Open.

126

Dog Writers' Association of America (DWAA) Writing Competition

Susan Jeffries, Second Vice-President
1616 13th Avenue S.W.
Great Falls, Montana 59404 U.S.A.
Tel: (406) 761-1871

February

International; entry open to all; annual; established 1940s. Purpose: to promote, honor excellence in writing about dogs. Sponsored and supported by DWAA, founded 1935. Average statistics: 300 entries, 50 awards. Held at DWAA annual banquet, New York City. Also sponsor grants to college students with background in dog activities; special Public Service Awards for educational or promotional efforts.

BOOK CONTEST: **Dog Fiction,** first published between November previous year and October current year, 3 entries maximum.

POETRY CONTEST: **Dog,** published in any medium, mounted on 8 1/2x11-inch paper. Other requirements same as for Book.

AWARDS: Certificates for "Best," Certificates of Merit, Honorable Mentions.

JUDGING: All entries read in entirety by dog journalism experts. May withhold awards. No entries returned. Not responsible for loss or damage.

ENTRY FEE: $5 each.

DEADLINES: Entry, October. Winners notified, January. Awards, February.

127

Freedoms Foundation National Awards

Freedoms Foundation at Valley Forge
Valley Forge, Pennsylvania 19481 U.S.A. Tel: (215) 933-8825

February

National; **entry open to U.S.;** annual; established 1949. Purpose: to recognize deeds that support America, contribute to citizenship, suggest solutions to problems. Sponsored by Freedoms Foundation at Valley Forge, nonprofit, nonpolitical, nonsectarian. Recognized by National Association of Secondary School Principals. Held during George Washington Birthday Celebration at Valley Forge and at local ceremonies. Have sermon, public-youth public addresses; college campus-community program; government-national activity; economic education; teacher, educator, individual contribution awards. Also sponsor other media contests; seminars; outreach programs; George Washington Plaque to Outstanding Individual; Principal School Award.

BOOK CONTEST: Americanism. Require comprehensive review or precis, 10 pages maximum.

AWARDS: George Washington Honor Medals, Certificates; Valley Forge Honor Certificates. One Award per person per category. Special Awards.

JUDGING: By national jury of state Supreme Court justices, patriotic, civic, service, veterans organization officers. May change classifications, amounts, withhold awards; retain or have access to winners for 3 years minimum for awards library research, display, convention, staff use.

ENTRY FEE: None.

DEADLINES: Entry, October. Judging, November. Awards, December. Event, February.

128

Gavel Awards

American Bar Association (ABA), Division of Communications
Dean Tyler Jenks, Special Events Director
77 South Wacker Drive
Chicago, Illinois 60606 U.S.A.
Tel: (312) 621-9249

August

National; **entry restricted to U.S. news and entertainment media;** annual; established 1958. Purpose: to recognize U.S. news, entertainment media that educate, increase public understanding of American legal and judicial system; promote correction, improvement of laws, courts, law enforcement, legal goals. Sponsored and supported by 270,000-member ABA. Average statistics: 378 entries, 235 entrants, 25 Gavel Awards, 42 Certificates. Held at ABA annual meeting. Tickets: $15-$20.

BOOK CONTEST: Legal and Judicial, published. Require 4 copies, synopsis, subject summary (including book review comments), biography. No legal publications or textbooks.

PLAY CONTEST: Legal and Judicial, produced. Require 4 copies of script, synopsis, objectives, biography.

ELIGIBILITY: Published or presented January to December of previous year, 5 entries maximum. Entries should relate to work of the bench, bar, law enforcement, law itself; current, historical, or futuristic.

AWARDS: Silver Gavel Awards (trophies and plaques) for outstanding contribution to public understanding of American law and justice, top executives, each winning organization. Gavel Awards Merit Certificate to noteworthy examples of distinguished public service.

JUDGING: By lawyers, judges, teachers. Based on informational value, educational merit, creativity, thoroughness, reportorial and technical skills, impact. May withhold awards.

ENTRY FEE: None.

DEADLINES: Entry, February. Awards, August.

129

Geographic Society of Chicago Publication Awards

Mildred F. Mitchell, Executive Secretary
7 South Dearborn Street
Chicago, Illinois 60603 U.S.A.
Tel: (312) 726-5293

Spring

International; entry open to all; annual; established 1951. Purpose: to encourage broader public interest in geography. Sponsored by Geographic Society of Chicago.

BOOK CONTEST: **Geography,** published.

ELIGIBILITY: Published during previous calendar year, of popular nature about geography.

AWARDS: 1-3 hand-made Scroll Awards.

JUDGING: By committee. Based on scientific merit, popular appeal.

ENTRY FEE: None.

DEADLINES: Entry, January. Awards, Spring.

130

Howard W. Blakeslee Awards

American Heart Association (AHA)
Howard L. Lewis, Chairman
7320 Greenville Avenue
Dallas, Texas 75231 U.S.A.
Tel: (214) 750-5340

December

National; **entry open to U.S.;** annual; established 1952. Named for Howard W. Blakeslee, founder of National Association of Science Writers. Purpose: to encourage mass communication reporting on heart and circulatory diseases. Sponsored by AHA. Held at AHA meeting.

BOOK CONTEST: **Heart Disease.** Require objectives, audience.

ELIGIBILITY: Published in U.S. or territories from March previous year to February current year. No employees or materials of AHA affiliates, local heart organizations.

AWARDS: Plaque and $500 for outstanding public reporting on heart and blood vessel diseases, each winner.

JUDGING: Based on accuracy, significance, skill, originality, achievements.

ENTRY FEE: None.

DEADLINES: Entry, May. Awards, December.

BOOK DESIGN

Book, Magazine, Publication, and Periodical Design, including BOOKMAKING, COVER, GRAPHICS, ILLUSTRATIONS, JACKET, TYPOGRAPHY.

131

Art Directors Club Annual Exhibtion
488 Madison Avenue
New York, New York 10022 U.S.A.

March

International; **entry open to U.S., Canada;** annual; established 1922. Purpose: to search for new expressions, techniques, breakthroughs, talents, directions. Sponsored by New York Art Directors Club. Publish *Art Directors Club Annual.* Also sponsor Newspaper-Magazine Advertising, Promotion-Graphic Design, Poster, Art-Illustration, Photography, and Television Contests.

BOOK DESIGN CONTEST: Book-Jacket Design. Categories: Trade, Children's (Book, Jacket).

ELIGIBILITY: First Produced in U.S. or Canada in current calendar year. No foreign market publications.

AWARDS: Gold, Silver Medals (1 per entry), Distinctive Merit Awards, each category. Merit Award and publication in Annual for each accepted for exhibition.

JUDGING: May withhold awards. No entries returned. Not responsible for loss or damage.

ENTRY FEE: $12 Single, $25 Campaign. $55 (Single), $85 (Campaign) Hanging Fee for entries accepted.

DEADLINES: Entry, November. Winners notified, March.

132

Communication Arts Magazine CA Design and Advertising Exhibition
Jean A. Coyne
410 Sherman Avenue
P.O. Box 10300
Palo Alto, California 94303 U.S.A.
Tel: (415) 326-6040

January

International; entry open to all; annual; established 1959. Sponsored by *Communication Arts Magazine* (bimonthly design publication, 52,000 circulation), considered largest juried competition. Average statistics: 19,000 entries.

BOOK DESIGN CONTEST: Design, printed between July previous and July current year, unmounted. Request English translation. No originals. Divisions: Single, Campaign (5 maximum). Categories: Complete Unit, Cover-Jacket.

AWARDS: Award of excellence Certificates, publication in *CA Annual* (November-December issue).

JUDGING: By designers, art directors, writers. No entries returned. Not responsible for loss or damage.

ENTRY FEE: $6 (single), $12 (campaign, series). Entrant pays postage (include SASE).

DEADLINES: Entry, June. Winners notified, October. Awards, January.

133

Creativity Awards Show
Art Direction Magazine
Ray Morrison, Director
10 East 39th Street, 6th Floor
New York, New York 10016 U.S.A.
Tel: (212) 889-6500

Fall

International; **entry restricted to professionals;** annual; established 1969. Purpose: to record trends in advertising design, art illustration, photography, TV commercials; reward, publicize talented art directors. Sponsored by *Art Direction Magazine,* founded 1949. Average statistics: 15,000 entries, 800 winners. Have Creativity Show (annual 1 week showcase at New York Coliseum for best work), exhibitions in major cities. Publish *Creativity* (international annual of awards show), *Advertising Techniques Magazine, Graphic Arts Buyer.*

BOOK-MAGAZINE DESIGN CONTEST: Cover Design, printed between May previous and May current year; unmounted; copies only. Categories: Book Cover Design; Magazine Cover Design.

AWARDS: Creativity Certificate of Distinction, exhibition at Annual Creativity Show.

JUDGING: Art Directors judged on concept, design. Artists, illustrators, photographers judged on excellence of various fields. No entries returned.

ENTRY FEE: $5 (single spread), $10 (3 or more), $9 (single), $18 (3 or more). Hanging Fee for winners.

DEADLINES: Entry, April. Winners notified, July.

134

DESI Awards Competition

Graphics Design: USA Magazine
Louis J. Boasi, Director
32 Gansvoort Street
New York, New York 10014 U.S.A.
Tel: (212) 675-5867

Spring

National; **entry open to U.S. citizens;** annual; established 1977. DESI is derived from "design." Purpose: to showcase excellent professional-academic graphic design. Sponsored by *Graphics Design: USA.* Exhibition held in New York City for 2 weeks. Publish awards issue of *Graphics Design: USA.* Second contact: Valerie Stewart, Graphics Design: USA, 120 East 56th Street, New York, New York 10022.

BOOK-PUBLICATION DESIGN CONTEST: Design, Cover, printed previous calendar year. Categories: Book Design, Cover; Publication Design, Cover.

AWARDS: DESI Certificates, each winner. Exhibition at Graphics Design Show.

JUDGING: By 4 judges in graphic design. No entries returned (unless requested). Not responsible for loss or damage.

ENTRY FEE: $8 (single piece, slide). $50 (single), $30 (slide) Hanging Fee required from winners. Entrant pays postage (include SASE).

DEADLINES: Entry, January. Judging, February-March. Awards, April.

135

Graphic Arts Awards Competition

Printing Industries of America
Katherine W. Rose, Assistant to Director
1730 North Lynn Street
Arlington, Virginia 22209 U.S.A.
Tel: (703) 841-8154

November

International; entry open to all; annual; established 1953. Purpose: to promote high standards in printed material production-design. Sponsored by Eastman Kodak Company, Harris Corporation, Printing Industries of America. Average statistics: 4500 entrants. Held in Arlington, Virginia. Have folder-broadside, booklet, catalog, direct mail, business-annual report, point-of-purchase, business form, greeting-pictorial postcard, carton-container, label-wrap, stationery, calendar, miscellaneous specialty, poster categories.

BOOK DESIGN CONTEST: **Graphics-Design,** published. Categories: Juvenile, Trade-Other, Yearbooks-School Textbooks, Book Jackets.

MAGAZINE DESIGN CONTEST: **Graphics-Design,** published. Categories: Magazines-House Organs (1-2 colors, 3 or more colors), Magazine Inserts.

ELIGIBILITY: Printed March previous to April current year. Divisions: National (U.S., Canada, Mexico), International (other countries).

AWARDS: Best of Category Plaque Award, each category. Award Certificates to Runners-Up.

JUDGING: By graphic arts experts. Based on technical reproduction quality, design, art, typography, general layout. May reclassify entries. No entries returned.

ENTRY FEE: $10 each. $35 additional, each winner.

DEADLINES: Entry, May. Judging, June. Awards, November.

136

Midwestern Books Competition
University of Kentucky
Lawrence S. Thompson, Project Director
Department of Classics
Lexington, Kentucky 40506 U.S.A.
Tel: (606) 266-4056

January

Regional; **entry restricted to Midwestern book publishers, printers, designers;** annual; established 1955. Purpose: to recognize outstanding typography and design of Midwest books. Sponsored by Department of Classics, University of Kentucky. Average statistics: 400 entries, 40 entrants.

BOOK-PERIODICAL DESIGN CONTEST: **Midwestern Design, Typography,** published in current year; pamphlet-periodical in paper covers acceptable, 1 copy each. Published or printed and designed in Ohio, Indiana, West Virginia, Illinois, Kentucky, Michigan, Minnesota, Wisconsin, Iowa, Missouri, Kansas, Nebraska, North and South Dakota, Pittsburgh (no other part of Pennsylvania). Submit (in triplicate) full production information.

AWARDS: Various Midwestern Books of the Year, exhibited internationally.

JUDGING: Based on typography, design, production quality; content considered only as design has aided in conveying spirit of books, aims of author. All entries kept in University of Kentucky Library. Winning publishers furnish additional copies for exhibition.

ENTRY FEE: $4 first, $2 each additional.

DEADLINES: Entry before Christmas. Awards, January.

137

Society of Illustrators Annual Exhibition
Terry Brown, Curator
128 East 63rd Street
New York, New York 10021 U.S.A.
Tel: (212) 838-2560

January-April

International; entry open to all; annual; established 1959. Purpose: to present best in illustration art. Sponsored by Society of Illustrators. Held in Society's Gallery in New York. Have advertising, institutional illustration categories. Also sponsor Student Scholarship Competition; Newspaper-Magazine Design, Film and Video Contests.

BOOK DESIGN CONTEST: Illustrations, published (submit proofs or tearsheets); unpublished (submit 35mm cardboard-mounted slides); 1 per entry. No stats, photos, original art. Categories: Paperback, Hardbound (Books and Covers).

ELIGIBILITY: Published or created October previous to October current year. Foreign entries submit slides only. Require original art work for exhibition and awards (except foreign entries).

AWARDS: Gold Medal, Silver Medals, Excellence Certificates to illustrators, art directors for Best, each category, and Best Unpublished in Show. Merit Certificates and reproduction with credit in *Illustrators Annual Book,* each exhibited.

JUDGING: By 6-9 judges, each category. Black and white, limited color, judged separate from full color. No entries returned.

ENTRY FEE: $8 per illustration or slide ($10 per slide, foreign entries). $25 Hanging Fee ($20 members) if accepted (except foreign).

DEADLINES: Entry, September. Exhibition, January-April.

138

Southern Books Competition

Southeastern Library Association
Frank J. Anderson, Project Director
Sandor Teszler Library, Wofford College
Spartanburg, South Carolina 29301 U.S.A. Tel: (803) 585-4821, ext. 355

Spring

Regional; **entry restricted to Southern publishers;** annual; established 1952. Purpose: to recognize excellence in book design, production. Sponsored and supported by Southeastern Library Association. Average statistics: 114 entries, 36 entrants, 19 awards. Publish Southern Books of the Year Handlist of winners.

BOOK DESIGN CONTEST: Southern Bookmaking, Design, published during previous calendar year by Southern publishers (Alabama, Arizona, Arkansas, Florida, Georgia, Kentucky, Louisiana, Mississippi, New Mexico, North Carolina, Oklahoma, South Carolina, Tennessee, Texas, Virginia, Washington, D.C., West Virginia, Puerto Rico). Submit 1 copy.

AWARDS: Recognition Certificate and national one-year exhibition.

JUDGING: By Publishers, printers, booksellers, librarians. Based on design, typography, materials, production quality. Request additional copies of winners for exhibition. Winners kept at University of Kentucky Library. Winning publishers furnish additional copies for traveling exhibit. No entries returned.

ENTRY FEE: $4 first, $2 each additional.

DEADLINES: Entry, January. Awards, Spring.

139

Type Directors Club (TDC) Search for Typographic Excellence

12 East 41st Street
New York, New York 10017 U.S.A.

Summer

International; entry open to all; annual; established 1954. Purpose: to recognize typographic excellence. Sponsored by TDC. Held in New

York City. Have traveling exhibitions (U.S., Europe, Far East).

BOOK-PUBLICATION DESIGN CONTEST: **Typography,** printed in previous calendar year, 1 copy (photographic prints but not slides), credits. Submit 4 copies if winner. Categories: Booklets, Book Jackets, Books.

AWARDS: Typographic Excellence Certificates to Type Director, Typographic Supplier, Calligrapher, Agency, Client, each winning entry. Winners exhibited, reproduced in published catalog.

JUDGING: By panel. Based on typographic excellence in type, type techniques, design, paper, print.

ENTRY FEE: $6 each (U.S., Canada), $3 each (foreign). Hanging fee, $50 each (U.S., Canada), $25 (foreign).

DEADLINES: Entry, January. Event, Summer

BOOK, PLAY, POETRY, SHORT STORY

Book, Play, Poetry, Script, Short Story and Publishing combinations, including FOR CHILDREN, JUVENILE, MYSTERY, SCIENCE FICTION, SMALL PRESS. (Also see BOOK, PLAY, POETRY, SCRIPT, SHORT STORY CATEGORIES.)

140

Broome Agency Literary Contest
Larry Parr, President
3080 North Washington Blvd.
Sarasota, Florida 33580 U.S.A.
Tel: (813) 355-3036

April

International; entry open to all; annual; established 1970. Purpose: to encourage, attract more and better writing. Sponsored by Broome Literary Service, authors' representatives and editorial service. Average statistics: 10,000 entries (both fiction and nonfiction). Also sponsor nonfiction book contest.

BOOK CONTEST: **Fiction,** unpublished, original, 50,000 words minimum. No carbons-photocopies, plays, scripts, poetry, or for children age 12 or under.

SHORT STORY CONTEST: **Any Subject,** unpublished, original, 5000 words maximum. No carbons-photocopies, or for children age 12 or under.

AWARDS: $1250 Best Book, $750 Best Short Story. Saleable manuscripts considered for commission marketing.

JUDGING: By Sherwood and Mary Ann Broome. All entries read in entirety. Sponsor may use names, titles in advertising-publicity. Not responsible for loss or damage.

ENTRY FEE: None. Entrant pays postage (include SASE).

DEADLINES: Entry, December. Awards, April.

141

Deep South Writers' Competition
Deep South Writers' Conference
John Fontenot
USL Box 4691
University of Southwestern Louisiana
Lafayette, Louisiana 70504 U.S.A.

September

International; entry open to all; annual; established 1960. Purpose: to discover, develop, promote literary and artistic talent. Sponsored by and held at Deep South Writers' Conference. Have workshops, panels, speakers. Tickets: $30 registration fee, $7.50 awards banquet. Also sponsor Nonfiction Book Contest and Article Contest.

BOOK CONTEST: Fiction, Juvenile, Science Fiction Novel, unpublished; typed double-spaced; limit 3 entries. Submit 2 chapters, synopsis, biographical statement.

SHORT STORY CONTEST: Various Categories, unpublished; any form, length; typed double-spaced; limit 3 entries. Categories: Any Form-Length, Juvenile *(Julia Collier Award For Fantasy),* Science Fiction. Other requirements same as for Book.

POETRY CONTEST: Various Categories, unpublished; typed double-spaced; limit 3 entries. Categories: Any Form *(John Z. Bennett Memorial Award);* Sonnet *(Harvey Hedge Award);* Southern Theme. Other requirements same as for Book.

PLAY CONTEST: One-Act, original, unpublished; typed double-spaced; limit 3 entries. Other requirements same as for Book.

AWARDS: $100 Special Novel Award (Book); Julia Collier Award (Juvenile Fantasy Short Story); $25 Prize, each contest.

JUDGING: By professional writers. No entries returned. Not responsible for loss or damage.

ENTRY FEE: None. Entrant pays postage (include SASE).

DEADLINES: Entry, July. Awards, September.

142

Edgar Allan Poe Awards
Mystery Writers of America
150 Fifth Avenue
New York, New York 10011 U.S.A.
Tel: (212) 255-7005

April-May

International; entry open to all; annual. Sponsored and supported by Mystery Writers of America.

BOOK CONTEST: Mystery, published. Categories: Mystery Novel Published in America; First Mystery Novel by American Author; Fact-Crime, Juvenile; Paperback; Book Jacket.

SHORT STORY CONTEST: Mystery, published.

SCRIPT CONTEST: Mystery Film, Television, produced. Categories: Mystery Motion Picture, Television Show (Special, Series Episode).

AWARDS: Edgar Allan Poe Statuette Awards.

ENTRY FEE: Not specified.

DEADLINES: Entry, January. Awards, April-May.

143

National Writers Club (NWC) Annual Writing Competition
Donald E. Bower, Director
1450 South Havana
Aurora, Colorado 80012 U.S.A.
Tel: (303) 751-7844

October

International; entry open to all; annual; established 1937. Purpose: to increase interest in writing. Sponsored and supported by NWC. Average statistics: 1000 entries. Publish *Authorship* (bimonthly), *NWC Newsletter.*

Also sponsor annual national and regional workshops, Nonfiction Book and Article Contests.

BOOK CONTEST: Novel, any subject, any length.

SHORT STORY CONTEST: Any Subject, 5000-word limit.

POETRY CONTEST: Any Type, any subject, 40-line limit.

AWARDS: Cash prizes and certificates, each contest: $800 (Book, including nonfiction), $500 (Short Story), $300 (Poetry).

JUDGING: By professionals, each category. All entries reviewed in entirety. Entrants retain all rights. Not responsible for loss or damage.

ENTRY FEE: $15 (Book), $10 (Short Story), $5 (Poetry). Entrant pays postage (include SASE).

DEADLINES: Entry, May. Judging, June-October. Awards, October.

144

Pacific Northwest Writers Conference (PNWC) Creative Writing Contests

Gladys Johnson, Executive Secretary
1811 N.E. 199th
Seattle, Washington 98155 U.S.A.
Tel: (206) 364-1293

July

International; entry open to all; annual; established 1956. Sponsored by PNWC, Pacific Lutheran University. Held during PNWC annual conference at Pacific Lutheran University (122nd and Park Avenue, Tacoma, Washington). Have seminars, workshops, personal meetings. Also sponsor High School Writing Contest for Northwest U.S.-Canada students (short story, poetry).

BOOK CONTEST: Fiction Novel, original, unpublished; 10,000-word maximum; typed double-spaced. Submit 1 entry, 1 photocopy (no originals), first chapter and maximum 5-page synopsis (plus additional chapters or excerpts).

SHORT STORY CONTEST: Fiction, any type, original, unpublished; 4000-word maximum; 1 entry; 1 photocopy (no originals); typed double-spaced.

POETRY CONTEST: Any Type, original, unpublished; 3 poems-pages maximum; 1 entry; 3 photocopies; typed double-spaced.

PLAY CONTEST: Various Categories, original, unproduced; 1 entry per category, 2 photocopies (no originals); typed double-spaced. Categories: One-Act, Intimate Theater (any length), Children's (1 1/2 hours maximum, small cast).

AWARDS: $200 First, $100 Second, $50 Third Prize in Novel, Short Story, Poetry Contest. $300 Memorial Grand Prize, Best Manuscript Overall (including nonfiction). PNWC Award, Best One-Act Play. Fletcher Cross Memorial Award, Best Intimate Theater Play (production). Seattle Junior Theatre Programs Award, $100 for Best Children's Play. Winning plays produced during Conference. All plays considered for production by La Pensee Discovery! Theater during following year.

JUDGING: By panel. Comments included when material returned. May withhold awards. Not responsible for loss or damage.

ENTRY FEE: $5 per entry plus $10 Conference dues ($5 senior citizens). Entrant pays postage (include SASE).

DEADLINES: Entry, April. Awards, July.

145

Pushcart Prize
Pushcart Press
Bill Henderson, Editor
P.O. Box 845
Yonkers, New York 10701 U.S.A.
Tel: (212) 228-2269

Spring

International; **entry restricted to small press publishers;** annual. Purpose: to publish best of small press literary work. Sponsored by Pushcart Press. Statistics: 4000 entries, 325 authors from 197 presses published to date. Also sponsor Nonfiction Book, Essay, Writing Contests. Second contact: P.O. Box 320, Stone Ridge, New York 12484.

BOOK CONTEST: **Small Press Any Subject,** short self-contained section, published.

POETRY CONTEST: **Small Press Any Type,** published.

SHORT STORY CONTEST: **Small Press Any Subject,** published.

WRITING CONTEST: **Small Press Any Type,** published.

ELIGIBILITY: Published during current calendar year; 6 entries maximum per small press publisher-editor.

AWARDS: Publication in *Pushcart Prize: Best of the Small Presses* (clothbound copy to each reprinted author, press). $100 to lead poem and short story.

JUDGING: By panel.

ENTRY FEE: None. Entrant pays postage (include SASE).

DEADLINES: Entry, October. Selection, January. Publication, Spring.

146

Southwest Writers' Conference Awards
University of Houston, Continuing Education Center
Marilyn R. Nerem
4800 Calhoun
Houston, Texas 77004 U.S.A.
Tel: (713) 749-4182

July

Regional; **entry restricted to Southwestern U.S. Conference participants;** annual; established 1952. $50 Golden Pen or Golden Palette Award to **Conference Novels, Short Stories, Poetry, Young Adult Novels, Children's Books, Juvenile Writing, Television Scripts.** Purpose: to create opportunity for writers to meet editors-publishers, have manuscripts critiqued. Sponsored by University of Houston Continuing Education Center, Houston Writers' Workshop. Average statistics: 200 entries, 10 finalists, 375 attendance. Held at Continuing Education Center, University of Houston for 3 days. Have workshops, discussions. Fees: $85 (before July), $95 (after). Awards, July.

147

Fellowship of Australian Writers (FAW) National Literary Awards
Victorian Fellowship of Australian Writers
J. S. Hamilton, President
1-317 Barkers Road
Kew 3101, Victoria, AUSTRALIA
Tel: 03-805243

March-April

National; **entry restricted to Australia;** annual; established 1965 (considered largest literary awards program in Australia). FAW Barbara Ramsden Award of Plaque for **Literature Book** (fiction-nonfiction). 2 $150

Australian Natives' Association Literature Awards for **Literary Work with Australian Theme.** $500, $200 Anne Elder Poetry Award for **First Book of Poetry.** FAW Christopher Brennan Award of Bronze Plaque to **Australian Poet for Quality Work over period of time** (formerly called ROBERT FROST AWARD). $100 Patricia Weickhardt Award to an **Aboriginal Writer.** Trophy for Shell Book of the Year. State of Victoria **Short Story** Awards of $700, $250, $200, $100 (3), $50 (4). $500 Alan Marshall Award for Best Manuscript with Strong **Narrative** Element (winning entry offered to publisher). $150, $30, $20 FAW John Shaw Neilson **Poetry** Awards. BHP-FAW **Publishing Project** Award to Australian not having fiction book previously published. 2 $125 Shell-Collection of **Creative Writing** Awards. $140, $40, $20 State of Victoria Awards. $80, $55 (4) FAW **Play, Radio, T.V. Script** Award. $80, $40, $30 FAW **Young Writers Poetry** Award. Sponsored and supported by Victorian Fellowship of Australian Writers. Recognized by Literature Board of Australia Council, state governments. Held at National Awards Dinner in Melbourne. Publish *FAW Bulletin* (monthly). Also sponsor workshops, conferences, seminars. Awards, March-April.

148

Canadian Authors Association (CAA) Awards

24 Ryerson Avenue
Toronto, Ontario M5T 2P3 CANADA
Tel: (416) 868-6916

Spring

National; **entry open to Canada;** annual; established 1975. Formerly called GOVERNOR-GENERAL'S MEDALS FOR LITERATURE (established 1937). Purpose: to honor literary excellence without sacrificing popular appeal. Sponsored by CAA. Supported by Harlequin Enterprises Ltd of Toronto. Publish *Canadian Author & Bookman* (quarterly). Also sponsor Vicki Metcalf Award, Nonfiction Book Contest.

BOOK CONTEST: Fiction, published, 5 copies.

POETRY CONTEST: Any Type, published, 5 copies.

PLAY-SCRIPT CONTEST: Drama Any Medium, produced, 5 copies.

ELIGIBILITY: Published-produced during current calendar year.

AWARDS: Silver Medal and $1000 to prose fiction, poetry, drama.

JUDGING: By trustees appointed by CAA National Executive. May withhold awards.

ENTRY FEE: None.

DEADLINES: Entry, December. Awards, Spring.

GRANTS (Aid, Emergency Assistance)

For Aid, Assistance to Writers in Financial Emergency. (Also see GRANTS.)

149

Carnegie Fund for Authors Emergency Grants-in-Aid

W. L. Rothenberg
330 Sunrise Highway
Rockville Centre, New York 11570
U.S.A.

Continous

International; entry open to all; continuous. Sponsored by Carnegie Fund for Authors.

WRITING GRANT: **Writing Emergency Assistance,** up to $500 to author with at least 1 book of reasonable length published commercially (which has received reader acceptance), for financial emergency due to illness or injury to self, spouse, dependent child, or other misfortune. Require published books listed in standard reference source, or commercial publication confirmation. No loans or project, publication grants.

DEADLINES: Open.

150

Change Inc. Emergency Assistance Grants

Susan Lewis, Secretary
Box 705, Cooper Station
New York, New York 10276 U.S.A.
Tel: (212) 473-3742

Continuous

National; **entry open to U.S.;** continuous; established 1970. Purpose: to award emergency grants to professional artists in all fields. Sponsored by Change Inc., P.O. Box 489927, Los Angeles, California 90048.

WRITING GRANTS: **Writing Emergency Assistance,** $100-$500 to professional writers in need of emergency assistance resulting from utility turn-off, eviction, unpaid medical bills, fire, illness. Require detailed letter, proof of professional status, recommendation letters (2 people in applicant's field), outstanding bills substantiating amount needed.

JUDGING: By Board of Directors.

DEADLINES: Open.

151

Mary Roberts Rinehart Foundation Grants-in-Aid

The Directors
516 Fifth Avenue, Room 504
New York, New York 10036 U.S.A.
Tel: (212) 840-6378

Continuous

National; **entry open to U.S. residents (nonnationals included);** continuous; established 1958. Named for writer Mary Roberts Rinehart. Purpose: to help creative people with no means to complete projects; encourage contributions to biography, autobiography, fiction, history, poetry, drama. Sponsored and supported by nonprofit Mary Roberts Rinehart Foundation.

WRITING GRANT: **Creative Writing Aid,** up to $500 (tax-free), payable in equal installments at quarterly intervals, to creative writer as financial assistance to complete work definitely projected; preference to new, relatively unknown writers. Require project plan-outline in English, 25% project sample (if already started), writing samples, evidence of financial need and ability; progress reports from recipient. No pedantic scholarship, experimental research, applicants with vague yearning to write but who cannot produce. No grants for criticism, instruction, printing, publishing.

JUDGING: All entries read in entirety by Foundation Directors and specialists. Entrant retains all rights. Not responsible for loss or damage.

ENTRY FEE: None. Entrant pays postage (include SASE).

DEADLINES: Open.

152

PEN Fund for Writers
PEN American Center
Karen Kennerly, Executive Secretary
47 Fifth Avenue
New York, New York 10003 U.S.A.
Tel: (212) 255-1977

Continuous

International; entry open to all; continuous. Sponsored and supported by 1800-member PEN American Center (founded 1922) of the 10,000-member, 80-country International PEN (Poets-Playwrights-Essayists-Editors-Novelists), founded 1921 as independent, nonprofit world association of writers. Also sponsor PEN Writing Award for Prisoners, PEN Literature Awards, PEN Translation Awards; Lucille J. Mednick Memorial Award ($500, annual) for distinguished service to the literary community and commitment to serve the young, unrecognized, and unpopular (candidates by monination only).

WRITING GRANTS: **Writing Emergency Assistance,** up to $500 to help established writers through financial emergency. Require professional, financial information.

ENTRY FEE: None.

DEADLINES: Open.

153

Abraham Woursell Prize
University of Vienna
Prof. Siegfried Korninger
Institut fuer Anglistik and Amerikanistik
Universitaetstrasse 7
A-1010 Vienna, AUSTRIA
Tel: (43-002567DW

Continuous

International; **entry restricted to writers aged 22-35 from noncommunist countries;** continuous. Purpose: to support young talented writers in economic need. Sponsored by University of Vienna, Institut fuer Anglistik und Amerikanistic.

WRITING GRANT: **Creative Writing Assistance,** 250,000 Austrian schillings to young creative writers, aged 22-35, in economic need, from noncommunist countries. No materials returned.

DEADLINES: Open.

GRANTS (General)

Primarily for CREATIVE WRITING and PUBLISHING, including Literary Magazine, Magazine Editing, Play, Poetry, Script, Small Press, Translation, and RESIDENCE GRANTS. (Also see RESIDENCE GRANTS, SCHOLARSHIPS, FELLOWSHIPS.)

154

Cintas Fellowship Program
Institute of International Education
Robert F. Morris, Arts Program Administrator
809 United Nations Plaza
New York, New York 10017 U.S.A.
Tel: (212) 883-8454

August

International; **entry restricted to Cuban citizen-lineage professional residing outside Cuba;** annual. Named for late Oscar B. Cintas, industrialist and former Cuban Ambassador to U.S. Purpose: to foster, encourage professional development-recognition of literature, other creative arts. Sponsored by Institute of

International Education (Wallace B. Edgerton, President), private non-profit organization in international educational, cultural exchange of students, scholars, leaders, specialists between U.S. and 100 countries. Supported by Cintas Foundation. Average statistics: 13 fellowships to creative artists. Also sponsor art, music fellowships.

WRITING FELLOWSHIP GRANT: Creative Writing-Literature, $5000 each (in quarterly payments for 12 consecutive months) to Cuban citizen-lineage professional (primarily to young writers with completed academic, technical training) for arts activities in U.S. or other approved countries. Require reference letters, samples of current or earlier work, press criticisms; reports and literary contributions, dedications at end of fellowship. No professional, academic study; research, scholary, academic writing. Not responsible for loss or damage.

ENTRY FEE: None. Entrants pay postage (include SASE).

DEADLINES: Entry, March. Notification, August. Fellowships, September.

155

Coordinating Council of Literary Magazines (CCLM) Grants and Fellowships

Jennifer Moyer, Executive Director
80 Eighth Avenue
New York, New York 10011 U.S.A.
Tel: (212) 675-8605

Semiannual, Annual

National; **entry open to U.S. noncommercial literary magazines;** semiannual (Literary Magazine Grants), annual (New Literary Magazines, Editing Fellowships); established 1967. Purpose: for general support, author payments, special need. Sponsored by CCLM, founded 1967 as nonprofit publicly supported organization for noncommercial literary (creative writing) magazines. Supported by NEA, NYSCA, private funds. Have regional meetings, literary magazine library, aid magazine distribution-promotion. Publish newsletter, resource materials for small press publishers-editors. Also sponsor Bookfairs Support Program (technical assistance and seed grants to encourage organization of bookfairs), College Contests (for undergraduate literary magazines).

MAGAZINE GRANT: Literary Magazines, $500-$4000 on matching basis for publication support, author payments, special development to U.S. noncommercial literary magazines, published 1 year minimum, 3 issues minimum. Tax-exempt status not required. Submit 6 copies each (2 most recent issues), editor biography, publication-production data, budget information, description of recent issues, grant fiscal report (if previous grantee). No scholarly, critical, social, cultural, political, high school, undergraduate college magazines.

New Literary Magazines *(Special Assistance Grants),* 10 available for seed money to new magazines 3 issues maximum, serving literary interest of isolated regions and-or ethnic minorities.

EDITING FELLOWSHIP GRANT: Literary Magazine Editing *(Editors' Fellowship Program),* 10 $5000 fellowships to editors of noncommercial literary magazines (5 issues minimum in 2 years) for excellence in editing.

JUDGING: By 5 editors, writers. Recommendation approved by Board of Directors.

DEADLINES: Not specified.

156

Corporation for Public Broadcasting (CPB) Program Fund

Lewis Freedman, Director
1111 Sixteenth Street N.W.
Washington, District of Columbia
20036 U.S.A. Tel: (202) 293-6160

July

National; **entry restricted to U.S. independent producers and writers, public TV stations;** periodic; established 1980. Purpose: to stimulate television dramas that express emotions, ideas of American people. Sponsored by CPB, private, nonprofit corporation, founded 1967 by Public Broadcasting Act. Supported by NEA, federal, private funds. Also sponsor media grants.

SCRIPT-WRITING GRANT: Public Television Script Development, up to $10,000 to public TV stations, independent writers, producers, for developing ideas, not yet in dramatic form, for 60-120 minute programs. Require proposal including basic information sheet, 5-page (or less) synopsis, samples on request, proof of rights, resume(s), script completion by 6 months after submission. Categories: Original, Literary Adaptation.

JUDGING: Program Fund staff checks for proposal completeness. Experts review, evaluate (deliberations confidential; names of panel members withheld until after final selections). Final selection by Program Fund Director. Based on audience appeal, value beyond entertainment, suitability for film or videotape, appropriateness for television. Not responsible for loss, damage, third party use-misuse of proposal.

ENTRY FEE: None. Entrant pays postage (include SASE).

DEADLINES: Entry, April. Notification, July.

157

Eben Demarest Trust Fund Grant

Anne Shiras, Secretary
4601 Bayard Street, Apt. 807
Pittsburgh, Pennsylvania 15213
U.S.A.

Summer

International; **entry restricted (nomination by organizations);** annual. Purpose: to free artist from livelihood dependence upon sale, approval of work. Sponsored by Eben Demarest Trust.

WRITING GRANT: Literature, 1 $5500 grant to gifted writer, artist who has produced work of recognized worth, has no other income equal to grant; nominated by organizations, institutions, or by Demarest Advisory Council member. No applications from individuals.

JUDGING: By 5-member council.

DEADLINES: Application, May. Notification, Summer.

158

Ludwig Vogelstein Foundation Grants

Douglas Turnbaugh, Treasurer
Box 537
New York, New York 10013 U.S.A.

Semiannual

International; entry open to all; semiannual; established 1940. Purpose: to support original projects by individuals in arts and humanities. Average statistics: 33 awards per year, $3000 average. Also sponsor art, music, photography, drama grants.

WRITING GRANT: Any Type,

$100-$5000 to individuals to support original project. Require evidence of achievement in field, importance of project to field; financial need.

DEADLINES: Open.

159

National Endowment for the Arts (NEA) Writing and Playwriting Fellowships and Grants
2401 E Street N.W.
Washington, District of Columbia
20506 U.S.A. Tel: (202) 634-6044

Various

National; **entry open to U.S. citizens-residents and nonprofit tax-exempt organizations;** various; established 1965. Sponsored by NEA (independent agency of federal government) to encourage and assist U.S. cultural resources; make arts widely available; strengthen cultural organizations; preserve cultural heritage; develop creative talent. Supported by annual appropriations from U.S. Congress, private donations. Address inquiries to program *italicized* in parentheses.

WRITING FELLOWSHIP GRANTS: **Creative Literature Writing** *(Literature Program),* $12,500 to writers for writing, research, general career advancement. Require previous publication of one of following: minimum 5 short stories or 5 literary essays-articles in 2 or more literary magazines; novel; volume of short fiction, poetry, or literary criticism, script publication or production. Submit samples. Application for only 1 genre. No playwrights. Application, December-February. Notification, following December.

Creative Literature Translation *(Literature Program),* $6250 or $12,500 (depending on project) to translators for translation-to-English projects. Require previous publication of book-length literary work or publication-production of play. Submit original work samples and translation. Preference to creative writers. Application, April-June. Notification, following June.

PLAY FELLOWSHIP: **Playwriting, Research, Travel** *(Theater Program),* $12,500 to produced playwright(s) for career advancement (collaborative work acceptable). Submit 4 copies of 1 play, any length or language. Application, October-January. Notification, September.

PLAY GRANT: **Playwriting, Translations, Adaptations** *(Theater Program),* limited grants of varying amounts on matching basis to theater organizations (magazines, publications, service organizations) for advancing careers of contemporary playwrights. Application, March. Notification, October.

PLAY RESIDENT GRANT: **Playwriting Development** *(Theater Program),* up to $10,000 on partial matching basis to professional theater companies, organizations for fee, travel, per diem expenses of playwright in residence. Application, March. Notification, October.

WRITING GRANTS: **Arts Development** *(Challenge Arts Grants),* $30,000-$1,500,000 on matching basis to media arts centers, public television-radio stations, cultural groups, groups consortia, for fund-raising, other activities contributing to organization's long-term financial stability. Application, June. Notification, February.

Folk Arts Documentation, Preservation *(Folk Arts Program),* up to $50,000 (usually $5000-$25,000) on matching basis to organizations, Native American tribes, media centers, educational institutions, state-local arts agencies for documentation, preservation, presentation of traditional folk arts. Have limited grants, heritage awards, apprenticeships, short-term advance learning opportunities ($1000-$5000) on nonmatching basis to individuals. Application 5-6 months prior to notification.

Literary Arts Education *(Expansion Arts Program),* $5000-$30,000 on matching basis to professionally directed, community-based organizations offering participation-training in literary arts (workshops, poetry festivals). Application, October. Notification, June.

Special Interdisciplinary Arts Projects *(Inter-Arts Program),* up to $50,000 on matching basis to organizations for collaborative projects, special events, career entry projects, services to field involving 2 or more arts ineligible for other NEA funding. Application 6 months prior to notification.

Special Literary Services *(Literature Program),* limited assistance grants to organizations for services to writers not funded under other NEA Programs. Deadlines: Open.

ELIGIBILITY: Programs may require project summary, audience benefits, budget, secured sources of matching grants, schedules, fiscal reports, resumes-biographies, recommendation letters, reviews, other supplementary information, evidence of nonprofit, tax-exempt status. Special consideration often given to projects involving minorities, women. Other requirements vary by program

JUDGING: Application review by Program Panel. Recommendation by National Council on the Arts. Final by NEA Chair.

DEADLINES: Vary by Program.

160

National Endowment for the Arts (NEA) Publishing and Residence Grants

2401 E Street N.W.
Washington, District of Columbia
20506 U.S.A. Tel: (202) 634-6044

Various

National; **entry open to U.S. citizens-residents and nonprofit tax-exempt organizations;** various; established 1965. Sponsored by NEA (independent agency of federal government) to encourage and assist U.S. cultural resources; make arts widely available; strengthen cultural organizations; preserve cultural heritage; develop creative talent. Supported by annual appropriations from U.S. Congress, private donations. Address inquiries to programs *italicized* in parentheses.

PUBLISHING GRANTS: Contemporary Literature Production, Distribution *(Literature Program),* grants on matching basis to organizations, book centers for audience development, distribution, promotion, exhibitions, bookfairs, review-media projects that provide public access to contemporary literature. No magazines promoting own work only. Categories: Audience Development ($1000-$20,000), Distribution ($1000-$40,000), Production and Design (unspecified), Review (up to $10,000). Application 7 months prior to notification.

Literary Magazine Development *(Literature Program),* $15,000-$30,000 on 2 or 3 to 1 matching basis to noncommercial literary magazines for securing continuing local-private financial support, implementing creative, editorial, distribution, promotion plans. Require 6 issues published in previous 3 years (submit 2 copies each). Application, August. Notification, April.

Literary Magazine Special Project *(Literature Program),* up to $6000 on partial matching basis to noncommercial literary magazines for special issues, creative literature collections, distribution-production expenses, payment to contributors. Require 3 issues published in previous 3 years (submit 2 copies each). No literary journals publishing reviews primarily. Apllication, August. Notification, April.

Small Press Project *(Literature Program),* $1000-$12,500 to noncommercial small presses for publication, promotion, distribution of books, anthologies, experimental work, contemporary translations. Require previous publication of minimum 5 volumes of creative literature in previous 3 years. Submit samples. No reprints. Author of NEA-supported publication receives minimum 10% royalties (cash or copies). Application, September. Notification, April.

WRITING RESIDENCE GRANTS: Artists' Colonies *(Inter-Arts Program),* up to $50,000 (usually $10,000-$30,000) on matching basis to artists' colonies for residency cost of artist unable to pay, fundraising, minority participation projects, colony's visibility. Application, December. Notification, June.

Creative Prose or Translation Writer *(Literature Program),* up to $10,000 on matching basis to organizations for fees, travel, per diem expenses of writers in residence. No playwrights. Application, January-March. Notification, October.

ELIGIBILITY: Programs may require project summary, audience benefits, budget, secured sources of matching grants, schedules, fiscal reports, resumes-biographies, recommendation letters, reviews, other supplementary information, evidence of nonprofit tax-exempt status. Special consideration often given to projects involving minorities, women. Other requirements vary by program.

JUDGING: Application review by Program Panel. Recommendation by National Council on the Arts. Final by NEA Chair.

DEADLINES: Vary by program.

161

National Endowment for the Humanities (NEH) Scriptwriting Grants

806 15th Street N.W.
Washington, District of Columbia
20506 U.S.A.

Summer, Fall

National; **entry open to U.S. nonprofit organizations;** semiannual; established 1965. Sponsored by NEH (independent federal grant-making agency) to support research, education, public activity in the humanities (modern, classical languages; linguistics; literature; history; jurisprudence; philosophy; archaeology; comparative religion; ethics; art history, criticism, theory, practice; historical, philosophical, social sciences with humanistic content, methods; human environment, condition; national life). Supported by annual appropriations from U.S. Congress, pivate donations. Address inquiries to programs *italicized* in parentheses.

SCRIPT GRANT: Humanities Scriptwriting *(Division of Public Programs, Projects in Media),* on matching basis to nonprofit organizations for writing 1 or more scripts on thought-provoking topics using humanities themes-resources. NEH approves project distribution, publicity; grantee retains rights.

ELIGIBILITY: U.S. nonprofit, tax-exempt organizations. Fresh approach to humanities subject, evidence of potential for new uses of humanities resources. Require statement of project need, summary, complete description, work plans, outreach-audience benefits; resumes, recommendations, reviews, budget, marketing plans; samples, manuscripts; other documentation, supporting materials.

JUDGING: By 4-stage review: NEH Panel (subject-area experts), Individual Review (external experts), National Council on the Humanities (26 presidential appointees), NCH Chair (makes final funding decisions). Based on proposal clarity, logic; use of humanities resources; interpretive nature; appeal to large audience (including English, Spanish speakers; blind; hearing-impaired); outreach potential to underserved social groups; feasibility, planning efficiency, budget.

DEADLINES: Application, January, July. Notification, June, December.

162

Translation Center Fellowships and Grants

Columbia University
307A Mathematics Building
New York, New York 10027 U.S.A.
Tel: (212) 280-2305

Fall

National; **entry open to U.S. citizens;** annual; established 1972. Sponsored by Translation Center, Columbia University. Supported by NEA, NEH, NYSCA. Average statistics: 200 entries, 5 finalists, 1 award. Publish *Translation Magazine,* chapbooks, anthologies.

TRANSLATION GRANT: **Literary Translation** *(Work-in-Progress Translation of Literature Awards),* $500 for translation completion. Require work-in-progress details, 10-20 pages of translation and original text, option letter or statement from university or small press indicating publishing interest. Occasional larger grants to multiple-translator projects.

Play Translation *(Translation of Theater),* for 20th-Century Western European Theater.

TRANSLATION FELLOWSHIP: **Translation Language Training** *(Translation Fellowships),* $10,000 for 1 year to American writers for training in lesser-known language as preparation for literary translation. Require 10-page minimum samples of original-translation work, proof of some knowledge of proposed language.

JUDGING: 5 judges read all entries in entirety. Not responsible for loss or damage.

ENTRY FEE: None. Entrant pays postage (include SASE).

DEADLINES: Entry, January (fellowship), February (grants). Awards, Fall.

163

Witter Bynner Foundation for Poetry Grant Award Program

Diana Abeyta, Administrator
660 East Garcia
P.O. Box 2188
Santa Fe, New Mexico 87501 U.S.A.
Tel: (505) 982-3583

Spring

National; **entry restricted to U.S. nonprofit poetry organizations;** annual; established 1972. Named after poet Witter Bynner (1881-1968). Purpose: to support poetry. Sponsored by Witter Bynner Foundation for Poetry. Average statsitics: 30 entrants, 9 grant awards.

POETRY GRANT: **Poetry Support,** 9 grants of $1000-$25,000 (averaging $8000) for support of poetry. Require formal application, closing report. Guidelines developed annually. Not for poetry reading projects or publications. No grants to individuals or for building endowments, capital improvement.

JUDGING: By 4-member Board of Trustees.

ENTRY FEE: None.

DEADLINES: Entry, not specified. Awards, Spring.

164

Writers Guild of America East (WGA) Foundation Fellowship Program

Craig Fisher, Executive Director
555 West 57th Street
New York, New York 10019 U.S.A.
Tel: (212) 245-6180

National; **entry open to U.S.;** annual; established 1980. Purpose: to encourage young writers working in film and television. Sponsored by WGA East Foundation. Supported by NEA, NYSCA. Average statistics: 400 entries, 40 semifinalists, 20 finalists, 8 awards. Also sponsor seminars for young film, television writers.

SCRIPTWRITING FELLOWSHIP GRANT: **Film, Television Scriptwriting,** $3500 fellowship to writers (Guild members and nonmembers) to complete material by end of current year. Submit 2 copies previous scripts (produced or unproduced) showing understanding of film medium; 2 copies outline or treatment.

JUDGING: By WGA members. Judges assigned to guide and assist in script completion. Entrants retain all rights. No entries returned.

ENTRY FEE: Entrant pays postage (include SASE).

DEADLINES: Not specified.

GRANTS (Regional-State)

Limited to specific Region, State. Primarily for CREATIVE WRITING and PUBLISHING, including Play, Poetry, Research, Script. Includes MASSACHUSETTS, MINNESOTA, NEW YORK, OHIO, and AUSTRALIA, CANADA, ENGLAND, WALES. (Also see RESIDENCE GRANTS, SCHOLARSHIPS, FELLOWSHIPS.)

165

Artists Foundation Artists Fellowship Program

Dale Stewart, Manager
100 Boylston Street
Boston, Massachusetts 02116 U.S.A.
Tel: (617) 482-8100

October

State; **entry restricted to Massachusetts independents, professionals;** annual; established 1975. Purpose: to recognize outstanding creative writers in Massachusetts; support future work of high merit. Sponsored and supported by Massachusetts Council on the Arts and Humanities. Average statistics: 4000 entries, 3500 entrants, 160 finalists, 75 winners (including nonwriting categories). Have film, photography, dance, music, craft divisions; workshops.

WRITING FELLOWSHIP GRANT: **Fiction Writing,** $3500 each grant. Submit work samples. Entrant pays postage (include SASE).

ELIGIBILITY: Massachusetts residents, over 18, no students.

JUDGING: By practicing out-of-state artists, anonymously. Not responsible for loss or damage.

DEADLINES: Entry, October.

166

Bush Foundation Fellowships for Artists

E-900 First National Bank Building
St. Paul, Minnesota 55101 U.S.A.
Tel: (612) 227-0891

March

State; **entry open to Minnesota residents;** annual; established 1975. Purpose: to assist writers to work full-time. Sponsored by Bush Foundation. Also have art, sculpture, photography categories.

WRITING FELLOWSHIP GRANT: **Fiction, Poetry Writing Work,** up to 10 grants ($12,000 maximum for 12-18 months, or $1000 per month for 6-12 months), up to $2000 program, travel expenses, for specific career, goal advancement, to 1-year minimum Minnesota resident writers, 25 or older. Require evidence of professional accomplishment through publication, recent work samples. No students.

JUDGING: Preselection by panels. Final by Interdisciplinary judges, based on demonstrated artistic quality, fellowship importance to creative growth.

DEADLINES: Application, October. Preliminary selection, January. Notification, March.

167

Creative Artists Public Service (CAPS) Program Fellowship Grants

Creative Artists Program Service
250 West 57th Street
New York, New York 10019 U.S.A.
Tel: (212) 247-6303

March

State; **entry open to New York;** annual; established 1970. Purpose: to aid individual writers in creating new work, completing work-in-progress. Sponsored by CAPS, nonprofit arts service organization. Supported by NEA, NYSCA. Average statistics: 200 awards (including art, film, painting, sculpture, graphics, choreography, music composition). Have community service program, visual arts and playwrights referral services. Also sponsor other media fellowship grants.

WRITING FELLOWSHIP GRANT: **Fiction, Subjective Prose,** $3500-$4000 for 12 months to create new work or complete work-in-progress. Submit 2 copies (30-50 pages), novel or short stories; double-spaced, typed on 8 1/2x11-inch white 20-pound paper in lightweight binder with metal fasteners.

Poetry: Submit 2 copies; maximum 25 pages, double-spaced; 15 pages, single-spaced. Other requirements same as for Fiction.

Playwriting-Screenwriting: Submit 2 copies full-length play or script, or 2 one-acts. Other requirements same as for Fiction.

ELIGIBILITY: New York residents willing to perform community-related service. No matriculated graduate, undergraduate students. No translations or adaptations. No proposals to travel, study, teach, publish-produce already complete work or purchase equipment.

JUDGING: By professionals (members change yearly). Work belongs to artists; CAPS requires 1 copy. Not responsible for loss or damage.

DEADLINES: Application, June.

Materials (on request), November. Notification, March.

168

Ohio Arts Council Aid to Individual Artists

Denny Griffith, Coordinator
727 East Main Street
Columbus, Ohio 43206 U.S.A.
Tel: (614) 466-2613

June

State; **entry open to Ohio residents;** annual; established 1978. Purpose: to provide direct, nonmatching grants to writers for creation of new work. Sponsored by Ohio Arts Council. Average statistics: 590 entries, 110 awards. Also have fellowships for visual artists, architects-designers, choreographers, composers, craftopersons. Second contact: 50 West Broad Street, Columbus, Ohio 43215; tel: (614) 466-2613.

WRITING GRANTS: **Creative Writing,** up to $6000 to Ohio residents for planning, supplies, facilities-services rental, research, presentation, reproduction, documentation, publication expenses for creating new work. Submit maximum 15 pages poetry, maximum 30-50 pages prose, minimum 1 full act of play (typed, double-spaced on 8 1/2x11-inch 20-pound bond) in triplicate.

ELIGIBILITY: No students. Not for out-of-state travel or over $500 equipment.

JUDGING: Based on creative, technical excellence of work. Preference to work advancing the arts.

DEADLINES: Application, January. Notification, June.

169

Australia Council Literature Grants

P.O. Box 302
168 Walker Street
North Sydney, New South Wales
2060, AUSTRALIA

Continuous

National; **entry restricted to Australia;** continuous. **Grants to Australian Creative Writers** ($6500-$37,-500), **Book Publishers** ($200,000 total; priority to adult fiction, drama, poetry), **Literary Magazine Publishers and Organizations** ($6000 average). Purpose: to encourage Australian creative writing through direct grants to writers; subsidize, promote resultant works. Sponsored by Australia Council. Supported by Australian government. Also sponsor other media grants.

170

Canada Council Grants

Robert Kennedy, Head, Arts Awards Service
P.O. Box 1047
255 Albert Street
Ottawa, Ontario K1P 5V8 CANADA
Tel: (613) 237-3400

September, March

National; **entry open to Canada;** semiannual; established 1957. Sponsored by Canada Council, founded 1957 by Act of Parliament to foster and promote study, enjoyment of art in Canada. Have architecture, arts criticism, dance, film, music, theater, visual arts, multidisciplinary and performance art sections. Also sponsor Aid to Arts Organizations.

WRITING GRANTS: **General,** (Under *Aid to Artists Branch)* to Canadian citizens, landed immigrants with 5 years residence. Categories: *Arts Grants A:* up to $19,000 for living expenses, project, travel costs for 4-12 months to senior artists with record of significant contribution. *Arts Grants B:* up to $11,000 for living expenses, project costs (possible added travel allowance) for 4-12 months to professional artists. *Short-Term Grants:* $800 per month and travel allowance (up to $800 possible project allowance) for 3 months to artists for specific project. *Project Costs Grants:* up to $2700 for goods, services, travel (no living) for completion of project. *Travel Grants:* for travel (up to $100 possible living expenses). Discipline divisions follow:

Creative Writing, to creative writers with a book professionally published (or equivalent in literary periodicals).

Film Script Writing, to 1-film-minimum, professionally produced scriptwriters for training, short film writing, critical research, postcompletion.

Playwriting, to 1-play-minimum, professionally produced playwrights. Require recent work sample.

Creative Writing Publication, to majority Canadian-owned publishers for publication, translation, promotion, distribution of books, periodicals.

Writers in Residence (called *Artist--in- Residence*), to institutions, groups for writer residencies and readings.

JUDGING: Preliminary by outside juries, based on artistic merit, potential, significance, project value, artistic quality, relevance. Secondary by 28-member Advisory Arts Panel. Final by 31-member Canada Council.

DEADLINES: Entry, April, October. Grants Awarded, September, March.

171

Phoenix Trust Grants
Society of Authors, Limited
84 Drayton Gardens
London SW10 9SD, ENGLAND
Tel: 01-373-6642

Continuous

National; **entry restricted to U.K. publishers;** continuous. 150-500 pound **Grants for Literature-Research Publication.** Purpose: to assist literature publication where publishers' advance does not cover research cost.

172

Welsh Arts Council Bursaries to Writers
Meic Stephens, Literature Director
9 Museum Place
Cardiff CF1 6QP, WALES Tel: Cardiff 394711

Continuous

National; **entry restricted to Welsh born, resident, or language published authors;** continuous. Up to 5000 pounds 1-year **Grants for Prose-Poetry Writing in Welsh-English.** Purpose: to give opportunity to write full-time during bursary tenure. Sponsored by Welsh Arts Council. Also sponsor Travel, Playwriting, Publisher Aid-Grants. Event, Continuous.

LITERARY

Usually for a series of literary-artistic achievements, or life's work (mostly not open to entry). Includes Book, Play, Poetry, and GRANTS FELLOWSHIPS, AID. (Also see BOOK CATEGORIES.)

173

American Academy and Institute of Arts and Letters Awards

633 West 155 Street
New York, New York 10032 U.S.A.
Tel: (212) 368-6361

May

International; **entry restricted (nomination by members);** annual. Academy-Institute Arts and Letters Award of $5000 to **Writers, Artists, Composers for Creative Work** (established 1941). Harold D. Vursell Memorial Award of $5000 to **Writer of Best Prose Book** (established 1978). E. M. Forster Award of $5000 to **Young English Writer for stay in U.S.** (periodic, established 1972). Richard and Hinda Rosenthal Foundation Awards of $3000 to **Writer for published American Fiction Novel,** and to Younger American Painter (established 1957). Morton Dauwen Zabel Award of $2500 (in 3-year rotation) to **American Poet, Fiction Writer, Critic** of progressive, original, experimental tendencies (established 1966). Russell Loines Award for Poetry of $2500 to **American-British Poet** (periodic). Marjorie Peabody Waite Award of $1500 (in 3-year rotation) to **Older Writer, Artist, Composer** for achievement-integrity of his-her art. Witter Bynner Poetry Prize of $1350 to **Poet** (established 1979). Award of Merit, Medal, $1000 to **American Novelist, Poet, Dramatist, Painter, Sculptor** (periodic). Sue Kaufman Prize of $1000 to **Writer for Best First Published Fiction** (may be novel, short story collection). Richard Rodgers Production Award subsidizing **Production of Musical Play in New York City** by authors, composers for work not commercially produced (open to application, established 1978). Distinguished Service to the Arts Award, Citation, cash to **U.S. Residents for Service to the Arts.** Gold Medals (as paired in 6-year rotation) to **Individual for Drama, Graphic Art; Belles Lettres, Criticism, Painting; Biography, Music; Fiction, Sculpture; History, Architecture; Poetry, Music.** William Dean Howells Medal to **Writer for American Fiction** (every 5 years). Sponsored by 250-U.S. member honorary American Academy and Institute of Arts and Letters, founded 1976 by merger of National Institute of Arts and Letters (founded 1898 to further U.S. literature-fine arts) and American Academy of Arts and Letters (founded 1904 of 50 members chosen from National Institute). Also sponsor Artists and Writers Revolving Emergency Aid Fund for writers, artists, composers in financial distress (nomination by members only), American Academy in Rome Fellowships in Creative Writing (prix de Rome); awards for nonfiction writers, music, architecture; scholarships for composers. Awards, May.

174

Neustadt International Prize for Literature

University of Oklahoma
Ivar Ivask, Chair
World Literature Today
630 Parrington Oval, Room 110
Norman, Oklahoma 73019 U.S.A.

February

International; **entry restricted (nomination by jury);** biennial; established 1969. $25,000 Silver Eagle Feather, Award Certificate to Individual for **Continuing Achievement in Fiction, Poetry, Drama.** Named after Ardmore, Oklahoma family who endowed the Prize. Formerly called BOOKS ABROAD-NEUSTADT INTERNATIONAL PRIZE FOR LITERATURE. Sponsored by University of Oklahoma and World Literature Today (quarterly international literary journal, founded 1927). Average statistics: 11 entries 1 award. Judging by 12-member international jury. Second contact: Donna Murphy, Media Information Office, University of Oklahoma, 900 Asp Avenue, Room 350, Norman, Oklahoma 73019; (405) 325-2335. Award announcement, February.

175

Australian Literature Society (ALS) Gold Medal
Alvie Egan
P.O. Box 55
Barooga 3644, AUSTRALIA Tel: 058 734426

National; **entry restricted to Australia (nomination by ALS members);** annual; established 1923. Cash award to published **Australian Literary Work.** Purpose: to develop, encourage Australian literature; honor best literary work published in Australia. Sponsored by ALS.

176

Canada Council Awards
P.O. Box 1047
255 Albert Street
Ottawa, Ontario K1P 5V8 CANADA
Tel: (613) 237-3400

Spring

National; **entry restricted (selection by Council);** annual; established 1936 (Governor General), 1963 (Molson), 1974 (Translation), 1975 (Children's), 1976 (Canada-Australia). $5000 Governor General's Literary Awards for **English and French-language Poetry and Fiction Literature** published by Canadian authors. $20,000 Molson Prizes for **Canadian Contributions to Arts, Humanities, Social Sciences** enriching cultural-intellectual heritage, contributing to national unity. $5000 Translation Prizes for **English into French, French into English Translations** by Canadian citizens or 1-year landed immigrants. $5000 Children's Literature Prizes for **English and French-Language Children's Literature** published by Canadian authors. $2500 Canadian-Australian Literary Prize to **English-Language Canadian-Australian Writers** (on alternating basis). $2500 Canada-Belgium Literary Prize to **French-Language Canadian-Belgian Writers** (on alternating basis). Sponsored by Canada Council, established by Act of Parliament in 1957 to foster, promote study, enjoyment, production of art-humanities-social science works. Also sponsor Nonfiction Book Awards. Awards, Spring.

177

Royal Society of Canada (RSC) Lorne Pierce Medal
E. H. P. Graneau, Executive Secretary
344 Wellington
Ottawa, Ontario K1A 0N4 CANADA
Tel: (613) 992-3468

May

National; **entry restricted to Canadian citizens, 5-year resident authors (nomination by members);** biennial; established 1926. Lorne Pierce Medal and $1000 for **Imaginative Literature in English or French,** to Canadian authors. Sponsored by RSC, established 1882 to promote learning, research in the arts and sciences. Held at annual RSC meeting. Also sponsor medals, scholarships for medical history, humanities, social sciences, research, critical literature. Award, May.

178

Bavarian Academy of Fine Arts Literature Prize
Max Joseph Platz 3
8 Munich 22
WEST GERMANY Tel: 29 46 22

July

National; **entry restricted (nomination by Academy);** annual. 10,000 DM to **German Writer for literary work.** Sponsored by Bavarian Academy of Fine Arts. Award, July.

179

Thomas-Dehler Prize for Literature
German Federal Ministry for Intra-German Relations
Dr. K. E. Murawski
Postfach 120 250
5300 Bonn 1, WEST GERMANY
(FRG) Tel: 228 3061

Triennial

National; **entry restricted to West Germany;** triennial; established 1968. 20,000 DM to **German Literature** to promote young writers, new talent. Purpose: to illustrate problems of divided Germany. Sponsored by German Federal Ministry for Intra-German Relations.

180

Nobel Prize for Literature
Swedish Academy
Kallargrand 4, Borshuset
111 29 Stockholm, SWEDEN

December

International; **entry restricted (nomination by Swedish Academy);** annual; established 1901. Gold Medal, Diploma and 725,000 Kronor to **author for total literary output.** Considered most prestigious literary award. Named after Alfred B. Nobel, inventor of dynamite. Purpose: to honor author producing distinguished literary work of idealistic tendency. Sponsored by Swedish Academy. Supported by Nobel Foundation. Second contact: Nobel Foundation, Nobel House, Sturegatan 14, 11436 Stockholm, Sweden. Award, December (aniversary of Nobel's death).

181

Nordic Literature Prize
Nordic Council
Inger Jagerhorn
Box 19506
10432 Stockholm, SWEDEN
Tel: 00946-8-143420

March

International; **entry restricted to Nordic countries;** annual. Prize to **Nordic Writer from Denmark, Finland, Iceland, Norway, Sweden.** Purpose: to recognize Nordic Writer and work. Sponsored by the Nordic Council. Held in March at Annual Session of Nordic Council in alternating Nordic capitals.

PLAY (Any Type-Subject)

Full-Length, One-Act and Short Plays. Includes Play Production, Script, and Residence Grants. (Also see other PLAY, PLAY PRODUCTION CATEGORIES.)

182

Charles H. Sergel Drama Prize
University of Chicago Theatre
5706 South University Avenue
Chicago, Illinois 60637 U.S.A.
Tel: (312) 753-3582

December

National; **entry open to U.S.;** biennial (even years). Purpose: to encourage writing of new American plays. Sponsored by University of Chicago.

PLAY CONTEST: Any Subject, original, unpublished, unproduced (where admission was charged), copyrighted. Submit 1 manuscript, typed, bound. No dramatizations, adaptations, translations, illustrations, music.

AWARDS: $1500.

JUDGING: May withhold award. Sponsor keeps winning copy. Not responsible for loss or damage.

ENTRY FEE: Not specified.

DEADLINES: Entry, June. Award, December.

183

Great American Play Contest
Actors Theatre of Louisville
Elizabeth King, Literary Manager
316 West Main Street
Louisville, Kentucky 40202 U.S.A.
Tel: (502) 584-1265

August

National; **entry open to U.S. citizens;** annual; established 1977. Purpose: to discover and support new playwrights. Sponsored and supported by State Theatre of Kentucky Actors Theatre of Louisville (LORT professional resident theater). Held in 638-seat Pamela Brown thrust-stage auditorium and 160-seat Victor Jory arena-stage auditorium. Have full season (19 productions), literary department, workshops, conferences. Also sponsor Festival of New American Plays, Literary Management Internship, Playwright-in-Residence program.

PLAY CONTEST: Any Subject, unproduced, 2 maximum per entrant. Submit typed, bound manuscript. Prefer 15 or fewer characters, no multiple full sets. No plays with equity waiver or equity productions. Categories: Full-Length, One-Act.

AWARDS: $5000 First Prize and production consideration, Full-Length. $1000 Heidemann Award, production consideration, One-Act. May split prizes. Playwrights receive royalties for production.

JUDGING: Prescreening by Literary staff; final by Producing-Director.

ENTRY FEE: None. Entrant pays postage (include SASE).

DEADLINES: Entry, April. Awards, August.

PLAY PRODUCTION: Any Subject, musicals should have small casts. No absurdist, sit com works.

184

Jacksonville University Annual Playwriting Contest
Jacksonville University College of Fine Arts
Davis Sikes, Director
Jacksonville University
Jacksonville, Florida 32211 U.S.A.
Tel: (904) 744-3950

March

International; entry open to all; annual; established 1971. Purpose: to encourage-support original writing; premiere selected scripts. Sponsored by Jacksonville University. Supported by Friends of the Fine Arts (Jacksonville University College of Fine Arts). Average statistics: 500 entries, 33 premiered to date. Held at Swisher Auditorium, Jacksonville University. Tickets: $4.50, free to writers.

PLAY CONTEST: Any Subject, full-length or bill of one-acts by same author; original, unproduced, any type or technique; 2 maximum. Prefer original, off-beat ideas. Submit typed, firmly bound script, brief resume.

AWARDS: $2000 and premiere production.

JUDGING: By university faculty, staff, students; community members. May withhold premiere or modify cash awards. Not responsible for loss or damage.

ENTRY FEE: None. Entrant pays postage (include SASE).

DEADLINES: Entry, December (accepted throughout year). Winner announced, April. Awards, June. Materials returned, April.

185

National Playwrights Conference and New Drama for Television Project Awards

Eugene O'Neill Theater Center
Lloyd Richards, Artistic Director
1860 Broadway, Suite 601
New York, New York 10023 U.S.A.
Tel: (212) 246-1485

July-August

National; **entry open to U.S. citizens;** annual; established 1965. At first Conference worked exclusively with stage plays; 1976 added New Drama for Television Project. Purpose: to develop talented writers through opportunity to work on plays with professional theater-media artists. Sponsored by National Playwrights Conference, founded 1966 to find new, original theater. Supported by ABC, NEA, Exxon; Jerome, Shubert, Rockefeller Foundations. Average statistics: 1300 entries, 100 finalists, 16 winners. Held at Eugene O'Neill Theater Center, Waterford, Connecticut, founded 1964 as nonprofit educational organization dedicated to restoring legitimate theater in America. Have 3 theaters, full productions, readings, staged readings, critiques, panel discussions, theater collection-library. Tickets: $3.50-$6. Also sponsor National Theatre of the Deaf, National Critics' Institute, National Theatre Institute Training Program, Choreographers' Conference, Composer-Librettist Conference, and Second Step Program for university, regional theater, educational television productions (with playwright in residence) of plays-scripts accepted for Conference. Second contact: 305 Great Neck Road, Waterford, Connecticut 06385.

PLAY CONTEST: Stage Any Subject, original, unproduced; any length; not currently optioned; 1 maximum per entrant. Submit 1 typed, bound copy, short biography. No adaptations.

SCRIPT CONTEST: Television Any Subject, original, unproduced; not currently optioned; 1 maximum per entrant. Submit 1 typed, bound copy script or extended outline. No adaptations.

AWARDS: ABC Theater Award, $10,000 and first option to television rights by ABC-TV, to Best. $200, room, board, transportation to Preconference weekend (reading of plays) and Conference to accepted entrants. During Conference authors rewrite plays, confer with dramaturges-story editors, rehearse actors, give 2 minimum staged readings (plays), videotape production (scripts). Possible full production during Conference.

JUDGING: All read in entirety by committee of television, theater experts. Final by 14-member selection committee. Not responsible for loss or damage.

ENTRY FEE: None. Entrant pays postage (include SASE).

DEADLINES: Entry, November. Acceptance, April. Preconference

Weekend, May. Conference, July-August.

186

Obie Awards
Village Voice
Judith Kruegler, Promotion Director
842 Broadway
New York, New York 10003 U.S.A.
Tel: (212) 475-3300

May

International; **entry restricted to plays produced in New York Off-Broadway or Off-Off-Broadway theaters;** annual; established 1956. Obie Certificate, $1000, for Best **New American Play, Playwriting,** direction, productions, performances, lifetime achievement. Sponsored and voted by *Village Voice* newspaper. Average statistics: 25 awards. Held in Greenwich Village (New York City). Judging by 6 *Village Voice* critics and 2 guest judges. Awards in May.

187

Pioneer Drama Playwriting Award
Pioneer Drama Service
Shubert Fendrich, Publisher
2172 South Colorado Blvd.
P.O. Box 22555
Denver, Colorado 80222 U.S.A.
Tel: (303) 759-4297

September

International; entry open to all; annual; established 1963. Purpose: to encourage playwrights in educational theater to submit quality scripts for publication. Sponsored and supported by Pioneer Drama Service. Average statistics: 1000 entries, 800 entrants, 4 countries, 15-20 finalists, 1-3 winners. Publish drama-related texts. Also sponsor Pioneer Drama and Ha'Penny Players National Children's Theatre Playwriting Awards. Second contact: Anne Fendrich, Managing Editor.

PLAY CONTEST: Any Subject, produced for educational or community theater, original or adaptations from literature in public domain, unpublished, one-act or full-length. Require performance proof, synopsis, cast balance, market. Categories: Comedy, Drama, Musical Comedy.

AWARDS: $1000 advance against royalties plus publication and catalog listing.

JUDGING: By editorial board; final by publisher. Based on set simplicity, cast balance, broad national appeal. Not responsible for loss or damage. All entries considered for publication.

ENTRY FEE: None. Entrant pays postage (include SASE).

DEADLINES: Entry, March. Acceptance, April. Winners announced, June. Awards, September.

188

Stanley Drama Award
Wagner College
Dr. J. J. Boies
631 Howard Avenue
Staten Island, New York 10301
U.S.A. Tel: (212) 390-3256

December

International; entry open to all; annual; established 1957. Named after Mrs. Alma Stanley. Purpose: to launch new playwrights. Sponsored and supported by Stanley-Timolat Foundation, Wagner College. Average statistics: 200-300 entries, 15 semifinalists, 4-5 finalists.

PLAY CONTEST: Any Subject, full-length or series of 2-3 thematically connected one-acts, unproduced, unpublished. Require professional recommendation; music on records or cassettes for musicals.

AWARDS: $1000 and possible production by sponsor.

JUDGING: Preliminary by 6-7 readers. Final by 1 theater professional. May use name in publicity.

ENTRY FEE: None. Entrant pays postage (include SASE).

DEADLINES: Entry, May. Winners announced, December.

189

Alberta Culture Playwriting Competition
Alberta Culture, Performing Arts
Gordon Gordey, Drama Consultant
11th Floor, CN Tower
1004-104 Avenue
Edmonton, Alberta T5J 0K5
CANADA

Spring

Regional; **entry restricted to Alberta residents;** annual; established 1968. Purpose: to provide recognition, financial assistance to Albertans with playwriting talent. Sponsored and supported by Alberta Culture. Have workshops, correspondence courses, consultative and financial services to authors, publishers. Publish *Alberta Authors Bulletin* (bimonthly newsletter). Also sponsor First Novel, Nonfiction, Regional History, and For Young People Book Contests, Literary Grants.

PLAY CONTEST: **Various,** original, unproduced. Adaptations accepted. Categories: Adult Full-Length, Adult One-Act, High School (any length), Television Drama, Radio Drama (2 divisions).

AWARDS: First, Second, Third Prize each category (except Radio Drama): $700, $350, $125 Adult Full-Length; $400, $150, $100 Adult One-Act; $200, $100, $75 High School; $1200, $300, $150 Television Drama. Radio Drama: $500 Division A, $1200 minimum Division B.

JUDGING: By independent judges. Sponsor may produce winners; withhold, alter prizes. No entries returned. Not responsible for loss or damage.

ENTRY FEE: None.

DEADLINES: Entry, February. Awards, Spring.

PLAY (Full-Length)

(Also see other PLAY, PLAY PRODUCTION CATEGORIES.)

190

Beverly Hills Theatre Guild Playwrights Award
Pamela Bohnert
704 North Alpine
Beverly Hills, California 90210 U.S.A.
Tel: (213) 552-1071 213-3161

January

National; **entry open to U.S.;** annual. Purpose: to find, encourage new dramatists; foster development of high-quality plays for theater. Sponsored and supported by Beverly Hills Theatre Guild.

PLAY CONTEST: **Full-Length,** original, unproduced (school productions excepted); minimum 90 minutes; any subject or genre; 1 per author or group. Submit bound copy. No translations, musicals.

AWARDS: $3000 First Prize. Additional $2000 financing for production in Los Angeles within one year.

JUDGING: By working professionals, academics. Author retains rights; sponsor may perform one script-in-hand rehearsed reading before non-paying audience on award night. Not responsible for loss or damage.

ENTRY FEE: None. Entrant pays postage (include SASE).

DEADLINES: Entry, May. Awards, January.

191

Carolina Regional Theatre First Stage Contest

Norman Ussery, Project Director
P.O. Drawer 1169
Chapel Hill, North Carolina 27514
U.S.A. Tel: (919) 933-5300

Summer

International; entry open to all; annual; established 1980. Purpose: to encourage contemporary drama by providing playwrights opportunity to experiment in risk-free final development. Sponsored by Carolina Regional Theatre and Cherokee Historical Association. Supported by May Duke Biddle Foundation, North Carolina Department of Cultural Resources. Recognized by Triangle Cities BBB, North Carolina Association of Professional Theatres. Average statistics: 40 entries, 6 semifinalists, 3 productions. Held in Cherokee, North Carolina. Tickets: $2-$4 per performance.

PLAY CONTEST: **Full-Length,** unproduced, unpublished.

AWARDS: Winners receive transportation, room, board in Cherokee for 3-week residency; fully mounted production.

JUDGING: 2 directors read all scripts in entirety; semifinalists judged by 4-member committee. Not responsible for loss or damage.

ENTRY FEE: None. Entrant pays postage (include SASE).

DEADLINES: Entry, February. Judging, March. Winners announced, April. Production, Summer.

192

Colonial Players Promising Playwright Award

Lee Williams, Contest Director
108 East Street
Annapolis, Maryland 21401 U.S.A.
Tel: (301) 268-7373

August

International; entry open to all; biennial (even years); established 1973. Formerly called HEFLER AWARD to 1973. Purpose: to encourage serious playwrights. Sponsored and supported by Colonial Players, organized in 1949 to develop appreciation of dramatic arts (present 6 productions a season at 179-seat theater-in-the-round). Tickets: $3.50-$4; $1 students, seniors. Have periodic special productions, workshops in acting, directing, other aspects of theater.

PLAY CONTEST: **Full-Length,** unpublished, typewritten, bound manuscript; 90-minute minimum, maximum cast 25 (prefer 12 or less). Two or more authors acceptable. Submit release of original copyright if adaptations used.

AWARDS: Best Entry $500 and possible full production. Merit Awards. Honorable Mentions.

JUDGING: Sponsor may produce play royalty-free within two years after award. Not responsible for loss or damage.

ENTRY FEE: Not specified. Entrant pays postage (include SASE).

DEADLINES: Entry, December

(even years). Winners announced, August (odd years).

193

Harold C. Crain Award in Playwriting
San Jose State University
Dr. Christopher Ostergren, Coordinator
Theatre Arts Department
125 South Seventh Street
San Jose, California 95192 U.S.A.
Tel: (408) 277-2763

February

International; entry open to all; annual; established 1977. Named after Dr. Harold C. Crain, late Chairman of San Jose State Theatre Arts Department. Average statistics: 200 entries, 40 semifinalists, 4 finalists.

PLAY CONTEST: **Full-Length Any Subject,** original, unproduced; in English; any theme-plot, 1 maximum per entrant. Submit 1 copy, typed and bound. Collaboration permitted. No adaptations, musicals, screenplays, works under option.

AWARDS: $500 and premiere production by sponsor. No royalties.

JUDGING: By university personnel, theater professionals. May withhold award.

ENTRY FEE: None. Entrant pays postage.

DEADLINES: Entry, November. Awards, February.

194

New Plays From Rutgers
Rutgers Theater Company
M.E. Comtois, Dramaturg
Rutgers State University of New Jersey
Mason Gross School of the Arts
New Brunswick, New Jersey 08903
U.S.A. Tel: (201) 932-9816, 932-9289

Summer

International; entry open to all; annual; established 1980. Sponsored by Rutgers Theater Company. Have public readings, workshop productions of selected scripts.

PLAY CONTEST: **Full-Length,** including adaptations and plays with music. No conventional musicals.

AWARDS: $1000 and production (with playwright in residence).

ENTRY FEE: Not specified. Entrant pays postage (include SASE).

DEADLINES: Entry not specified. Production, Summer.

195

Oglebay Institute Towngate Theatre Playwriting Contest
Oglebay Institute Performing Arts Department
Jennifer Coffield, Performing Arts Specialist
Oglebay Park
Wheeling, West Virginia 26003
U.S.A. Tel: (304) 242-4200

Fall

International; entry open to all; annual; established 1976. Purpose: to provide opportunity for producing a good play rejected by others. Sponsored and supported by Oglebay Institute. Average statistics: 75 entries, 4 countries, 1 winner, 7 performances, 900 attendance. Held at 171-seat Towngate Theatre, 2118 Market Street, Wheeling, West Virginia. Tickets: $2.50-$4.

PLAY CONTEST: **Full-Length,** unproduced, unpublished; unlimited entry; in English; nonmusical.

AWARDS: $300 plus limited run production. $200 travel expenses for author to attend production.

JUDGING: Drama specialists, critics review all entries. Author retains rights, but sponsor may determine final staging and responsibility for production-promotion. Not responsible for loss or damage.

ENTRY FEE: None. Entrant pays postage (include SASE).

DEADLINES: Entry, December. Winner notified, May. Production, Fall.

196

Open Circle Theatre Playwriting Prize

Goucher College
Barry Knower, Director
Towson, Maryland 21204 U.S.A.
Tel: (301) 825-3300

June

International; entry open to all; annual; established 1977. Sponsored and supported by Open Circle Theatre, Goucher College.

PLAY CONTEST: **Full-Length Any Subject,** original, unproduced; at least half of major roles can be played by women. Adaptations of noncopyrighted material acceptable.

AWARDS: $200 and production. Winner receives travel, residency expenses.

ENTRY FEE: None.

DEADLINES: Entry, December. Winner announced, June.

197

Ruth Martin-C. Brooks Fry Award

Theatre Americana
Melva Campbell, President
P.O. Box 245
Altadena, California 91011 U.S.A.
Tel: (213) 790-5006

June

International; entry open to all; annual; established 1934. Theme: Americana. Sponsored and supported by nonprofit Theatre Americana, oldest little theater in nation dedicated to presentation of original scripts by American authors. Average statistics: 300 entries, 4 finalists. Held at Farnsworth Park, Altadena, California. Have workshops. Tickets: $3.50. Publish *The Prompter* (monthly newspaper). Also sponsor awards for acting, directing.

PLAY CONTEST: **Full-Length,** original, unpublished; 2-3 acts, minimum 90-minute performance time. Submit bound manuscript; include piano score or tape if musical. Preference to American authors, plays of American scene. No movie, TV scripts, obscenity for shock value.

AWARDS: $500 to Best Written Play. Full production of 4 finalists.

JUDGING: By 3 professionals. Based on manuscript, viewing of play in production.

ENTRY FEE: $10. Entrant pays postage (include SASE).

DEADLINES: Entry, April. Awards, June.

PLAY (Short, One-Act)

Short and One-Act Plays, and Book, Poetry, including BY WOMEN, CONTEMPORARY. (Also see other PLAY, PLAY PRODUCTION CATEGORIES.)

198

John Gassner Memorial Playwriting Award
New England Theatre Conference (NETC)
Marie L. Philips, Executive Secretary
50 Exchange Street
Waltham, Massachusetts 02154
U.S.A. Tel: (617) 893-3120

October

National; **entry open to U.S.;** annual; established 1967. Formerly called NEW ONE-ACT PLAY CONTEST, founded 1963. Purpose: to encourage new playwrights; produce new one-act plays. Sponsored and supported by NETC, nonprofit association of individuals, educational institutions, theater-producing oriented groups and organizations. Founded 1952 to develop, expand, assist theater activity in New England and beyond. Average statistics: 175-225 entries, 20 semifinalists, 2 awards. Have annual convention, contests, workshops, conferences, training programs, seminars, auditions, talent registry, placement and speakers' bureau, consultant services. Publish *NETC News* (bimonthly) and *Design and Technology Exchange* supplement, special publications, *New England Theatre Directory.* Also sponsor annual Moss Hart Memorial Award (to full-length plays dealing with courage and dignity); drama competitions; special achievement awards to performers, theater-supporting groups, publications.

PLAY CONTEST: One-Act Any **Subject,** original, unpublished, unproduced; any form; 1-hour maximum; limit 1 entry. Require 3 typed, bound copies; synopsis; cast list; character description.

AWARDS: $200 First, $100 Second Place. Winners given script-in-hand performance at NETC New Scripts Showcase, with audience-critic critiques.

JUDGING: By 4-member panel of educators, professionals. All entries read in entirety. May withhold awards. Not responsible for loss or damage.

ENTRY FEE: None. Entrant pays postage (include SASE).

DEADLINES: Entry, April. Judging, April-August. Winners announced, September. Awards, October. Materials returned, November.

199

Mortimer Fleishhacker Playwriting Award: Best New Plays by Women
One Act Theatre Company of San Francisco
Michael Lynch, Coordinator
430 Mason Street
San Francisco, California 94102
U.S.A. Tel: (415) 421-6162

Spring-Summer

National; **entry restricted to U.S. women;** annual; established 1980. Purpose: to encourage one-act plays by women playwrights. Sponsored by One Act Theatre Company (OATC). Supported by Mortimer Fleishhacker Foundation, OATC. Recognized by TCG, *Writer,* NEA, BATC. Average statistics: 500 entrants, 50 semifinalists, 15 finalists, 5 winners. Held in San Francisco. Have 2 99-seat theaters. Tickets: $6.50. Publish monthly newsletter.

PLAY CONTEST: One-Act By Women, in English, any theme, 60 minutes maximum; typed, 2 copies, 1 play per entrant. No collaborations, musicals, children's, adaptations.

AWARDS: $500 First, $300 Second, $200 Third Place. 2 Honorable Mentions of $100, plus production.

JUDGING: Preliminary by 10 OATC judges. Final by 5 nationally prominent actors, critics, playwrights. Sponsor may produce plays. Not responsible for loss or damage.

ENTRY FEE: None. Entrant pays postage (include SASE).

DEADLINES: Entry, January. Event, judging, February-June. Awards, June.

200

Religious Arts Guild Drama, Poetry, Book Awards

Unitarian Universalist Association (UUA)
Barbara M. Hutchins, Executive Secretary
25 Beacon Street
Boston, Massachusetts 02108 U.S.A.
Tel: (617) 742-2100

Summer

International; entry open to all; annual (book, poetry), biennial (play); established 1923. Purpose: to create, foster interest in church fine arts, increase beauty appreciation in lives of religious liberals. Sponsored by Religious Arts Guild of the UUA. Have Anthem loan library. Publish *U U World* (130,000 circulation house paper), religious drama, worship services. Also sponsor $100 Try Works Prize for creative performable Unitarian Universalist Church service celebrating great occasion.

PLAY CONTEST: Contemporary One-Act Drama (called *One-Act Drama Playwright Competition),* unpublished, 20-40 minutes running time, 5 players maximum, contemporary setting; 1 entry, 2 copies, bound, typed. No costumed period pieces.

POETRY CONTEST: Human Spirit (called *Dorothy Rosenberg Poetry Award),* any style, length, unpublished, typed (no carbon, copies), 1 poem per page. Limit 3 poems per entrant.

BOOK CONTEST: Religious Liberalism (called *Frederic G. Melcher Book Award),* published in U.S. in previous calendar year. Submission by publishers only.

AWARDS: $200 Best Play. $50 First Prize, $25 Second Prize, Poem. $1000 and Bronze Medallion, Best Book.

JUDGING: UUA may reproduce winning poem in *U U World* house paper; may publish and perform plays royalty-free for nonprofit occasions. Not responsible for loss or damage.

ENTRY FEE: Entrant pays postage (include SASE).

DEADLINES: Entry, January (play, book), March (poetry). Awards, Summer.

201

Russell Sharp Drama Fair

The Theater Guild of Webster Groves
517 Theater Lane
Webster Groves, Missouri 63119
U.S.A. Tel: (314) 962-0876

Spring-Summer

International; entry open to all; annual; established 1926. Named after Russell A. Sharp, charter member of Theater Guild. Purpose: to further creative efforts of world's playwrights. Sponsored by The Theater Guild of Webster Grove, oldest community theater west of Mississippi River (100-member nonprofit organization). Have 144-seat theater. Also sponsor full-length and Children's Theater productions.

PLAY CONTEST: **One-Act,** unpublished; typed on 8 1/2x11-inch white paper, stapled or in binder; 3 maximum per year per entrant. No huge casts, elaborate stagings.

AWARDS: $75 First, $50 Second Place. Winners produced by Guild.

JUDGING: By Guild members. No critiques provided. Not responsible for loss or damage.

ENTRY FEE: None. Entrant pays postage (include SASE).

DEADLINES: Entry, April. Judging, June. Event, awards, August.

202

San Mateo County Fair One-Act Playwriting Competition

San Mateo County Fair Arts Committee
Lois Kelley, Administrator
171 Flying Cloud Isle
Foster City, California 94404 U.S.A.
Tel: (415) 349-2787

July-August

International; entry open to all; annual; established 1957. Purpose: to provide showcase for emerging trends in arts. Sponsored and supported by San Mateo County Fair Arts Committee. Average statistics: 200,000 attendance. Held at San Mateo County Fair (2495 S. Delaware, San Mateo, California) for 19 days. Tickets: $3. Also sponsor San Mateo County Fair Poetry Competition. Second contact: San Mateo County Fair Association, P.O. Box 1027, San Mateo, California 94403.

PLAY CONTEST: **One-Act,** unpublished, unproduced, property of entrant or with copyright release; 30-60 minutes; 3 entries maximum; 2 copies each script, bound, stapled, double-spaced on one side of paper. Categories: One-Act Comedies, Melodramas, Romances, Dramas (other than tragedies).

AWARDS: $250 First Prize. Second, Third, Merit Awards. Ribbons, each category. $100 Special Subject Award (for Thoroughbred Race Horse Interpretation).

JUDGING: By 2 readers from Bay Area theater arts community. Based on structure, characterization, dialog, concept, plot, theatricality. May withhold awards, read excerpt of play on royalty-free basis until end of Fair. Not responsible for loss or damage.

ENTRY FEE: $5 each. Entrant pays postage (include SASE).

DEADLINES: Entry, June. Winners announced, July.

203

Texas Community Theater Original One-Act Play Contest

StageCenter, Inc.
P.O. Box 3377
College Station, Texas 77841 U.S.A.
Tel: (713) 822-5511

Summer

National; **entry open to U.S.;** biennial (odd years); established 1979. Purpose: to recognize, encourage original one-act plays suitable for production by small community-theater. Sponsored and supported by StageCenter, Inc. Average statistics: 50 entrants, 10 finalists, 3 winners, 300 attendance, 4 productions. Held at Bryan, College Station, Texas, for 6 months. Have thrust stage in 100-seat community theater. Tickets: $3.

PLAY CONTEST: One-Act, suitable for small community-theater production on thrust stage, any style or content; 40 minutes maximum; typed or photocopied on 8 1/2x11-inch white paper, bound.

AWARDS: $100 each to 3 winning plays, maximum. Winners produced by StageCenter.

JUDGING: By 3-4 judges selected by StageCenter from Bryan-College Station area. Based on originality, community audience appeal, creative use of thrust stage. Sponsor may produce winners during summer following contest. Not responsible for loss or damage.

ENTRY FEE: None. Entrant pays postage (include SASE).

DEADLINES: Entry, not specified. Acceptance, February. Judging, March-April. Awards, materials returned, May. Event, June-August.

204

Virginia Z. Weisbrod One-Act Playwriting Competition

Little Theatre of Alexandria (LTA)
Donald R. Williams, Chairman
600 Wolfe Street
Alexandria, Virginia 22314 U.S.A.
Tel: (703) 683-5778

July

International; entry open to all; annual; established 1979. Named after Virginia Z. Weisbrod, active member of the theater. Purpose: to recognize original scripts and playwrights; bring plays to LTA audiences. Sponsored and supported by LTA. Average statistics: 140 entrants, 8 finalists, 1000 attendance, 3 productions, 5 performances. Have full season (7 productions) for public; 200-seat theater. Held at LTA for 1 week.

PLAY CONTEST: One-Act, original, unpublished, unproduced, 20-60 minutes, 1 copy, in English; multiple entries from same author acceptable.

AWARDS: $250 First Place and production. Honorable Mention, all finalists. Production, selected finalists.

JUDGING: Prescreening by 4 judges minimum; final by 12. Based on dramatic action, concept, dialog, stageability. May produce winner without royalty. Not responsible for loss or damage.

ENTRY FEE: None. Entrant pays postage (include SASE).

DEADLINES: Entry, March. Judging, April-June. Awards, July.

PLAY (Specific Subject)

One-Act, Short, and Full-Length Plays, on various subjects, including CHILDREN, GAY, HAWAII-PACIFIC CULTURE, HISPANIC, JEWISH, MUSICAL, POETIC DRAMA. (Also see other PLAY, PLAY PRODUCTION CATEGORIES.)

205

American College Theatre Festival (ACTF) Playwriting Awards

Producing Director
John F. Kennedy Center for the Performing Arts
Washington, District of Columbia 20566 U.S.A. Tel: (202) 254-3437

April

International; **entry restricted to student plays produced in festival;** annual. National Playwriting Award of $2500, National Festival production, William Morris Agency management contract, Dramatists Guild Membership, publishing by Samuel French, August residence scholarship at O'Neill Theatre Center (Waterford, Connecticut) to author, and $1000 to producing college-university theater department for Best **Original Student Full-Length Play-Musical.** Norman Lear Award of $3108, teleplay writing contract, Los Angeles round-trip transportation, living expenses, $500 Writers Guild of America membership for **Comedy Play.** Lorraine Hansberry Award of $2500 First, $1000 Second Place to student authors; $750 and $500 grants to producing theater departments for **American Black Experience Play** (established 1975). David Library of the American Revolution Playwriting Awards of $2000 First, $100 Second Place to authors for **American Freedom Full-Length Plays** (sponsored by David Library of the American Revolution, Box 48, River Road Route 32, Washington Crossing, Pennsylvania 18977, 215-493-6776; established 1974). Warner Brothers Writers Award of $6043 (60-minute) or $3323 (30-minute) teleplay writing contract, $500 Writers Guild of America membership, reasonable travel expenses to Los Angeles to student author, $500 to producing drama department for **Student Play** (established 1980). Authors must be graduate-undergraduate students at accredited junior-senior colleges. Plays must be produced within 2 years of student's enrollment, by U.S. colleges-universities, or foreign ATA member colleges-universities (in countries contiguous with continental U.S.). Sponsored by American Theater Association. Average statistics: 430 entries. Also sponsor awards, scholarships for acting, theatrical design. Judging at local, 13 U.S. regional, and 10-top-play national festivals. National Festival-Awards at John F. Kennedy Center (Washington, D.C.), April.

206

American Jewish Theatre Production of New Plays Program

American Jewish Theatre
Stanley Brechner, Producer
1395 Lexington Avenue
New York, New York 10028 U.S.A.
Tel: (212) 427-6000

September-June

International; entry open to all; annual; established 1980. Purpose: to select plays for theater season. Sponsored by American Jewish Theatre. Supported by 92nd Street Young Men's, Young Women's Hebrew Association. Held at Studio Theatre. Average statistics: 200 entries, 5 countries, 15 semifinalists, 5 finalists, 1 award.

PLAY CONTEST: **Jewish Theme,** in English.

AWARDS: $500-$750 for best play plus professional production during regular season (September-June).

JUDGING: By 5 professionals.

ENTRY FEE: None. Entrant pays postage (Include SASE).

DEADLINES: Not specified.

207

Community Children's Theatre Playwriting for Children Awards

Madalene Woodbury, Chair
1015 West 55th Street
Kansas City, Missouri 64113 U.S.A.
Tel: (816) 444-4832

May

International; entry open to all; annual; established 1951. Founded 1947 by nonprofessional women. Purpose:

to bring live theater to Kansas City area public school children; entertain, educate, broaden horizons; train audiences to appreciate theater. Sponsored by Community Children's Theatre of Kansas City. Tickets: Free. Have 8 women's volunteer trouping units performing at 250 elementary schools yearly (100,000 attendance).

PLAY CONTEST: **Short For Children** (grades 1-6), unpublished, 30-page minimum, typed, double-spaced, bound, 55-60 minutes; 8 characters or less, parts performable by adult women. Wholesome action interspersed with humor, minimum dialog, simple for easy trouping from school to school. No cursing, excess slang, storyteller approach, virile roles, love stories, seasonal plays.

AWARDS: $500 to Best Script.

JUDGING: By 6-8-member committee. Based on capacity to stimulate children's imagination, clarity, forward-moving story, humor, appropriate subject matter. May divide, withhold award. Sponsor keeps winning scripts, may produce winners royalty-free for 2 years. Not responsible for loss or damage.

ENTRY FEE: None. Entrant pays postage (include SASE).

DEADLINES: Entry, January. Judging, January-March. Materials returned, April-May. Awards, May.

208

David B. Marshall Award in Musical Theatre

University of Michigan Professional Theatre Program
Jean B. Galan
227 South Ingalls
University Michigan League
Ann Arbor, Michigan 48109 U.S.A.
Tel: (313) 763-5213

June

National; **entry open to U.S.;** annual; established 1976. Named after University of Michigan alumnus David B. Marshall. Purpose: to stimulate playwrights, lyricists, composers to collaborate on original works for musical theater. Sponsored and supported by Professional Theatre Program at University of Michigan and Contempo Communications Foundation for the Arts. Average statistics: 30-50 entries, 3 awards.

PLAY CONTEST: **Musical Full-Length,** original, unproduced, in English; may be co-authored; typed on one side of paper. Submit 3 copies, 3 audiotapes of music-songs.

AWARDS: $2000 (may be divided among several winners) and possible production at University of Michigan. Consideration for professional production.

JUDGING: Preliminary by University panel. Final by 3 national judges. May withhold awards. Sponsor reserves right to keep for files one copy each manuscript and tape entered. Not responsible for loss or damage.

ENTRY FEE: $25 reader's fee. Entrant pays postage (include SASE).

DEADLINES: Entry, January. Awards, June.

209

Fendrich Playwriting Award

National Foundation for Jewish Culture
Susan Merson
122 East 42nd Street, Room 1512
New York, New York 10168 U.S.A.
Tel: (212) 490-2280

April

International; entry open to all; annual; established 1980. Named after Shubert and Anne Fendrich. Purpose: to encourage playwrights to investigate Jewish heritage; offer new works reflecting fresh perspective on Jewish life-culture. Sponsored and supported by National Foundation for Jewish Culture, Jewish Theatre Association. Average statistics: 160 entries. Publish quarterly newsletter; *Plays of Jewish Interest.* Also sponsor Jewish Ethnic Music Festival.

PLAY CONTEST: **Full-Length Jewish Life and Culture,** original, unpublished; in English; nonmusical.

AWARDS: $1000 advance against royalties and publication by Pioneer Drama Service.

JUDGING: All read in entirety by committee member. Finalists read and winner selected by 3-member professional panel. Not responsible for loss or damage.

ENTRY FEE: None. Entrant pays postage.

DEADLINES: Entry, December. Winner announced, April.

210

Forest A. Roberts-Shira Institute Playwriting Award Competition

Forest Roberts Theatre of Northern Michigan University (NMU)
James A. Panowski, Director
Marquette, Michigan 49855 U.S.A.
Tel: (906) 227-2553, (800) 682-9797

April

International; entry open to all; annual; established 1977. Named after Forest A. Roberts, former Head, NMU Department of Speech. Formerly called FOREST A. ROBERTS PLAYWRITING AWARD COMPETITION. Purpose: to encourage, stimulate artistic growth among playwrights; provide students creative opportunity to produce original work on university stage. Sponsored and supported by Shiras Institute Philanthropic organizations, Forest Roberts Theatre, NMU. Average statistics: 300 entries, 5 countries, 17 finalists, 3 awards, 4 performances, 1600 attendance. Held at Forest Roberts Theatre, NMU. Tickets: $1-$3. Have workshops, seminars.

PLAY CONTEST: **Full-Length Changing Themes,** unproduced unpublished, 1 copy; finalists provide additional copies if requested. May be coauthored, based on factual information, or adaptation. Various yearly themes. No musicals, one-act plays.

AWARDS: $1000 and partially mounted production. Winner is Artist-in-Residence during run of show, including classroom appearances, conducting seminars and workshops; room, board, transportation provided.

JUDGING: Screening committee reads plays in entirety twice. Final by students, faculty, community leaders. Sponsor may present world premiere, negotiate with author for ACTF production. Not responsible for loss or damage.

ENTRY FEE: None. Entrant pays postage (include SASE).

DEADLINES: Entry, July. Materials, November. Judging, July-December. Production, April.

211

Harry & Luci Wolpaw Playwriting Competition

Jewish Community Center of Cleveland
Dorothy Silver, Director of Cultural Arts Department
3505 Mayfield Road
Cleveland Heights, Ohio 44118
U.S.A. Tel: (216) 382-4000, ext. 275

May

National; **entry open to U.S.;** annual; established 1970. Purpose: to encourage writing of original plays. Theme: American Jewish Experience. Sponsored by Jewish Community Center of Cleveland, Wolpaw Playwriting Competition Fund. Supported by contributions to Wolpaw Competition Fund. Average statistics: 50 entries, 1200 attendance. Held at Jewish Community Center of Cleveland for 11 performances. Tickets: $2.50-$4.50.

PLAY CONTEST: **American Jewish Theme,** unpublished, not previously used.

AWARDS: $1000. Winner produced at Jewish Community Center.

JUDGING: By small committee, supervised by Director of Cultural Arts at Jewish Community Center. Sponsor claims right to produce.

ENTRY FEE: None. Entrant pays postage (include SASE).

DEADLINES: Entry, November. Winners announced, February. Play produced, May.

212

Honolulu Theatre for Youth (HTY) Ayling Playwriting Competition

Pepi Nieva, Public Relations Director
P.O. Box 3257
Honolulu, Hawaii 96801 U.S.A.
Tel: (808) 521-3487

Spring

International; entry open to all; biennial (odd years); established 1978. Named after Mildred and Edmond Ayling, art patrons. Purpose: to encourage new material on Hawaii and Pacific Basin cultures-settings. Sponsored and supported by Edmond and Mildred Ayling. Have theater conservatory, 5 plays annually. Also sponsor HTY Theatre for Schools Program.

PLAY CONTEST: **Short Hawaii and Pacific Basin Culture,** unpublished; approximately 60 minutes, typewritten, bound. Require release for copyrighted works.

AWARDS: $500 Best. Honorable Mentions.

JUDGING: 3 judges view all entries. May withhold awards. Sponsor may produce winning play royalty-free up to one year (and any other entry with royalty payment).

ENTRY FEE: None. Entrant pays postage (include SASE).

DEADLINES: Entry, December. Judging, March. Awards, Spring.

213

International Gay Playwriting Contest

Gay Theatre Alliance
Terry Helbing, Northeast Coordinator
P.O. Box 294, Village Station
New York, New York 10014 U.S.A.
Tel: (212) 255-4713

December

International; entry open to all; annual; established 1980. Formerly cosponsored by The Glines and called NATIONAL GAY PLAYWRITING CONTEST. Purpose: to locate, encourage writing of new gay plays. Sponsored and supported by Gay Theatre Alliance. Average statistics: 200 entrants, 5 semifinalists, 2 awards. Have workshops, plays. Publish *Directory of Gay Plays* and newsletter (quarterly). Second contact: Allan Estes, Northwest Coordinator, 1115 Geary, San Francisco, California 94109; tel: (415) 776-1848.

PLAY CONTEST: **Gay Character**

or Theme, unpublished, unproduced (except staged readings or workshop productions), one-act or full-length, in English; 1 entry, typed, bound with folder. Submit tape of score for musicals. Particularly interested in women's materials.

AWARDS: $500 First, $250 Second Prize. Will assist winners in securing production.

JUDGING: Screening by regional coordinator. Final by international panel of gay theatre experts. All entries read in entirety. Entrant retains all rights. Not responsible for loss or damage.

ENTRY FEE: None. Entrant pays postage (include SASE).

DEADLINES: Entry, September (not before June). Awards, December.

214

Living Playwrights Competition

Dragon's Teeth Press
El Dorado National Forest
Georgetown, California 95634 U.S.A.

December

International; entry open to all; annual. Purpose: to encourage renaissance of poetic drama. Sponsored and supported by Dragon's Teeth Press. Publish *New Poetic Drama* (quarterly).

PLAY CONTEST: **Poetic Drama,** original, unproduced, unpublished; 30-90 pages typed and bound in covers. Experimental or traditional, free or metric verse, preferably with 1 set, 24-hour action, 2-12 characters. Leading character may be dramatic figure from ancient to modern world history.

AWARDS: Cash award, publication in *New Poetic Drama,* and presentation to leading theatre groups in U.S. and abroad for Best New Verse Play.

JUDGING: By panel. Based on treatment originality, depth of conception, character revelation, historical accuracy, dramatic and poetic power. Entrant retains all rights except first publication.

ENTRY FEE: $10 each. Entrant pays postage (include SASE).

DEADLINES: Entry, September. Winners announced, December. Winner published, Spring.

215

National Repertory Theatre (NRT) Play Awards

Nancy Cunningham, Michael Dewell
P.O. Box 71011
Los Angeles, California 90071 U.S.A.
Tel: (213) 629-3762

April

International; entry open to all; annual; established 1977. Purpose: to encourage, support new plays, playwrights. Sponsored and supported by NRT Foundation, nonprofit, public, tax-exempt organization for new playwriting, development of Hispanic-American theater. Average statistics: 630 entries, 41 states, 4 winners. Also sponsor Academy of Stage and Cinema Arts (ASCA), professionally oriented drama school training actors, directors, playwrights; Bilingual Foundation of the Arts (BFA); Pasadena Community Arts Center.

PLAY CONTEST: **Any Subject, Hispanic,** original, unproduced, unpublished; any style-length; in English; designed for living stage presentation. Submit script, biography, history; include original Spanish work with English translation. No musicals or adaptations.

AWARDS: $5000 NRT Play Award, round-trip transportation to presentation ceremony, and possible production (Any Subject). 2 $1000 BFA Special Prizes, Best Original dealing with Hispanic experience in U.S., Best Translation major Spanish-language play. Second, Third Prizes; Honorable Mentions.

JUDGING: Prescreened by reader committee; final by 7 judges.

ENTRY FEE: None. Entrant pays postage (include SASE).

DEADLINES: Entry, September. Winners announced, January. Awards, April.

216

Pioneer Drama & Ha'Penny Players National Children's Theatre Playwriting Award
Pioneer Drama Service
Shubert Fendrich, Publisher
2172 South Colorado Blvd.
Box 22555
Denver, Colorado 80222 U.S.A.
Tel: (303) 759-4297

September

International; entry open to all; annual; established 1980. Purpose: to encourage playwrights in educational theater to submit quality children's scripts for publication. Sponsored and supported by Pioneer Drama Service and Ha'Penny Players (an activity of City of Long Beach, California Recreation Department). Also sponsor Pioneer Drama Playwriting Award. Second contact: Dave Barton.

PLAY CONTEST: **For Children,** original or adaptation; produced or unproduced; unpublished; 60-90 minutes performance time. Include prior performance information. Categories: Comedy, Musical.

AWARDS: $500 advance against royalties plus publication and production by sponsors.

JUDGING: By editorial board; final by publisher. Based on simplicity of sets, balanced cast, broad national appeal. All entries considered for publication. Not responsible for loss or damage.

ENTRY FEE: None. Entrant pays return postage (include SASE).

DEADLINES: Entry, March. Acceptance, April. Winners announced, June. Awards, September.

PLAY PRODUCTION (Any Type-Subject)

U.S. theaters producing new plays and playwrights. One-Act, Short, and Full-Length, including INTERNSHIPS, PRODUCTION WORKSHOPS, POETRY PERFORMANCE. (Also see PLAY and PLAY PRODUCTION CATEGORIES.)

217

Academy Theatre New Scripts Program
Keith B. Crofford, Literary Manager
P.O. Box 77070
581 Peachtree Street N.E.
Atlanta, Georgia 30309 U.S.A.
Tel: (404) 873-2518

Continuous

International; entry open to all; continuous. Academy Theatre (formerly Center Stage) is Atlanta's oldest and only professional resident theater company. Purpose: to find and produce new works for theater. Sponsored and supported by Academy

Theatre. Average statistics: 75 entrants, 50,000 attendance. Publish production brochures. Also sponsor School of Performing Arts (founded 1956 by Frank Wittow), with Lab Theatre for student actors, technicians.

PLAY PRODUCTION: Any Subject.

JUDGING: All entries reviewed by literary staff.

ENTRY FEE: None. Entrant pays postage (include SASE).

DEADLINES: Entry, open.

218

Alaska Repertory Theatre Production of New Plays
Robert J. Farley, Artistic Director
705 West 6th Avenue, Suite 201
Anchorage, Alaska 99501 U.S.A.
Tel: (907) 276-2327

Continuous

International; entry open to all; continuous; established 1977. Sponsored by Alaska Repertory Theatre. Average statistics: 50% of mainstage season devoted to new plays (3).

PLAY PRODUCTION: Any Subject. Categories: Full-Length, One-Act, Musical.

ENTRY FEE: None.

DEADLINES: Entry, open (February-April preferred). Materials returned in 5 months.

219

American Conservatory Theatre (ACT) Production of New Plays
Raye Birk, Director
450 Geary Street
San Francisco, California 94102
U.S.A. Tel: (415) 771-3880

Continuous

International; entry open to all; continuous. Purpose: to encourage development of new playwrights and new plays. Sponsored by ACT. Average statistics: 40% of mainstage season devoted to new plays, 5 second stage, 8 workshops-readings. Have Plays-in-Progress (production, performance, staged readings), new play workshops. Also sponsor PLAYWRIGHT FELLOWSHIPS. Second contact: Edward Hastings.

PLAY PRODUCTION: Any Subject(full-length, one-act). No children's, musicals.

ENTRY FEE: None. Entrant pays postage (include SASE).

DEADLINES: Entry, open. Materials returned in 2-6 months.

220

Arkansas Repertory Theatre Production of New Plays
Steven J. Caffery
712 East 11th Street
Little Rock, Arkansas 72202 U.S.A.
Tel: (501) 378-0405

Continuous

International; entry open to all; continuous. Sponsored and supported by Arkansas Repertory Theatre. Average statistics: 25% of mainstage season devoted to new plays. Have workshops.

PLAY PRODUCTION: Any Subject, any type, full-length, one-act, musicals. Prefer small cast, realistic, absurd, poignant dialog. Seek short, experimental pieces for workshop productions.

ENTRY FEE: None. Entrant pays postage (include SASE).

DEADLINES: Entry, open (best months December-February). Materials returned in 6 months.

221

Barter Theatre Production of New Plays

Rex Partington, Producing Director
P.O. Box 867
Abington, Virginia 24210 U.S.A.
Tel: (703) 628-2401

Continuous

International; entry open to all; continuous; established 1932. Sponsored and supported by Barter Theatre (state theater of Virginia), nonprofit organization. Held at Barter Theatre, oldest, longest-running professional theater in U.S. Have 99-seat training theater for works-in-progress performances by intern actors (on 2-year, 10-member program), Short Plays for Children.

PLAY PRODUCTION: **Any Subject,** full-length, one-act, musical, children's plays. Prefer small cast. Must be considered good theater. Require synopsis, query letter (include SASE).

ENTRY FEE: None.

DEADLINES: Entry, open. May-August preferred. Materials returned in 6-12 months.

222

Berkeley Stage Company Production of New Plays

Tony Taccone
P.O. Box 2327
Berkeley, California 94702 U.S.A.
Tel: (415) 548-4728

Continuous

International; entry open to all; continuous; established 1974. Purpose: to produce new plays. Sponsored by Berkeley Stage Company. Supported by California Arts Council, City of Berkeley, CETA, Ford Foundation, NEA. Average statistics: 300 entries, 12-14 semifinalists, 5-7 finalists. Held at Berkeley Stage Company, 1111 Addison, Berkeley. Tickets: $4 (students, seniors), $6 (Thursdays, Sundays), $7 (Fridays, Saturdays).

PLAY PRODUCTION: **Any Subject** public reading, performance.

JUDGING: All scripts read in entirety by at least 1 judge of 7-member committee. May be returned with comments, held for staged readings or full production. Not responsible for loss or damage.

ENTRY FEE: None. Entrant pays postage (include SASE).

DEADLINES: Entry, open.

223

Circle Repertory Company Production of New Plays

B. Rodney Marriott, Literary Manager
161 Avenue of the Americas
New York, New York 10013 U.S.A.
Tel: (212) 691-3210

Continuous

International; entry open to all; continuous. Sponsored by Circle Repertory Company. Average statistics: 2000 entries, 6 new plays, 5 second stage, 45 workshop readings. Held at Circle Repertory Theater, 99 Seventh Avenue South, New York City. Also sponsor one-act play festival of Projects-in-Progress, miniproduction of new scripts, Playwrights' Workshop (by invitation only).

PLAY PRODUCTION: **Any Subject,** any type (one-act, full-length, adaptations, translations, etc.). Prefer plays in lyrical naturalism style. No musicals, children's plays.

JUDGING: All plays read in entirety by Literary Department staff. Prior to mainstage production, each play given reading, workshop production, discussion.

ENTRY FEE: None. Entrant pays postage (include SASE).

DEADLINES: Entry, open. Materials returned in 3 months.

224

Folger Theatre Group Production of New Plays

Robert Stevens, Literary Manager
201 East Capitol Street S.E.
Washington, District of Columbia
20003 U.S.A. Tel: (202) 547-3230

Continuous

International; entry open to all; continuous; established 1970 as division of Folger Shakespeare Library for professional production of Shakespeare, classics, new plays. Named after Henry Clay Folger, first president of Standard Oil of New York. Purpose: to balance works of Shakespeare and classical writers with current dramatic themes, issues. Sponsored and supported by Folger Shakespeare Library (administered by Trustees of Amherst College). Average statistics: 550 entries, 5 plays (regular season), 2 new plays (theater-in-residence season), 240 performances, 50,000 attendance. Held at Elizabethan-style 219-seat Folger Theatre, Kennedy Center's Terrace Theatre. Have privately endowed, independent library, housing finest collection of Shakespeare in world, other book collections, concerts, art collections, exhibitions, Shakespeare film collection. Also sponsor play workshops, internships in theatrical technical training, administration, design. Second contact: Eileen S. Cowel, Assistant to Producer.

PLAY PRODUCTION: Any Subject, any style, original, full-length, one-act, musicals. Prefer plays highly contemporary in theme or treatment, especially incorporating music, movement, big dramatic moments. No new translations, adaptions of classics, children's or radio-television style plays.

JUDGING: All scripts read in entirety by Literary Manager and assistant. All reviewed at least in part by producer. No individual evaluations.

ENTRY FEE: None. Entrant pays postage (include SASE).

DEADLINES: Entry, open. Materials returned in 2 months.

225

Goodman Theatre Production of New Plays

Gregory Mosher, Artistic Director
200 South Columbus Drive
Chicago, Illinois 60603 U.S.A.
Tel: (312) 443-3800

Continuous

International; entry open to all; continuous; established 1925. Sponsored and supported by Chicago Theatre Group, nonprofit organization. Average statistics: 50% mainstage season devoted to 3 new plays, 3 second stage productions. Held at 683-seat Mainstage Theatre, 135-seat Studio Theatre. Have Writers-in-Performance Series (authors read own works and others'). Second contact: Roche Schulfer, Managing Director.

PLAY PRODUCTION: Any Subject, one-act, full-length, musicals, adaptations, translations, cabaret. Prefer maximum 16 cast for mainstage, 10 for studio, serious intent regardless of genre. No children's plays.

ENTRY FEE: None. Entrant pays postage (include SASE).

DEADLINES: Entry, open. Materials returned in 6-8 months.

226

Hippodrome Theatre Workshop Production of New Plays
Kerry McKenney, Codirector
25 S.E. 2nd Place
Gainesville, Florida 32601 U.S.A.
Tel: (904) 373-5968

Continuous

International; entry open to all; continuous; established 1973. Grown from 100-seat to 2-stage theater with combined 390 seats; began state touring 1978. Purpose: to provide center for creative theatrical experience in atmosphere of artistic freedom and professional discipline. Motto: "Theater can provide impetus to improve society, raise important social issues, demonstrate values and ideals." Sponsored by Hippodrome Theatre. Supported by NEA, Florida Fine Arts Council, Alachua County Community Education Department. Recognized by Theatre Communications Group, Alternate Roots, FEDAPT, Equity Seed Theatre. Average statistics: 31,000 (mainstage), 50,000 (touring, education) attendance. Held at 270-seat main stage, 120-seat second stage, 25 S.E. 2nd Place, Gainseville, Florida. Have workshops, one-act play festival of established or new plays, in English. Tickets: $4.50-$7.50. Also sponsor film series, theatrical, dance, musical events. Second contact: Dan Schay, Executive Director.

PLAY PRODUCTION: Any Subject, new, unproduced; full-length, one-act, children's plays (for tour in schools, 30-minute maximum); in English.

JUDGING: Rights negotiable. Copy fee reimbursed if script lost.

ENTRY FEE: None. Entrant pays postage (include SASE).

DEADLINES: Entry, open.

PLAY INTERNSHIP: Play Production,15 interns (3 technical, 2 management, 10 acting-directing).

227

Magic Theatre Production of New Plays
Suresa Dundes, Script Reader
Building 314
Fort Mason
San Francisco, California 94123
U.S.A. Tel: (415) 441-8001

Continuous

International; entry open to all; continuous. Sponsored by Magic Theatre. Average statistics: 100% of mainstage season devoted to 5 new plays, 3 second stage productions.

PLAY PRODUCTION: Any Subject, new plays, full-length, one-act; especially surreal, absurd, experimental, but will consider wide spectrum of material. Prefer small cast (2-10); stylized sets. Interested in mixed media performance pieces. No musicals, commercial comedies, caberet, children's plays.

ENTRY FEE: None. Entrant pays postage (include SASE).

DEADLINES: Entry, open. Materials returned in 1 year.

228

Manhattan Theatre Club
Jonathan Alper, Literary Manager
321 East 73rd Street
New York, New York 10021 U.S.A.
Tel: (212) 288-2500

Continuous

International; entry open to all; continuous. Sponsored and supported by Manhattan Theatre Club, nonprofit off-off Broadway theater center. Average statistics: 90% mainstage season devoted to 5 new plays, 10 second stage productions. Have 12 workshops.

PLAY PRODUCTION: Any Subject, full-length, one-act, cabaret. Prefer plays about contemporary American life. No large historical dramas, children's or contemporary verse plays.

PLAY INTERNSHIPS: Play Literary Management and Production. Emphasizes audience development, business, casting, general administration, literary, production; for 3 months, nonpaid.

ENTRY FEE: None.

DEADLINES: Entry, open. Materials returned in 6 months.

229

New Dramatists Production Workshop

Stephen Harty, Administrative Director
424 West 44th Street
New York, New York 10036 U.S.A.
Tel: (212) 757-6960

Continuous

International; entry open to all; continuous; established 1949. Purpose: for playwrights to test skills before offering plays to producers. Sponsored by New Dramatists, Inc. (Kathleen Norris, Executive Director), nonprofit educational workshop for playwrights (membership free). Supported by NEA, NYSCA. Average statistics: 250 entries, over 400 total members accepted to date. Have craft discussions, free tickets to new Broadway and Off Broadway plays, observership of Broadway plays from first reading through opening night; 30-40-seat theater, conference rooms, duplicating equipment, pianos, rehearsal hall, writing rooms.

PLAY PRODUCTION WORKSHOP: Playwriting, workshop readings, productions, critiques of new plays (30-40 per season) with professional actors, directors, technicians before audience, so member playwrights may develop plays in unrestricted, professional atmosphere. Playwright must live or intend to live in Greater New York City area, have written 2 full-length plays. No adaptations, collaborations, musicals.

JUDGING: Read by 3 judges. After membership, playwrights submit new work, major revisions for annual reevaluation.

ENTRY FEE: None.

DEADLINES: Entry, open.

230

New Playwrights' Theatre of Washington Production of New Plays

Robert M. Bowen, Script Coordinator
1742 Church Street N.W.
Washington, District of Columbia
20036 U.S.A. Tel: (202) 232-1122

Continuous

National; **entry open to U.S. citizens;** continuous; established 1972. Purpose: to foster creation, development, production of new works by American playwrights; give Washington, D.C. a center for such purpose. Sponsored and supported by New Playwrights' Theatre, nonprofit, charitable, professional theater-educational institution. Average statistics: 5-6 productions, 20 workshops per year. Have regular open readings, staged readings, rehearsals, performances. Also sponsor Dramathon (festival of new plays with open readings), NPT School (to provide training for beginning playwrights, actors).

PLAY PRODUCTION: Any Subject, any style, full-length, one-act, musical; 20 cast maximum, flexible staging; thoroughly bound with cover. Playwrights must be willing to do further developing-refining on selected plays even if previously produced. No children's plays.

AWARDS: Royalties and full production with 4-6 weeks rehearsal time, at least 20 preformances.

JUDGING: Each script read by qualified evaluators. Rejected scripts returned with 2 critiques.

ENTRY FEE: None. Entrant pays postage (include SASE).

DEADLINES: Entry, open. Materials returned in 6-8 months.

231

Northwest Writers Conference New Play Production

The Empty Space Theater
Bill Partlan, Director, New Play Development
919 East Pike Street
Seattle, Washington 98122 U.S.A.
Tel: (206) 325-6801

April

Regional; **entry open to Idaho, Montana, Oregon, Washington, Wyoming residents;** annual. Founded 1970 as not-for-profit theater. Purpose: to stage professional readings of new plays by emerging Northwest playwrights. Sponsored by The Empty Space Theater. Have 6-7 primary shows, midnight shows, Summer Park Show, professional colloquia, intimate theater with flexible stage-audience seating plan. Also sponsor New Playwrights Forum (staged readings and development of plays-in-progress written by Northwest region and other invited playwrights). Second contact: M. Burke Walker, Artistic Director.

PLAY PRODUCTION: Any Subject, unproduced or significantly rewritten plays or musicals, 10-cast maximum; typed and bound, with lyrics in proper textual place and cassette tape (musicals), title page showing character-setting breakdown. Interested in full-length plays, off-beat and zany comedy, newest dramatic literature. No children's plays.

AWARDS: Stage Readings of plays selected for development.

ENTRY FEE: None. Entrant pays postage (include SASE).

DEADLINES: Entry, January (best submission date, March to August). Event, April. Materials returned in 2 months.

232

Old Log Theater Production of New Plays

Don Stolz, Producer-Director
Box 250
Excelsior, Minnesota 55331 U.S.A.

Continuous

International; entry open to all; continuous. Sponsored and supported by Old Log Theater, oldest continuously running proscenium theater in U.S.

PLAY PRODUCTION: Any Subject.

JUDGING: Each entry read in entirety.

ENTRY FEE: None. Entrant pays postage (include SASE).

DEADLINES: Entry, open.

233

Palisades Theatre Company Production of New Plays
Bobbie Seifer, Artistic Director
P.O. Box 10717
St. Petersburg, Florida 33733 U.S.A.

Continuous

International; entry open to all; continuous. Sponsored and supported by Palisades Theatre Company. Average statistics: 100% of mainstage season devoted to 7 new plays. Have 3 workshops.

PLAY PRODUCTION: **Any Subject,** full-length, one-act, musicals, children's plays (prefer 2-4 performers, 1 musician, 45 minutes maximum), adaptations, translations, cabaret, collage-compilations. Minimum technical requirements, small cast, suitable for touring or in-house production.

ENTRY FEE: None. Entrant pays postage (include SASE).

DEADLINES: Entry, open. Materials returned in 3 months.

234

St. Nicholas Theater Production of New Plays
Cynthia Sherman, Artistic Director
2851 North Halsted Street
Chicago, Illinois 60657 U.S.A.

Continuous

International; entry open to all; continuous; established 1976. Purpose: to bring new life to theater through new playwrights, designers, actors, directors. Sponsored and supported by St. Nicholas Theater Company. Average statistics: 80% mainstage season devoted to 3 new plays, 4 second stage productions. Have workshops, readings, New Works Ensemble productions, children's programs.

PLAY PRODUCTION: **Any Subject,** full-length, one-act, musicals (small cast), children's, adaptations. Prefer realism, good characterization, clear dramatic objectives. No abstract works, mysteries, commercial comedies, large musicals.

ENTRY FEE: None.

DEADLINES: Entry, open. Scripts returned in 4 months.

235

Seattle Repertory Theatre Production of New Plays
Daniel Sullivan, Resident Artistic Director
Seattle Center
P.O. Box B
Seattle, Washington 98109 U.S.A.
Tel: (206) 447-4730

Continuous

International; entry open to all; continuous; established 1962. Sponsored by Seattle Repertory Theatre. Supported by Mobil Foundation. Have second stage "New Plays in Process" series of 5 plays, bringing authors to Seattle to develop their plays (7-day rehearsal sessions, with minimal sets, props, costumes). Second contact: Marta Mellinger, PR Director.

PLAY PRODUCTION: **Any Subject,** No restrictions on cast size or scale.

ENTRY FEE: None.

DEADLINES: Entry, open.

236

South Coast Repertory Production of New Plays
Jerry Patch, Literary Manager
P.O. Box 2197
Costa Mesa, California 92626 U.S.A.
Tel: (714) 957-2602

Continuous

International; entry open to all; continuous. Sponsored and supported by South Coast Repertory. Average statistics: 15% of mainstage season devoted to new plays, second stage. Held at South Coast Repertory Theatre, 655 Town Center Drive, Costa Mesa. Have workshops, readings. Second contacts: David Emmes, Marin Benson, Artistic Directors.

PLAY PRODUCTION: Any Subject, new plays, full-length, one-act. Interested in plays that are overtly theatrical; show knowledge, control of dramatic structure; use language imaginatively. No restrictions.

ENTRY FEE: None.

DEADLINES: Entry, open. January to March best months to submit. Materials returned in 3 months.

237

Theater for the New City Production of New Plays
Crystal Field, Director
162 Second Avenue
New York, New York 10003 U.S.A.
Tel: (212) 924-1109

Continuous

International; entry open to all; continuous; established 1970. Purpose: to encourage production of new plays. Sponsored by Theatre for the New City. Recognized by Off-Off Broadway Alliance, Theatre Communications Group. Tickets: $3. Have workshop productions. Also sponsor theater management, technical internships.

PLAY PRODUCTION: Any Subject, especially full-length, one-act, musicals, children's plays. Prefer experimental, noncommercial works.

AWARDS: None.

ENTRY FEE: None.

DEADLINES: Entry, open.

238

University Theatre Production of New Plays
Ronald A. Willis
317 Murphy
University of Kansas
Lawrence, Kansas 66045 U.S.A.
Tel: (913) 864-3981

Continuous

International; entry open to all; continuous. Sponsored by University Theatre, University of Kansas. Held at Inge Theatre (100 seats), University Theatre (1188 seats). Circulate scripts to other theater directors. Tickets: $2-$4. Second contact: Jack B. Wright.

PLAY PRODUCTION: Any Subject. Require attendance by entrant (Fall).

ENTRY FEE: None. Entrant pays postage (include SASE).

DEADLINES: Entry, open.

239

Writers Theatre Workshop Production Program
American Writers Theatre Foundation (AWTF)
Linda Laundra, Artistic Director
P.O. Box 810, Times Square Station
New York, New York 10108 U.S.A.
Tel: (212) 581-5295

Continuous

International; entry open to all; continuous; established 1975. Purpose: to encourage poets, novelists, essayists, playwrights to write new stage works, adaptations. Sponsored by AWTF, nonprofit tax-exempt performing, literary arts organization. Have staged readings, developmental workshops, full staged productions.

PLAY PRODUCTION: **Any Subject,** new contemporary plays, adaptations of literary masterpieces.

POETRY PERFORMANCE: **Any Subject,** fully staged performance with professional actors, designed around specific theme or single poet's work. Some prose included.

JUDGING: Each read by 3 judges. If playwright is unable to attend performance, tape is sent.

ENTRY FEE: None.

DEADLINES: Entry, open.

PLAY PRODUCTION (Full-Length)

U.S. Theaters producing Full-Length new plays and playwrights. Includes Apprentice-Internships. (Also see PLAY and PLAY PRODUCTION CATEGORIES.)

240

Alley Theatre Production of New Plays

George Anderson, Assistant to the Director
615 Texas Avenue
Houston, Texas 77002 U.S.A.

Continuous

International; entry open to all; continuous. Sponsored by Alley Theatre.

PLAY PRODUCTION: **Full-Length Any Subject,** no musicals.

ENTRY FEE: None.

DEADLINES: Entry, open.

241

American Place Theatre Production of New Plays

Wynn Handman, Director
111 West 46th Street
New York, New York 10036 U.S.A.
Tel: (212) 246-3730

Continuous

National; **entry open to U.S.;** continuous; established 1964. Purpose: to give American writers opportunity for play production. Sponsored by American Place Theatre. Also sponsor Women's Project, lunchtime series. Second contact: Julia Miles, Associate Director.

PLAY PRODUCTION: **Full-Length Any Subject,** original, bound, small casts. Interested in musicals. No translations, adaptations.

AWARDS: Fees to writers accepted.

JUDGING: By literary adviser, artistic director. Not responsible for loss or damage.

ENTRY FEE: None. Entrant pays postage (include SASE).

DEADLINES: Entry, open.

242

American Stage Festival Production of New Plays

Will Maitland Weiss, Managing Director
P.O. Box 225

Milford, New Hampshire 03055
U.S.A. Tel: (603) 673-7515

Summer

International; entry open to all; annual; established 1975. Purpose: to provide professional performing arts; train young people as professional performers. Sponsored by American Stage Festival. Supported by ticket sales, private contributors. Recognized by Actors Equity Association. Average statistics: 200 entrants, 75 performances, 40,000 attendance. Held in southern New Hampshire for 12-13 weeks. Have 500-seat, 40-foot proscenium stage theater. Tickets: $6-$9.50. Second contact: Harold DeFelice, Artistic Director.

PLAY PRODUCTION: Full-Length, any style-subject.

PLAY APPRENTICE-INTERNSHIPS: Play Production. Require audition and-or interview, over age 18. Submit photo, resume. Categories: Acting, Stage Management, Administration, Design.

AWARDS: Noncompetitive (play production). Credit toward Equity union card for 25 Apprentice-Interns.

JUDGING: By American Stage Festival staff.

ENTRY FEE: None.

DEADLINES: Entry, April (best months to submit scripts, November-January). Acceptance, May. Event, Summer. Materials returned in 2 months.

243

American Theatre Arts (ATA) New Plays Program

Rebecca Westberg, Director of Play Development
6240 Hollywood Blvd.
Hollywood, California 90028 U.S.A.
Tel: (213) 466-2462

Continuous

International; entry open to all; continuous; established 1976. Purpose: to provide creative performing experiences and conservatory for actor development; offer highest attainable quality to widest audiences. Sponsored by and held at ATA. Second contact: Don Eitner, Artistic Director.

PLAY PRODUCTION: Full-Length Any Subject, by new or experienced playwrights, any type or style, one copy.

AWARDS: Flat fee or box-office percentage, and participation in production process. ATA gets 1% of subsequent production proceeds from premiering plays for 7 1/2 years.

ENTRY FEE: None. Entrant pays postage (include SASE).

DEADLINES: Entry, open. Materials returned in 4-6 weeks.

244

Arena Stage Production of New Plays

Douglas C. Wager, Literary Manager
6th Street and Maine Avenue S.W.
Washington, District of Columbia
20024 U.S.A. Tel: (202) 554-9066

September-June

International; entry open to all; continuous; established 1976. Founded 1950 in old movie theater, moved to permanent home 1961, won "Tony" Award 1976. Purpose: to produce new American plays, important European premieres, classics, new musicals. Sponsored by and held at Arena Stage. Supported by foundation grants, contributions, ticket sales. Average statistics: 1000 entries, 30 countries, 5 new play productions, 250,000 attendance, 15 total productions. Have 3 theaters, workshops, postproduction discussions, new play development series *(In-the-Process)* with informal critiques for script revision. Tickets: $7.-50-$12. Also sponsor Living Stage Theatre Company outreach arm bringing live theater to poor, elderly, disabled, incarcerated, other disenfranchised audiences (Robert Alexander, Founder-Director). Second contact: Zelda Fichandler, Producing Director.

PLAY PRODUCTION: Full-Length, Any Subject, any style or genre, unpublished, in English, 1 entry at a time, 1 copy. Well-written plays on universal and contemporary issues, suited to any of 3 theaters (800-seat in-the-round, 500-seat modified thrust, 200-seat workshop-cabaret). Also interested in musicals (include sample of score), one-acts, adaptations, new translations, cabaret material. Require preliminary letter, plot synopsis. Request resume, production history. No children's or nonthematic "commercial" musicals.

AWARDS: 5% of gross per performance. Playwright's attendance at rehearsals, performances may be required.

JUDGING: By 2-5 readers.

ENTRY FEE: None. Entrant pays postage (include SASE).

DEADLINES: Entry, open. In-Process Productions, April-June. Materials returned in 2-4 months.

245

Chelsea Theater Center Production of New Plays

James Harris, Literary Manager
407 West 43rd Street
New York, New York 10036 U.S.A.
Tel: (212) 541-8616

Continuous

International; entry open to all; continuous; established 1964. Sponsored by Chelsea Theater Center. Supported by NEA, NYSCA, foundations. Recognized by TCG, FEDAPT. Average statistics: 1200 entries (plays), 16,000 attendance, 76 performances. Tickets: $3-$16. Second contact: Edward Callaghan, Marketing Director.

PLAY PRODUCTION: Full-Length Any Subject, new, unproduced in U.S.; cast size, physical requirements not restricted. Submit synopsis, cover letter first. All scripts read.

AWARDS: Payment based on Off-Broadway standard contract.

ENTRY FEE: None.

DEADLINES: Open.

PLAY INTERNSHIP: Theater Management, Production, including development, public relations-marketing.

246

Circle in the Square Theatre Production of New Plays

Garrison Fishgall, Director of Play Development
1633 Broadway
New York, New York 10019 U.S.A.
Tel: (212) 581-3270

Continuous

International; entry open to all; continuous; established 1951. Purpose: to present American, European plays. Sponsored by nonprofit Circle in the Square. Statistics: 100 major productions to date. Held in 650-seat theater. Also sponsor accredited Circle in the Square Theatre School for 22 actors per year. Second contact: Theodore Mann, Artistic Director.

PLAY PRODUCTION: **Full-Length Any Subject,** prefer small cast (under 10) with star roles appropriate for theater-in-the-round. Request letter outlining premise, content. No one-acts.

ENTRY FEE: None.

DEADLINES: Entry, open. March-August preferred.

247

Cleveland Play House Production of New Plays

Peter Sander, Dramaturg
P.O. Box 1989
Cleveland, Ohio 44106 U.S.A.
Tel: (216) 795-7000

Continuous

International; entry open to all; continuous. Sponsored by and held at Cleveland Play House (2040 E. 86th Street, Cleveland, Ohio 44106). Average statistics: 10 productions per year. Also sponsor apprentice program in art-craft of theater for actors, technicians, managers. Second contact: Nadine Buchanan, Assistant to the Director.

PLAY PRODUCTION: **Full-Length Any Subject,** prefer small cast, relevant, well-crafted, with simple unit sets. Interested in adaptations, translations, musicals, children's plays.

AWARDS: Playwrights receive expenses while in rehearsal, royalties.

ENTRY FEE: None.

DEADLINES: Entry, open. Best date, April-August. Materials returned in 2-8 months.

248

Cricket Theatre Production of New American Plays

John Orlock, Literary Manager
528 Hennepin Avenue
Minneapolis, Minnesota 55104
U.S.A. Tel: (612) 333-1411

Continuous

National; **entry open to U.S.;** continuous. Sponsored by Cricket Theatre. Statistics: 14 produced in Works-in-Progress Series, 3 on main stage. Also sponsor commissions to playwrights of promise.

PLAY PRODUCTION: **Full-Length Any Subject,** preference to new American playwrights, small cast (6 or less). Interested in musicals, conventional, unconventional works. Require letter, synopsis. No children's plays.

ENTRY FEE: None. Entrant pays postage (include SASE).

DEADLINES: Entry, September-June. Reports in 6 months.

249

Dallas Theater Center Production of New Plays

Eleanor Lindsay, New Plays Development
3636 Turtle Creek Blvd.
Dallas, Texas 75219 U.S.A.
Tel: (214) 526-8210

Continuous

International; entry open to all; continuous; established 1959. Sponsored by Dallas Theater Center. Have workshops, main and second stage productions. Also sponsor Eugene McKinney New Play Reading Series. Second contact: Paul Baker, Managing Director; tel: (214) 526-0107.

PLAY PRODUCTION: **Full-Length Any Subject,** including children's plays. For second stage, 8 maximum cast, single-level unit set. No musicals.

ENTRY FEE: None.

DEADLINES: Entry, open. Best submission, September-March. Materials returned in 3 months.

250

The Empty Space Theater New Playwrights Forum
Bill Partlan, Director, New Play Development
919 East Pike Street
Seattle, Washington 98122 U.S.A.
Tel: (206) 325-6801

Various

Regional; **entry open to Idaho, Montana, Oregon, Washington, Wyoming residents or invited writers;** annual; established 1977. Founded 1970 as not-for-profit theater. Purpose: to assist promising playwrights; expose audience to play-creation process. Sponsored by The Empty Space Theater. Have 6-7 primary shows, midnight shows, Summer Park Show, professional colloquia, intimate theater with flexible stage-audience seating plan. Also sponsor Northwest Writers Conference New Play Production for emerging Northwest playwrights. Second contact: M. Burke Walker, Artistic Director.

PLAY PRODUCTION: **Full-Length Any Subject,** unproduced or significantly rewritten plays or musicals, 10-cast maximum; typed and bound, with lyrics in proper textual place and cassette tape (musicals), title page showing character-setting breakdown. Interested in off-beat, zany comedy, newest dramatic literature. No children's plays.

AWARDS: Recommended scripts go to 1 of 5 developmental stages with professional actors, directors: Consultation, Cold Reading, Staged Reading, Workshop Production, Mainstage Production.

JUDGING: By readers.

ENTRY FEE: None. Entrant pays postage (include SASE).

DEADLINES: Entry, July. Event, various. Materials returned in 2 months.

251

Invisible Theatre Production of New Plays
1400 North First Avenue
Tucson, Arizona 85719 U.S.A.
Tel: (602) 882-9721

September-May

International; entry open to all; annual; established 1970. Begun as playwright's theater; in 1979 included reinterpretation of classics. Purpose: to provide alternative theater; encourage local artistic growth. Sponsored by and held at Invisible Theatre. Supported by public, private sources. Recognized by Arizona Arts Commission. Average statistics: 50 entries, 100 performances. Have workshops, tours, children's theater, outdoor Shakespeare. Tickets: $4-$4.50. Second contact: Vera Marie Badertscher, Publicity Director, 5734 Paseo Cimarron, Tucson, Arizona 85715.

PLAY PRODUCTION: **Full-Length Any Subject,** including children's plays, 10 maximum cast, simple technical requirements, good female roles. Submit synopsis first.

AWARDS: Box-office share.

JUDGING: All scripts read by staff. Sponsor owns one-time production rights.

ENTRY FEE: None. Entrant pays postage (include SASE).

DEADLINES: Entry, open. Best submission, October-March. Materials returned in 6 months.

252

Long Wharf Theatre Production of New Plays

John Tillinger, Literary Manager
222 Sargent Drive
New Haven, Connecticut 06511
U.S.A.

Continuous

International; entry open to all; continuous. Sponsored by Long Wharf Theatre.

PLAY PRODUCTION: **Full-Length Any Subject,** no musicals.

ENTRY FEE: None.

DEADLINES: Entry, open.

253

Milwaukee Repertory Theater Company Production of New Plays

John Dillon, Artistic Director
Play Development Office
929 North Water Street
Milwaukee, Wisconsin 53202 U.S.A.

Continuous

International; entry open to all; continuous. Sponsored by Milwaukee Repertory Theater Company.

PLAY PRODUCTION: **Full-Length Any Subject.** Prefer synopsis first. No children's plays.

ENTRY FEE: None.

DEADLINES: Entry, open. Best submission, September-March.

254

New Jersey Shakespeare Festival Production of New Plays

Drew University
Paul Barry, Artistic Director
Madison, New Jersey 07940 U.S.A.

Continuous

International; entry open to all; continuous. Sponsored by New Jersey Shakespeare Festival.

PLAY PRODUCTION: **Full-Length Any Subject,** no musicals or children's plays.

ENTRY FEE: None.

DEADLINES: Entry, open.

255

Performance Community Production of New Plays

Byron Schaffer, Jr., Artistic Director
1225 West Belmont Avenue
Chicago, Illinois 60657 U.S.A.

Continuous

National; **entry open to U.S.;** continuous; established 1974. Purpose: to develop new American plays. Sponsored by Performance Community, founded 1969 as Dinglefest Theatre Company, incorporated 1974 as Performance Community. Average statistics: 16,000 annual attendance, $50,000 total sales. Held at Theatre Building, 1225 West Belmont Avenue, Chicago. Tickets: $5-$10.

PLAY PRODUCTION: **Full-Length Any Subject,** any style, preferably small cast, simple set. Submit typed, bound script.

AWARDS: Production plus 5% of gross.

ENTRY FEE: None. Entrant pays return postage (include SASE).

DEADLINES: Entry, open.

256

Playhouse on the Square Production of New Plays
Jackie Nichols, Director
2121 Madison
Memphis, Tennessee 38104 U.S.A.
Tel: (901) 725-0776

Continuous

International; entry open to all; continuous. Sponsored by Playhouse on the Square. Have workshops, readings, works-in-progress series.

PLAY PRODUCTION: **Full-Length Any Subject,** prefer small cast, single-set plays (including musicals). No sit coms.

ENTRY FEE: None.

DEADLINES: Entry, open. Materials returned in 4 months.

257

Playwrights' Center New Play Production
Kevin Berigan, Public Relations Director
2301 East Franklin Avenue
Minneapolis, Minnesota 55406 U.S.A. Tel: (612) 332-7481

Continuous

International; entry open to all; continuous; established 1971. Purpose: to assist playwrights in producing new works. Sponsored by Playwrights' Center (formerly Minnesota Playwriting Laboratory, Playwrights' Lab). Supported by Jerome Foundation, Minnesota State Arts Board. Have workshops, classes, national touring program of open play readings. Publish monthly newsletter. Also sponsor Playwrights' Center Residence Grants.

PLAY PRODUCTION: **Full-Length Any Subject,** preference to plays from Minnesota and Midwest; others read and critiqued for fee.

ENTRY FEE: Not specified.

DEADLINES: Open. Materials returned in 4-6 months.

258

Repertory Theatre of St. Louis New Play Production
Wallace Chappell, Artistic Director
P.O. Box 28030
St. Louis, Missouri 63119 U.S.A.
Tel: (314) 968-7340

Continuous

International; entry open to all; continuous; established 1971. Formerly called LORETTO-HILTON REPERTORY THEATRE to 1981. Sponsored by Repertory Theatre of St. Louis. Supported by NEA, Ford Foundation, subscribers. Recognized by NEA, Missouri Arts Council. Average statistics: 5 new plays per season. Tickets: $4.50-$11.50. Publish newsletter. Second contact: Addie Walsh, Literary Manager.

PLAY PRODUCTION: **Full-Length Any Subject,** any style; prefer small cast, two-act, low production demands; suitable for large, varied audience. Interested in adaptations, contemporary dramas.

AWARDS: 4 weeks performance, residency and royalty fees for produced plays.

ENTRY FEE: None. Entrant pays postage (include SASE).

DEADLINES: Entry, open. Best submission, February-June. Materials returned in 3 months.

259

Soho Repertory Theatre New Play Readings and Production
Jerry Engelbach, Artistic Director
19 Mercer Street
New York, New York 10013 U.S.A.
Tel: (212) 925-2588

October-June

International; **entry restricted to playwrights, directors;** annual; established 1975. Purpose: to stage rarely produced classics, high-quality modern plays; hold readings of high-quality new plays not ready for production. Sponsored by Soho Repertory Theatre. Supported by audience, NYSCA, foundations. Member of OOBA, TCG. Average statistics: 60-100 per night attendance, 13 productions, 196 performances. Held in Manhattan's Soho area for 5 weeks (each production), 1 night (reading). Have 100-seat theater, high-ceiling 3-sided thrust stage, largest off-off-Broadway subscription audience. Tickets: $5. Second contact: Engelbach, 224 Centre Street, New York, New York 10013.

PLAY PRODUCTION: **Full-Length Any Subject,** of high theatrical-literary quality, complete script, resume (if available). Seek nonrealistic contemporary plays. Directors submit resume, brief play description first. No sit coms, happenings, poetry readings.

AWARDS: $50-$200 directing and option fees for productions. No royalties, reading fees.

JUDGING: By 2 artistic directors and freelance play readers. Sponsor holds standard limited option agreement for produced plays, receives royalty from playwright if subsequently produced under professional contract (not applicable to readings). Not responsible for loss or damage.

ENTRY FEE: None. Entrant pays postage (include SASE).

DEADLINES: Entry, open. Scripts returned in 3-6 months.

260

Theatre by the Sea Production of New Plays
Jon Kimbell, Producing Director
91 Market Street
Portsmouth, New Hampshire 03801 U.S.A.

Continuous

International; entry open to all; continuous. Sponsored by Theatre by the Sea. Second contact: Theatre by the Sea, 25 Bow Street, Portsmouth, New Hampshire 03801.

PLAY PRODUCTION: **Full-Length Any Subject,** prefer small-cast contemporary drama (including musicals), simple unit sets, plays with universal merit sensitive to New England tastes.

ENTRY FEE: None.

DEADLINES: Entry, open. Best submission, April-August. Materials returned in 3 months.

261

Victory Gardens Theater Production of New Plays
Dennis Zacek, Artistic Director
3730 North Clark
Chicago, Illinois 60613 U.S.A.
Tel: (312) 549-5788

Continuous

International; entry open to all; continuous. Sponsored by Victory Gardens Theater. Have reader's theater series for new plays.

PLAY PRODUCTION: Full-Length Any Subject, small cast, single set. Interested in Black, Hispanic, musicals, good female roles.

ENTRY FEE: None.

DEADLINES: Entry, open.

262

Virginia Museum Theatre Production of New Plays

Tom Markus, Artistic Director
Boulevard and Grove Avenue
Richmond, Virginia 23221 U.S.A.
Tel: (804) 257-0831

Continuous

International; entry open to all; continuous; established 1955. Purpose: to provide high-quality professional theater, educational services and opportunities. Sponsored by Virginia Museum Theatre, founded as community theater; became professional 1972.

PLAY PRODUCTION: Full-Length Any Subject, small-cast new plays or small musicals. No excessive, strong language or dinner theater comedy.

ENTRY FEE: None.

DEADLINES: Entry, open. Materials returned in 6 months.

PLAY PRODUCTION (Special Type-Subject)

U.S. theaters producing One-Act, Short and Full-Length new plays and playwrights, ABOUT BLACKS, ASIAN-AMERICAN, FOR CHILDREN-YOUTH, MUSICAL. (Also see other PLAY, PLAY PRODUCTION.)

263

AMAS Repertory Theatre Musical Theatre Program

Jerry Lapidus, Administrative Director
AMAS Repertory Theatre
1 East 104th Street
New York, New York 10029 U.S.A.
Tel: (212) 369-8000

Continuous

International; entry open to all; continuous; established 1969. AMAS means "you love." Purpose: to promote community theater where people can work together with respect for individual skills and talents. Sponsored by AMAS Repertory Theatre. Supported by NEA, NYSCA, New York City Department of Cultural Affairs. Recognized by OOBA, TCG, TDF, AEA. Average statistics: 125 entries, 6 countries, 4 works chosen (12 performances each), 4200 attendance. Have workshops. Tickets: $6 adults, discounts available.

PLAY PRODUCTION: Musical, original, finished script with tape cassette of music score. No profanity, nudity.

JUDGING: Entries read in entirety if quality warrants. Final by Artistic Director and Founder, assisted by dramaturg, Board of Directors. If show moves to Broadway, authors, composers, lyricists are contractually obligated to pay AMAS percentage of weekly gross. Not responsible for loss or damage.

ENTRY FEE: None. Entrant pays postage (include large SASE).

DEADLINES: Entry, open. Production, 9-12 months after acceptance (season is September-May). Materials returned in 1 month.

264

East West Players New Play Production

Mako Iwamatsu, Artistic Director
4424 Santa Monica Blvd.
Los Angeles, California 90029 U.S.A.

Continuous

International; entry open to all; continuous. Sponsored and supported by East West Players. Average statistics: 80% of mainstage season devoted to 2 new plays. Have 2 workshops-readings.

PLAY PRODUCTION: **Asian American Life** (contemporary, abstract, period), full-length, one-act, musicals, children's, adaptations, translations.

ENTRY FEE: None. Entrant pays postage (include SASE).

DEADLINES: Entry, open. Materials returned in 2 months.

265

Honolulu Theatre for Youth Production of New Plays

Jane Campbell, Managing Director
P.O. Box 3257
Honolulu, Hawaii 96801 U.S.A.
Tel: (808) 521-3487

Continuous

International; entry open to all; continuous; established 1955. Honolulu Theatre for Youth is the major cultural resource in Hawaii dedicated to family. Purpose: to create best in theater for young people, families. Sponsored by Honolulu Theatre for Youth, nonprofit, private, cultural, educational organization producing quality theater. Supported by Hawaii State Foundation on Culture and the Arts, Hawaii State Legislature, NEA, Leeward College, foundations. Average statistics: 50% mainstage season devoted to 4 new plays, attendance nearing 2 million in 25 years. Held at Leeward Community College Theatre. Have theater for schools, state tours. Tickets: $1.50 (students), $3 (adults).

PLAY PRODUCTION: **Youth.** Prefer 1-hour plays that can tour, with history, related themes; legends of Pacific countries; strong characters. Prefer one-acts. Require letter of inquiry before script submission.

JUDGING: By staff.

ENTRY FEE: None. Entrant pays postage (include SASE).

DEADLINES: Entry, open. September-March best submission. Materials returned in 4 months.

266

Hyperion Theatre Children's Theatre Project

Barbara Haig, Director of Children's Theatre Project
1835 Hyperion Avenue
Los Angeles, California 90024 U.S.A.
Tel: (213) 661-9188

Continuous

International; entry open to all; continuous; established 1979. Purpose: to present thought-provoking alternatives to children; open communication between parents and children. Theme: Quality Theater for Young Audiences. Sponsored and supported by Hyperion Theatre, member of Los Angeles Theatre Alliance (LATA). Average statistics: 3 productions, 250 attendance per show. Held at Hyperion Theatre for 6 weeks each production. Tickets: $3 adults, $2.50 children.

PLAY PRODUCTION: **For Chil-**

dren, any appropriate subject, 50-60 minutes, live actors. May include music.

JUDGING: All entries read by Project Director, Artistic Director. Based on adherence to goals in Children's Theatre. Cast and director selected by winning playwright and producer. Sponsor gets 6 month exclusivity in Los Angeles County. No royalties paid.

ENTRY FEE: None. Entrant pays postage (include SASE).

DEADLINES: Entry, open.

267

National Black Theatre Production of New Plays
Zuri McKie, Managing Director
9 East 125th Street
Harlem, New York 10035 U.S.A.
Tel: (212) 427-5615

Continuous

International; entry open to all; continuous; established 1968. Purpose: to transform theater into celebration of life; improve quality of living for people. Sponsored by National Black Theatre. Supported by NYSCA, NEA, foundation gifts (60% of income derived from contributions). Recognized by FEDAPT, OOBA, AAA, BTA. Average statistics: 65% of mainstage season devoted to 1-3 new plays. Held at 9 East 125th Street and touring sites. Have workshops. Second contact: Keibu Faison, Tour Coordination.

PLAY PRODUCTION: **One-Act About Blacks,** musicals. Prefer plays that raise awareness and present timely, positive image of Black life.

ENTRY FEE: None.

DEADLINES: Entry, open. September-December best submission. Materials returned in 1 month.

268

The New York Cast New Original One-Act Plays Program
Dick Rizzo, Co-Producer
131 Thompson 6D
New York, New York 10012 U.S.A.

Periodic

International; entry open to all; periodic; established 1978. Purpose: to showcase acting talents of members to casting directors. Sponsored and supported by The New York Cast. Tickets: up to $3.

PLAY PRODUCTION: **One-Act Any Subject.**

ENTRY FEE: None. Nominal fee charged if play accepted for production (all persons involved with production contribute to cost).

DEADLINES: Entry, open.

POETRY (Any Type-Subject)

Any type-subject. Includes Writing, Play. (Also see other POETRY CATEGORIES.)

269

Billee Murray Denny Poetry Award
Lincoln College
Dave Hawkinson, Development Office
300 Keokuk
Lincoln, Illinois 62656 U.S.A.
Tel: (217) 732-3155

October

International; **entry restricted to independents, amateurs;** annual; established 1980. Purpose: to promote amateur poetry. Average statistics: 580 entries. Sponsored by Lincoln College. Supported by Lynn C. Denny estate.

POETRY CONTEST: **Any type,** any subject; by amateurs or independents; typed double-spaced on 8 1/2x11-inch paper; 100 lines maximum, limit 3 entries. No vulgar, obscene, suggestive, or offensive word-phrase.

AWARDS: $1000 First, $450 Second, $200 Third Prize. Winners published in *Lincoln Log* and college literary magazine, *Spectrum;* may be submitted to other journals.

JUDGING: By 6-member panel of educators, poets. No entries returned.

ENTRY FEE: $10. Entrant pays postage (include SASE).

DEADLINES: Entry, April. Winners announced, October.

270

Bitterroot Poetry Contest

Bitterroot Magazine
Menke Katz, Editor-in-Chief
Blythebourne Station, P.O. Box 51
Brooklyn, New York 11219 U.S.A.

Various

International; entry open to all; annual; established 1962. Sponsored by *Bitterroot Magazine* (quarterly, Henry F. Beechhold, Executive Editor, Trenton State College, Trenton, New Jersey 08625). Publish *Bitterroot International Poetry Quarterly.*

POETRY CONTEST: **Any Type,** unpublished, original, 30-line limit, 3 entries maximum, each entry on separate page, in separate envelope. Need not be a subscriber.

AWARDS: First, Second, Third Place Kaitz Awards ($50, $35, $15), Kushner Awards ($60, $40, $25), Dovid-Badonneh Awards ($100, $60, $40). Winners published in *Bitterroot Magazine.*

ENTRY FEE: None.

DEADLINES: Entry, December.

271

Bollingen Prize in Poetry of the Yale University Library

Beinecke Rare Book and Manuscript Library
David E. Schoonover, Secretary
Box 1603A Yale Station
New Haven, Connecticut 06520
U.S.A. Tel: (203) 436-0236

January

National; **entry restricted (selection by sponsor);** biennial. $5000 Award to **Published American Poet** (born, naturalized U.S. citizen). Sponsored by Yale University Library (Beinecke Rare Book and Manuscript Library, Louis L. Martz, Director). Award, January.

272

Daniel Varoujan Award

New England Poetry Club
Diana Der Hovanessian, President
2 Farrar Street
Cambridge, Massachusetts 02138
U.S.A.

Fall

International; entry open to all; annual; established 1980. Purpose: to honor Armenian poet Daniel Varoujan, killed 1915 in his prime. Sponsored by New England Poetry Club. Supported by royalties from *Anthology of Armenian Poetry* (Hovanessian and Margossian, editors,

Columbia University Press). Publish *Ararat Magazine* (quarterly). Also sponsor Golden Rose Award for poetry (selection by Club). Second contact: Mildred Nash, Chair, 39 Sunset Blvd., Burlington, Massachusetts 01803.

POETRY CONTEST: Any Type, any form, worthy of the art of Daniel Varoujan; unpublished, in English, 2 copies. No translations.

AWARDS: $200 to Best Poem. Winner published (if entrant wishes) in *Ararat Magazine.*

JUDGING: By editorial board of *Ararat Magazine.*

ENTRY FEE: Not specified.

DEADLINES: Entry, April. Awards, Fall.

273

"Discovery": The Nation Poetry Contest

Poetry Center of the 92nd Street YM-YWHA
Shelley Mason, Managing Editor
1395 Lexington Avenue
New York, New York 10028 U.S.A.
Tel: (212)427-6000

May

International; **entry open to unpublished (book) poets;** annual; established 1968. Sponsored by *The Nation* magazine, Poetry Center of the 92nd Street YM-YWHA (founded 1939). Average statistics: 3000 entries, 4 awards, 900 attendance. Tickets: $2. Also have readings, lectures, classes, workshops.

POETRY CONTEST: Any Type, original, in English; 10 poems, 500 lines total maximum. Submit 4 sets each entry. Require biography, publication information. Poet must not have published own book of poetry, including chapbooks and self-publications.

AWARDS: 4 $50 winners, invitation to read at Poetry Center. 1 poem each winner printed in *The Nation* (may publish other poems for pay).

JUDGING: By panel. No entries returned. Sponsor may publish previously unpublished work.

ENTRY FEE: Not specified.

DEADLINES: Entry, February. Judging, April. Event, May.

274

Encore International Poetry Contests

Encore Magazine
Alice Briley, Editor
1121 Major Avenue N.W.
Albuquerque, New Mexico 87107
U.S.A. Tel: (505) 344-5615

Spring, Fall

International; entry open to all; semiannual (General), annual (Student); established 1966. Sponsored by *Encore Magazine* (quarterly of verse and poetic arts). Average statistics: 350-500 entries, over 300 entrants, 2-3 countries, 19-22 awards.

POETRY CONTEST: Any Type, unpublished, original; 24 lines maximum; single-spaced on 8 1/2x11-inch paper (bond); 2 copies. Categories: General (open to all, unlimited entries); Student (open to students, 1 entry); Subscribers (open to subscribers only, 1 entry); Book Purchasers (open to buyers of *Encore Anthology* or *From Weaver's Shuttle,* 2 poems per each book purchase); Catherine A. Waldraff Contest (formerly called *Anonymous Donor Contest,* open to all, unlimited entries).

ELIGIBILITY: Unpublished, original poems, not under consideration for publication elsewhere. No winners of $5 or more in other contests.

AWARDS: General: $25, $10, $5. Student: $15, $10, $5. Subscribers: $25, $10, $5. Book Purchasers: $15, $5. Waldraff: $100 First Prize, 10 Honorable Mentions, $5 each. Winners published in Spring and Fall *Encore*.

JUDGING: By qualified judges not connected with magazine. No entries returned.

ENTRY FEE: $1, General; $5 for 1-5 poems, Waldraff.

DEADLINES: Entry, May (General), November (Student). Awards, August and February.

275

Harian Creative Press Poetry Awards Series

Dr. Harry Barba, Writing Director
47 Hyde Blvd.
Ballston Spa, New York 12020
U.S.A. Tel: (518) 885-7397

Continuous

International; entry open to all; continuous; established 1967. Harian Creative Press founded 1967 by Harry Barba. Purpose: to encourage, teach, publish, promote socially functional writing, education, art, culture. Motto: "One world is better than none." Sponsored and supported by Harian Creative Press. Recognized by MLA, CEA, NEA, AWP, COSMEP. Also sponsor Short Story-Novella Contest.

POETRY CONTEST: Any Type, original, unpublished; single poems, groups, or collections; length and style functionally suitable to contents; simple poetry that sings, might be set to music, shows heart and mind, for, by, of the people. No obscenity, violence, scrambled writing.

AWARDS: $50 to Best Poem, $200 Best Collection. Will critique entries, consider for publication.

JUDGING: By Harry Barba. May withhold awards. All entries read in entirety. Sponsor owns first publication rights. Not responsible for loss or damage.

ENTRY FEE: $5 per poem (up to 20 lines), $25 per collection. Entrant pays postage (include SASE).

DEADLINES: Entry, open. Materials returned in 6-8 weeks.

276

Indiana State Federation of Poetry Clubs Poetry Contest

Louise Nelson, Contest Chair
302 North 3rd Street
Marshall, Illinois 62441 U.S.A.

Quarterly

International; entry open to all; quarterly. Sponsored by Indiana State Federation of Poetry Clubs.

POETRY CONTEST: Any Type, in English, typewritten on one side 8 1/2x11-inch paper; limit 1 entry.

AWARDS: First ($15), Second ($10), Third ($5) Place. 3 Honorable Mentions.

JUDGING: Poems destroyed after judging; none returned or published.

ENTRY FEE: None.

DEADLINES: Entry, January, April, July, October.

277

Kay Snow Writing Contest

Willamette Writers, Inc.
Mrs. Philip C. Herzog,
Treasurer-Agent
3622 S.E. Lambert Street

Portland, Oregon 97202 U.S.A.
Tel: (503) 777-1236

August

International; **entry open to U.S. and Canada;** annual; established 1969. Purpose: to honor founder of Willamette Writers Club, nonprofit educational organization established 1965 to encourage, provide meeting place for writers. Sponsored and supported by Willamette Writers. Held during annual Willamette Writers Conference in Portland, Oregon for 2 days; 150-200 attendance. Have workshops, speakers. Tickets: approximately $65. Publish monthly bulletin. Also sponsor Nonfiction Writing Contest. Second contact: Jim White, P.O. Box 808, Portland, Oregon 97207.

POETRY CONTEST: **Any Type,** original, unpublished; 10-30 lines, 1 entry, double-spaced (photocopies acceptable). No photos, illustrations.

WRITING CONTEST: **Fiction,** original, unpublished, 1500 words maximum, 1 entry per category, double-spaced (photocopies acceptable). No photos, illustrations. Categories: General, Juvenile.

AWARDS: $100 First, $50 Second, $25 Third Prize, Best Poetry, Best General Fiction, Best Juvenile Writing. 1 prize per entrant.

JUDGING: Based on originality, significance, effectiveness of style, artistry. May withhold awards; print winners in monthly bulletins. Entrants retain all rights. No entries returned.

ENTRY FEE: Free (members), $5 each (nonmembers).

DEADLINES: Entry, June. Awards, August.

278

L.A. Advertiser Poetry Contest
Arnie Lutz, Publisher & Editor
7313 Earldom Avenue
Playa Del Rey, California 90291
U.S.A. Tel: (213) 827-0302

Continuous

International; entry open to all; continuous; established 1977. Purpose: to promote poetry in world. Sponsored by L.A. Advertiser, Inc. Average statistics: 1300 entries, 500 entrants, 6 semifinalists, 3 winners.

POETRY CONTEST: **Any Type,** any number.

AWARDS: $100 First, $50 Second, $25 Third Place.

JUDGING: By 3 poetry editors. Not responsible for loss or damage.

ENTRY FEE: None. Entrant pays postage (include SASE).

DEADLINES: Entry, open. Awards, June.

279

Leroy Memorial Poetry Awards
Crossroads Newsletter
Zinita Fowler
2014 Palo Alto
Carrollton, Texas 75006 U.S.A.
Tel: (214) 245-1026

December

International; entry open to all; annual. Sponsored by *Crossroads Newsletter.* Also sponsor Viola Hayes Parsons Poetry Awards and Crossroads Mini-Contest.

POETRY CONTEST: **Any Type,** style, form, visual format, length; in English; 1 copy; previously published (poet must retain full rights) or original. Unlimited entries.

AWARDS: $300 Grand Prize, 3 $100 First Prizes, 3 $50 Second Prizes, 3 $25 Third Prizes, 5 $10 Special Merit Awards. Winners published in Christmas newsletters.

JUDGING: By 3 judges of different ages, ideologies. No entries returned.

ENTRY FEE: 1 poem, $3; 2 poems, $5; 3, $8; 4, $10; etc.

DEADLINES: Entry, November. Awards, December.

280

Marie-Louise d'Esternaux Poetry Scholarship

Brooklyn Poetry Circle (BPC)
Gabrielle Lederer, Contest Chair
61 Pierrepont Street, #51
Brooklyn, New York 11201 U.S.A.
Tel: (212) 875-8736

May

International; **entry restricted to students age 16-21;** annual; established 1960. Named after founder of BPC. Purpose: to encourage young people to study, compose poetry to enrich themselves and others. Sponsored and supported by BPC. Average statistics: 75 entries, 1-2 countries, 1-2 winners. Held at annual BPC dinner. Also sponsor poetry-writing workshop (October-May), monthly meetings.

POETRY CONTEST: Any Type, original, unpublished; 24-line limit; 4 copies, typewritten, double-spaced; 1 per entrant, 2 entrants maximum per school (school's English Department selects entries, if by high school students).

AWARDS: $50 to winner plus 1 year BPC membership (including monthly poetry criticisms).

JUDGING: By BPC President, 2 poetry critics. Sponsor keeps winning poems, others destroyed. Not responsible for loss or damage.

ENTRY FEE: None. Entrant pays postage (include SASE).

DEADLINES: Entry, April. Judging, April-May. Awards, May.

281

McKendree Writers' Conference Writing Contests

Evelyn Best, Director
105 Florence Street
Lebanon, Illinois 62254 U.S.A.
Tel: (618) 537-2568

May

International; entry open to all; annual; established 1954. Purpose: to promote writing inspiration, encouragement, fellowship. Sponsored by McKendree Writers' Conference, Illinois Arts Council. Held at McKendree College, Lebanon, Illinois, for 1 day. Publish quarterly newsletter. Also sponsor Nonfiction Writing Contest. Second contact: Helen Church, President, St. Louis Street, Lebanon, Illinois 62254.

POETRY CONTEST: Any Type, unpublished; 40-line limit; 3 entries. Categories: Light, Serious.

PLAY CONTEST: Any Subject, unpublished; 3000-word limit.

WRITING CONTEST: Fiction, unpublished; 3000-word limit.

AWARDS: $50 Prize, each category.

ENTRY FEE: $1 each category.

DEADLINES: Entry, March. Awards, May.

282

National League of American Pen Women (NLAPW) New Mexico State Board National Poetry Contest

Alice Briley, Contest Chair
1121 Major Avenue N.W.
Albuquerque, New Mexico 87107
U.S.A.

August

National; entry open to all; annual. Sponsored by NLAPW New Mexico.

POETRY CONTEST: Any Type, original, unpublished; in English; typed, on 8 1/2x11-inch paper; 24 lines maximum; unlimited entries; 2 copies each.

AWARDS: $50 First, $15 Second, $10 Third Place.

JUDGING: No entries returned.

ENTRY FEE: $1 each. Entrant pays postage (include SASE each entry).

DEADLINES: Entry, May. Winners notified, August.

283

Nethers Poetry Contest

Nethers Farm Retreat for Poets & Chamber Musicians
Carla Eugster, Director
Box 41
Woodville, Virginia 22749 U.S.A.
Tel: (703) 987-8913

April

International; entry open to all; annual; established 1980. Motto: "To create without losing awareness of nature, and the world." Sponsored by Nethers Farm Retreat for Poets and Chamber Musicians, founded 1978 to provide congenial work-living space for artists within context of socially aware farm. Also sponsor Work Scholarship at Retreat ($2.50 fee reduction per work hour).

POETRY CONTEST: Any Type, 3 poems or pages of poetry maximum, double-spaced, on 8 1/2x11-inch paper.

AWARDS: Best Poem (2 winners), 1 week free at Nethers Retreat and publication in *As Is.*

JUDGING: By professional poet and editor. All entries reviewed in entirety.

ENTRY FEE: $3. Entrant pays postage (include SASE).

DEADLINES: Entry, February. Awards, April.

284

New Poetry Contest

World of Poetry
Joseph Mellon, Contest Director
2431 Stockton Blvd.
Sacramento, California 95817 U.S.A.

August

International; entry open to all; annual; established 1974. Sponsored by *World of Poetry* (quarterly; John Campbell, Editor-Publisher).

POETRY CONTEST: Any Type, any subject, original, unpublished; hand-printed or typed; no line limit; 6 maximum per entrant.

AWARDS: $1000 Grand, $500 First Prize; 6 $200 Second Prizes, 10 $100 Third Prizes, 82 Fourth Prizes (two poetry anthologies worth $79). All entrants receive 1-year *World of Poetry* subscription.

ENTRY FEE: $6 each.

DEADLINES: Entry, June. Awards, August.

285

North American Mentor Magazine Annual Poetry Contest

Westburg Associates Publishers
John Westburg, Publisher-Editor
1745 Madison Street
Fennimore, Wisconsin 53809 U.S.A.
Tel: (608) 822-6237

September

International; entry open to all; annual; established 1964. Purpose: to provide and encourage writing, reading, critical comparison of poetry. Sponsored by John and Mildred Westburg. Average statistics: 2500 entries, 550 entrants, 4-6 countries, 12 awards. Publish *North American Mentor Magazine.*

POETRY CONTEST: **Any Type,** 50 lines or less, in English, 5 entries maximum.

AWARDS: First, $50; Second, $25; 10 Honor Awards, $5; 100 Merit Certificates. Published in *North American Mentor Magazine* and in Mentor anthologies.

JUDGING: By editors, poets, professors, previous winners. Sponsor claims all rights to all entries. Entrants may publish elsewhere upon request.

ENTRY FEE: $11 (includes 1-year subscription to *Mentor Magazine).* Free to paid subscribers. Entrant pays return postage for unused poems.

DEADLINES: Entry, September.

286

Poetry Magazine Awards

Modern Poetry Association
John Frederick Nims, Editor
601 South Morgan Street
P.O. Box 4348
Chicago, Illinois 60680 U.S.A.
Tel: (312) 996-7803

November

International; **entry restricted to poetry published in Poetry Magazine;** annual. $100-$1000 **Awards for Poetry** published in monthly *Poetry Magazine,* founded 1912. Sponsored by nonprofit Modern Poetry Association, founded 1941. Awards, November.

287

River City Arts Festival Poetry Competition

Arts Assembly of Jacksonville
632 May Street
Jacksonville, Florida 32204 U.S.A.
Tel: (904) 633-3748

April

National; **entry open to U.S.;** annual; established 1972. Formerly called JACKSONVILLE ARTS FESTIVAL. Purpose: to encourage appreciation for literary arts; provide quality juried poetry event. Sponsored by Arts Assembly of Jacksonville, Fine Arts Council of Florida. Supported by community businesses and organizations, City of Jacksonville. Held in Jacksonville for 2 days. Average statistics: 100 entries, 85 entrants, 7 awards, 400 attendance. Second contact: Jeff Driggers, Jacksonville Public Library, 122 Ocean Street, Jacksonville, Florida 32202.

POETRY CONTEST: **Any Type,** unpublished; no line limit; maximum 3 per entrant. Categories: Adult (18 and over), Student (17 and under).

AWARDS: Adult: $150 Grand, $125 Second, $100 Third Prize. Student: $60 Grand, $40 Second, $25 Third Prize.

JUDGING: Preliminary by educators, writers, critics. Final by 1 judge.

Festival may reproduce entry for publicity. No entries returned.

ENTRY FEE: Adults, $2 each; students, $1 each.

DEADLINES: Entry, February. Event, April.

288

San Mateo County Fair Fairworld Poetry Competition
San Mateo County Fair Arts Committee
Lois Kelley, Administrator
171 Flying Cloud Isle
Foster City, California 94404 U.S.A.
Tel: (415) 349-2787

July-August

International; entry open to all; annual; established 1957. Purpose: to provide showcase for emerging arts trends. Sponsored and supported by San Mateo County Fair Arts Committee. Average statistics: 200,000 attendance. Held at San Mateo County Fair (2495 S. Delaware, San Mateo, California) for 19 days. Tickets: $3. Also sponsor San Mateo County Fair Playwriting Competition. Second contact: San Mateo County Fair Association, P.O. Box 1027, San Mateo, California 94403.

POETRY CONTEST: Any Type, unpublished, original; not submitted for publication or to another contest; in English; 2 maximum per entrant; 24 lines maximum; 3 copies, typed double-spaced on 8 1/2x11-inch paper.

AWARDS: $100 Robert Frost Award Top Prize. $50 Carl Sandburg Award. Other prizes $25, $15, $10; 7 book prizes. Special Youth Award 1 book, 2 ribbons. $100 Special Subject Award (Thoroughbred Race Horse Interpretation). Winners displayed at fair.

JUDGING: By published poet-critic. Author retains rights.

ENTRY FEE: $2 each. No entries returned.

DEADLINES: Entry, June. Event, July-August.

289

Seed-in-Hand Poetry Series Competitions
June Owns, Editor-Publisher
P.O. Box 541
Richmond, Virginia 23204 U.S.A.

Continuous

International; entry open to all; continuous (6 times a year). Purpose: to acknowledge, Award creative poets.

POETRY CONTEST: Any Type. Requirements not specified.

AWARDS: Cash Prizes (amounts not specified). Winners Published in copyrighted chapbook.

ENTRY FEE: Not specified. Entrant pays postage (include SASE).

DEADLINES: Entry, July-September.

290

Sinclair Community College Creative Writing Contest
Gary Mitchner
Department of English
444 West Third Street
Dayton, Ohio 45402 U.S.A. Tel: (513) 226-2594

March

International; entry open to all; annual; established 1967. Purpose: amateur writers meet and gather advice from professional writers. Sponsored by Sinclair Community College, Ohio Arts Council. Held at annual Writers'

Workshop at the college, for 2 days; 250 attendance. Tickets: $2 (presentation), $20 (workshop). Also sponsor Nonfiction Writing Contest.

POETRY CONTEST: Any Type, unpublished; 100-line limit; 2 poems make 1 entry.

WRITING CONTEST: Fiction, unpublished; typed double-spaced on 8 1/2x11-inch paper; 5000-word limit.

AWARDS: $60 First Place, each adult category. $30 Second, $20 Third Place. Scholarship to high school First Place, each category. Merit Certificates. Winners published in writers' Workshop booklet.

JUDGING: By Sinclair English Department. No entries returned. Not responsible for loss or damage.

ENTRY FEE: $4, adults. $2, high school students.

DEADLINES: Entry, January. Judging, February. Awards, March.

291

Southern California Chapter, California State Poetry Society (CSPS) National Contest

Ernestine Emrick, Contest Chair
13517 East Mar Vista, Apt. B
Whittier, California 90602 U.S.A.
Tel: (213) 332-3742

November

National; **entry open to U.S.;** annual; established 1974. Sponsored by Southern California CSPS Chapter. Second contact: Sally Herres, Treasurer, Southern California Chapter of California State Poetry Society, 374 E. Cypress Street, Covina, California 91723.

POETRY CONTEST: Any Type, original, unpublished; in English; 40-line limit; any number of entries; on 8 1/2x11-inch paper, single- or double-spaced. Submit original and 2 copies. No previous money award winners or other contest-publisher submissions.

AWARDS: $75 First, $50 Second, $25 Third Place. 5 $5 Special Recognition Prizes.

JUDGING: No entries returned. Author retains rights.

ENTRY FEE: $1 each.

DEADLINES: Entry, August. Awards, November.

292

Sri Chinmoy Poetry Awards

Committee for Spiritual Poetry
Jonathan Roberts
86-16 Parsons Blvd.
Jamaica, New York 11432 U.S.A.
Tel: (212) 523-3692

November

International; entry open to all; annual; established 1977. Named in honor of spiritual Master and poet Sri Chinmoy, whose work represents poetic ideal of contest. Purpose: to encourage writing of poetry that expresses spiritual aspirations of mankind. Sponsored by Committee for Spiritual Poetry.

POETRY CONTEST: Any Type, unpublished, in English; limit 3 poems, 100-lines maximum, 3 copies.

AWARDS: $500 First, $250 Second, $100 Third Prize. 40 Honorable Mentions. Winners published in spring anthology.

JUDGING: No entries returned.

ENTRY FEE: Not specified.

DEADLINES: Entry, October. Awards, November.

293

Stanley Kunitz Award for Poetry

Columbia, A Magazine of
Poetry-Prose
Nancy Schoenberger, Co-Editor
404 Dodge Hall
Columbia University
New York, New York 10027 U.S.A.
Tel: (212) 280-4391

Spring

International; entry open to all; annual; established 1979. Purpose: to publish high-quality poetry by new and established writers. Sponsored by Columbia University Writing Division, School of the Arts. Average statistics: 20 entries, 1 award.

POETRY CONTEST: Any Type, unpublished.

AWARDS: $100 Stanley Kunitz Award and publication in *Columbia.*

JUDGING: 10-15-member board reads all entries in entirety. May publish winning poem.

ENTRY FEE: None.

DEADLINES: Entry, February. Awards, Spring.

294

Viola Hayes Parsons Poetry Awards

Crossroads Newsletter
Zinita Fowler
2014 Palo Alto
Carrollton, Texas 75006 U.S.A.
Tel: (214) 245-1026

July

International; entry open to all; annual. Sponsored by *Crossroads Newsletter.* Also sponsor Crossroads Mini-Contest and Leroy Special Poetry Contests.

POETRY CONTEST: Any Type, style, form, visual format; in English; 36-line limit; 1 copy typed or printed on 8 1/2x11-inch paper. Unlimited entries. No previously published entries; however, winners of not over $10 may be entered if poet retains full rights.

AWARDS: Grand Prize, $1000; Second Place, $500; Third, $200. 5 $20 Special Merit Awards. 20 $10 Honorable Mention Awards. Crossroads Choice, $100. Winners published in *Crossroads Anthology* (copy to winners).

ENTRY FEE: 1 poem, $5; 3, $10; 4, $15; 6, $20; etc. No poems returned.

DEADLINES: Entry, awards, July.

295

White Mountain Press Poetry Competition

L.E. Hayes, Editor
5 Kirock Place
Westport, Connecticut 06880 U.S.A.

May

International; entry open to all; annual; established 1981. Purpose: to encourage young and upcoming poets. Sponsored by White Mountain Press. Publish 1-2 chapbooks per year.

POETRY CONTEST: Any Type, unpublished in book-chapbook form (magazines excepted); 50 lines maximum.

AWARDS: $200 First, $100 Second, $50 Third, $10 Fourth to Tenth Place. All finalists invited to submit manuscript for chapbook series consideration.

JUDGING: All entries read in entirety. Not responsible for loss or damage. No entries returned.

ENTRY FEE: $2 each.

DEADLINES: Entry, April. Awards, May.

296

William Stafford-Lake Oswego Festival of Arts Poetry Contest

P.O. Box 368
Lake Oswego, Oregon 97034 U.S.A.

June

International; entry open to all; annual; established 1977. Sponsored by Lake Oswego Festival of Arts.

POETRY CONTEST: Any Type, any style, subject matter; original, unpublished; 3 maximum per entrant, 30 lines maximum. submit 3 typed, double-spaced copies each entry. No base language, Haiku, Cinquain; no previous award winning poems.

AWARDS: $200 in prizes and possible publication in anthology.

ENTRY FEE: $5.

DEADLINES: Entry, May. Awards, June.

297

C.S.P. World News Poet of the Year Contest

Canadian Society of Poets (CSP)
Guy F. Claude Hamel, Editor
P.O. Box 2608, Station D
Ottawa, Ontario K1P 5W7 CANADA

October

International; entry open to all; annual; established 1975. Purpose: to encourage unpublished poets. Sponsored and supported by *C.S.P. World News.* Publish *C.S.P. World News* (monthly).

POETRY CONTEST: Any Type, original, unpublished, typed, 16 lines maximum, unlimited entries. No pornography. Require recent photo of entrant.

AWARDS: Publication in *C.S.P. World News,* lifetime subscription, other magazine exposure.

JUDGING: By editor-publisher. Not responsible for loss or damage.

ENTRY FEE: Not specified.

DEADLINES: Entry, Open. Judging, October. Winners announced, January.

298

Cheltenham Festival of Literature Poetry Competition

Cheltenham Arts Festivals Ltd
Jeremy Tyndall, Festival Organizer
Town Hall, Cheltenham, Glos. GL50 1QA
ENGLAND Tel: (0242) 21621

October

International; entry open to all; annual. Sponsored and supported by Cheltenham Festival of Literature and *Telegraph Sunday Magazine.*

POETRY CONTEST: Any Type, original, unpublished, in English, typed on one side of paper, 30-line maximum, 3-poem limit. Require entry blank with each poem. No translations; no families or persons connected with Festival.

AWARDS: 3 prizes, 200 pounds each.

JUDGING: All entries read by 3 judges. Winners announced in *Telegraph Sunday Magazine.* Sponsor may publish; has first refusal rights to purchase any entry for broadcasting. Copyrights remain with authors. No entries returned. Not responsible for loss or damage.

ENTRY FEE: 40 pence per poem.

DEADLINES: Entry, June. Judging, August. Awards, October.

POETRY (Various Categories)

Includes Book, Short Story, Grants. (Also see other POETRY CATEGORIES.)

299

Arizona State Poetry Society (ASPS) National Poetry Contest

Georgene S. Collins, Contest Chair
Route 4, Box 475
Phoenix, Arizona 85043 U.S.A.

Fall

International; entry open to all; annual; established 1968. Sponsored by ASPS. Publish *Sandcutters* (quarterly). Recognized by NFSPS, AAP.

POETRY CONTEST: Various Categories, unpublished; not under consideration elsewhere; no previous winners of over $10; unlimited entries; original and 1 copy, typed single-spaced, 1 poem per page. Categories: Grand Prize, Varying Theme (40-line limit, any form); Haiku (modern or traditional); Cinquain (Crapsey style, any subject); Traditional (28-line limit, rhymed forms and blank verse, any subject); Free Verse (16-40 lines, any subject); Humor (16-line limit, any form); For Children (16-line limit, any form); Southwest (28-line limit, any form); Mountains (32-line limit, any form); Tall Tales (50-line limit, narrative form).

AWARDS: $50 Grand Prize and Honorable Mention Certificates, Best Theme. $25 First, $15 Second, $10 Third Place, Honorable Mention Certificates, all other categories. Winners published in Winter issue *Sandcutters*.

JUDGING: By judges not affiliated with ASPS. Honorable Mentions returned; nonwinning entries destroyed.

ENTRY FEE: $1 each. Entrant pays postage (include SASE).

DEADLINES: Entry, September. Winners announced, November.

300

Chabot College Spring Arts Festival Poetry and Short Story Contest

Chabot College Valley Campus
Jerald T. Ball, Poetry Chairman,
Humanities Faculty
3033 Collier Canyon Road
Livermore, California 94550 U.S.A.

Spring

International; entry open to all; annual. Sponsored and supported by Chabot College. Publish annual anthology. Second contact: David Wright, Short Story Chairman, Language Arts Faculty, Chabot College.

POETRY CONTEST: Various Categories, original, unpublished; typed on 8 1/2x11-inch white paper; 1 poem per page, 2 copies each; unlimited entries. Not under consideration for other contests at time of submission. No prize-winning poems (honorable mentions acceptable). Categories: Free Verse (free style, 32-line maximum); Sonnet (Shakespearean or Pertrarchan); Short Form (8-line maximum); Narrative (any subject or style, 50-line maximum); Student Division (under 21, may also enter other categories).

SHORT STORY CONTEST: Any Subject, 800-word maximum. Requirements same as for Poetry.

AWARDS: Grand Prizes and Short Story: $25 First, $15 Second, $5 Third Place each. Poems: $15 First, $5 Second Place each. Honorable Mentions. Special Award to students.

JUDGING: May one-time publish prize-winning poems or short story. Students judged separately.

ENTRY FEE: $1 each. Provide SASE for winners list.

DEADLINES: Entry, March. Winners notified, Spring.

301

Ina Coolbrith Circle Poetry Contest

Lewis Baer, President
P.O. Box 621
Penngrove, California 94951 U.S.A.

October

State; **entry open to California residents;** annual. Sponsored by Ina Coolbrith Circle, founded 1919 as tribute to California's first Poet Laureate, for promotion of poetry, art, California history-literature study. Held at Ina Coolbrith Circle National Poetry Day Banquet at Spenger's (1919 Fourth Street, Berkeley, California). Also have biennial Newspaper Verse Contest.

POETRY CONTEST: Various Categories, original, unpublished, not submitted to another editor or contest; 42-line limit, 3 copies, typed double-spaced on 8 1/2x11-inch paper; 2 maximum per entrant. Categories: Serious in Traditional Form, Serious in Free Verse, Light or Humorous Verse (any form), Short (12-line limit, any form), California History (any form).

AWARDS: $50 Grand Prize. $25 First, $15 Second, $10 Third Place, each category.

ENTRY FEE: Nonmembers $1.

DEADLINES: Entry, September. Awards, October.

302

Iowa Poetry Association (IPA) Poetry Contest

Dr. Loren C. Gruber, President
P.O. Box 121
Indianola, Iowa 50125 U.S.A.
Tel: (515) 961-8926

April-May

State; **entry open to Iowa;** annual; established 1946. Purpose: to encourage, promote writing and appreciation of poetry in Iowa. Sponsored and supported by IPA. Affiliate of AAP and NFSPS. Average statistics: 7400 entries, 300 finalists. Held in Des Moines. Have poetry workshops (spring and fall). Publish *Lyrical Iowa* (annual). Second contact: Pat King, Vice-President, 218 South Main, Albia, Iowa 52501.

POETRY CONTEST: Various Categories, unpublished. Divisions: K-8, High School, College, Adult. Categories (adult): General, National-World Events, Humorous, Light, Memorial.

AWARDS: $5-$15, including school entries. Best poems, winners, published in *Lyrical Iowa.*

JUDGING: Prescreening by editors committee. Final by nationally known (non-Iowa resident) poet or critic. Permission to reprint must be secured through sponsor. Not responsible for loss or damage.

ENTRY FEE: None. Entrant pays postage (include SASE).

DEADLINES: Entry, February. Judging, March-April. Event, April-May.

303

Kansas Poetry Contest

Ossie E. Tranbarger, Contest Sponsor
619 West Main Street
Independence, Kansas 67301 U.S.A.
Tel: (316) 331-1283

December-January

International; **entry restricted to adults;** annual; established 1968. Purpose: to promote, encourage poets. Sponsored and supported by Ossie E. Tranbarger. Average statistics: 207 entries. Have Haiku workshop. Publish *Kansas Poetry Contest* paper.

POETRY CONTEST: Various Categories, unpublished; unlimited entries. Categories: Open (8-24 lines), Haiku (traditional).

AWARDS: $50 First, $25 Second, $10 Third Prize, each category. 4-5 Honorable Mentions. Winners published in sponsor's paper, receive copy.

JUDGING: By 2 judges (1 per category). Winners retain rights after publication. Not responsible for loss or damage.

ENTRY FEE: $1 each. Entrant pays postage (SASE).

DEADLINES: Entry, October. Judging, November. Awards, December-January.

304

Kentucky State Poetry Society (KSPS) Poetry Contests

James W. Proctor, Contest Chairman
505 Southland Blvd.
Louisville, Kentucky 40214 U.S.A.
Tel: (502) 368-8248

Summer

International; entry open to all; annual; established 1950. Purpose: to encourage poets, further learning and enjoyment of poetry. Sponsored by KSPS. Recognized by NFSPS. Average statistics: 2500 entries, 600 entrants, 4 countries, 130 awards, 150 attendance. Held at Mammoth Cave National Park in Kentucky for 2 days. Publish *Pegasus* (KSPS magazine), and quarterly newsletter.

POETRY CONTEST: Various Categories, original, unpublished; most limited to 28 lines; 2 copies, typed on 8 1/2x11-inch paper; 1 entry per category. Grand Prix Award category: Any Subject. Other categories: Contemporary, Students (Grades 1-3, 4-6, 7-8, 9-12, College), Any Subject, Senior Citizens, Traditional, Illini Sonnet, Haiku (single or sequence), Shakespearean Sonnet (iambic pentameter), Miscellaneous, Theme, Humorous, Philosophies, Sentimental, World Peace, Natural Order, Cinquain Sequence (2-5), Kentucky.

ELIGIBILITY: No entries submitted to another source, or previous first-third place winners in other contests. Poems by children must be own work (teacher may suggest, advise). May be handwritten, if legible, on oversized paper.

AWARDS: $100 Grand Prix. Books and cash awards ($1-$25) in other categories. Honorable Mentions. Winners published in *Pegasus*.

JUDGING: By separate judges, each category. All entries read in entirety. May publish First Prize winners; copyright reverts to author thereafter. No poems returned.

ENTRY FEE: Varies (none or $1-$2). $5 for Grand Prix entries. Entrant pays postage.

DEADLINES: Entry, June. Awards, October.

305

Louisiana State Poetry Society (LSPS) National Poetry Day Contest

Golda F. Walker, Chair
915 Aberdeen Avenue
Baton Rouge, Louisiana 70808
U.S.A. Tel: (504) 344-9932

October

International; entry open to all; annual; established 1979. Named after National Poetry Day. Purpose: to encourage, promote poetry writing. Sponsored by LSPS, individuals, businesses. Average statistics: 675 entries, 375 entrants, 75 awards. Held at National Poetry Day Celebration for 1-2 days. Have workshops, poetry readings.

POETRY CONTEST: Various Categories, original, unpublished; typed, on 8 1/2x11-inch paper, original and 1 copy. Not entered simultaneously in other contests; no pornographic or subversive material. One per category (except Grand Prix). Categories: Varying Theme (Grand Prix Award; any form, 75-line limit; 2 entries maximum), Shakespearean Sonnet, Book Review Poem (any form, 75-line limit), Prose Poem (2 pages), Portrait of Black Woman (any form, 32-line limit), Love (any form, 36-line limit), Narrative (48-line limit), Lyric (24-line limit), Inspirational (28-line limit), Sonnet, Gems (36-line limit), Religious (30-line limit), Petrarchan Sonnet, Nostalgia (14-line limit), Philosophical (20-60 lines), The Infinite (60-line limit), Humorous Light Verse (16-line limit), Living, Golda Design Rhyme (12-line limit), Haiku, Villanelle, Swamp Scene (28-line limit), Free Verse (16-60 lines), Children (16-line limit), Folklore (48-line limit), Rocking Chair Scene (classical ballad, 60-line limit, Louisiana residents only).

AWARDS: $100 Grand Prix. $50-$5 cash prizes other categories.

JUDGING: By nationally selected poets. May withhold awards. May reserve first publication rights to winners for anthology.

ENTRY FEE: $1 each. Grand Prix: $5 (1), $8 (2 poems). Shakespearean Sonnet, $2. Entrant pays postage (include SASE); only winners returned.

DEADLINES: Entry, September. Awards, October.

306

National Federation of State Poetry Societies (NFSPS) Annual Poetry Contests

Amy Jo Zook, Contest Chair
3520 State Route 56
Mechanicsburg, Ohio 43044 U.S.A.
Tel: (513) 834-2666

June

International; entry open to all; annual; established 1959. Incorporated as nonprofit 1966. Purpose: to promote excellence in poetry; bring poets together for mutual support. Sponsored by NFSPS. Supported by member societies' dues, patron donations. Recognized by AAP. Average statistics: 10,000 entries, 3000 entrants, 6 countries, 500 finalists, 150 money awards, 200-250 attendance. Held in member state for 3-4 days. Have workshops, readings, lectures, films, speakers, book display, sale tables. Tickets: $15-$20. Publish *Strophes* (quarterly). Second contact: Alice Briley, President and *Strophes* Editor, 1121 Major Avenue N.W., Albuquerque, New Mexico 87107.

POETRY CONTEST: Various Categories, unpublished; in English; 1 maximum per category (except NFSPS Award); 2 copies each original typed single-space, one side only, on 8

1/2x11-inch white paper. Categories: Any Subject NFSPS Grand Prize (100-line limit, 4 maximum per entrant, any form), Family Relationships (40-line limit, any form), Spiritual Impact of Great Music (sonnet), Random Rhyme (32-line limit, free form with rhymes interspersed), Growing Older (40-line limit, any form), Humorous (12-line limit, light verse, rhymed), humorous (16-line limit, any form), Shakespearean Sonnet (any subject), Brotherhood (40-line limit, any form), Bible (40-line limit, any form), Haiku (traditional), Beymorlin Sonnet (Shakespearean or Italian), Artist's Creative Life (20-line limit, any form), West Virginia Subject (24-line limit, any form), Flight (42-line limit, any form), 20th-Century Painters or Painting (40-line limit, free form), American Frontier (40-line limit, any form), Creative Mind (40-line limit, any form), By High School Students (32-line limit, any form), Poet's Choice (32-line limit), Any Subject (Shakespearean Two-Sonnet Sequence), Any Subject (40-line limit, free verse), Any Subject (40-line limit, free style), Any Subject (40-line limit, 5 divisions, any form). Also have 22 membership categories.

ELIGIBILITY: Not presented on radio, television, or stage; printed for distribution; published; under consideration or accepted for publication; having won prize worth $10 or more in previous contest; or currently submitted in another contest.

AWARDS: First, Second, Third Place Cash Awards, each category. Grand Prize ($1000, $400, $200). Family Relationships ($100, $30, $20). Spiritual Impact of Great Music ($50, $25, $15). Any Subject (any form, 1 division only, $100, $35, $15). Other categories ($50, $30, $20; or $25, $20, $15; or $25, $15, $10). Up to 7 or more Honorable Mentions. First and Second Place printed in NFSPS *Prize Poems Anthology;* winners listed in *Strophes.*

JUDGING: By 1-2 poets each category, selected by committee. May withhold awards; no ties. May print cash award winners in *Prize Poems Anthology.* No entries returned.

ENTRY FEE: $1 each (nonmembers), $3 total handling fee (members), free (student category). NFSPS Grand Prize category, $5 each. Entrant pays postage.

DEADLINES: Entry, January-March. Judging, April-May. Awards, June.

307

National League of American Pen Women (NLAPW), Alexandria Branch Poetry Contest

Virginia Gallahue
1201 Shenandoah Road
Alexandria, Virginia 22308 U.S.A.
Tel: (703) 765-9418

October

International; entry open to all; annual; established 1972. Sponsored and supported by NLAPW, Alexandria Branch. Recognized by NLAPW. Average statistics: 1000 entries, 300 entrants. Held in Alexandria, Virginia. Have writers' conference. Second Contact: Lolete Barlow, 5403 Ludlow Drive, Temple Hills, Maryland 20031.

POETRY CONTEST: **Various Categories,** unpublished; in English; unlimited entry; 2 copies, typed, double-spaced. Categories: Sonnet, Free Verse, Lyric, Traditional, Humorous. Other categories change yearly.

AWARDS: $35 First Prize, all categories but Lyric. $25 First Prize, Lyric. $20 Second, $10 Third, all categories. Other awards may be added.

JUDGING: All entries read in entirety by well-known poets, then destroyed at close. Not responsible for loss or damage.

ENTRY FEE: $1 each.

DEADLINES: Entry, July. Materials, August. Awards, October.

308

National League of American Pen Women (NLAPW), Philadelphia Branch, National Poetry Contest
Pansye Powell, Contest Chair
210 Larch Circle
Doylestown, Pennsylvania 18901
U.S.A. Tel: (215) 345-7176

March

National; **entry open to U.S.;** biennial (odd years); established 1978. Purpose: to encourage development of young writers, composers, artists. Sponsored and supported by NLAPW-Philadelphia Branch. Average statistics: 200 entrants, 250 entries, 20 semifinalists, 12 awards. Also sponsor annual scholarships. Second contact: Abby Reese, President, 17 Derwin Road, Bola Cynwyd, Pennsylvania.

POETRY CONTEST: Various Categories, original, unpublished, not submitted for publication at time of entry; no previous cash award winners; typed, double-spaced, on 8 1/2x11-inch paper; unlimited entries. Send 1 original, 2 carbon copies. Categories: Serious Poetry (16-line limit), Light Verse (8-line limit, no limericks).

AWARDS: $25 First, $15 Second, $10 Third Place, 3 Honorable Mentions, each category.

JUDGING: By 3 members of NLAPW-Philadelphia (2 preliminary, 1 final). Entrants retain all rights. Unreturned entries except winners destroyed.

ENTRY FEE: $1 each ($5 for 6 poems). Include SASE if return requested.

DEADLINES: Entry, February. Awards, March.

309

National League of American Pen Women (NLAPW) Pikes Peak Branch Poetry Contest
Frances E. Trapp, Chair
714 South Nevada Avenue
Colorado Springs, Colorado 80903
U.S.A.

October

International; entry open to all; annual. Sponsored by NLAPW, Pikes Peak Branch.

POETRY CONTEST: Various Categories, original, unpublished, typewritten, double-spaced on one side of 8 1/2x11-inch paper. No previous NLAPW contest winning poems. Categories: Shakespearean Sonnet, Optional (16-line limit).

AWARDS: $15 First, $10 Second, $5 Third Prize, each category.

JUDGING: By independent judges. Entrant retains all rights.

ENTRY FEE: $1 each. Entrant pays postage (include SASE).

DEADLINES: Entry, September. Awards, October.

310

National League of American Pen Women (NLAPW), San Diego Branch National Poetry Contest
Contest Chairman
4001 Hope Street
San Diego, California 92115 U.S.A.

May

National; **entry open to U.S. age 18 and over;** annual. Sponsored by NLAPW, San Diego Branch.

POETRY CONTEST: Various Categories, original, unpublished, not entered in another contest; 3 original copies, typed, double-spaced on one side 8 1/2x11-inch paper, one poem per page, 24-line limit per poem. Categories: Theme (any form), Free Verse (any theme), Any Form (rhymed or metered, any theme).

AWARDS: $15 First Place to Theme. $15 First, $10 Second, $5 Third Place to Free Verse and Any Form. Honorable Mention Certificates.

JUDGING: By independent judges. Entrant retains all rights; all entries destroyed after contest.

ENTRY FEE: $1 each. Entrant pays postage (include SASE).

DEADLINES: Entry, March. Winners announced, May.

311

New Mexico State Poetry Contest

New Mexico State Poetry Society (NMSPS)
Jeanne Bonnette, Contest Chair
6801 Ina Drive N.E.
Albuquerque, New Mexico 87109
U.S.A. Tel: (505) 822-1113

May

International; entry open to all; annual; established 1969. Purpose: to encourage interest in poetry. Sponsored and supported by NMSPS. Recognized by NFSPS. Average statistics: 300 entrants, 12 awards. Held at NMSPS annual meeting (May). Publish poetry collections.

POETRY CONTEST: Various Categories, in English; maximum 30 lines per poem; unlimited entry. Submit 2 copies. Categories: Rhymed Verse, Free Verse, Traditional, General.

AWARDS: $15 First, $10 Second, $5 Third Prize. 3 Honorable Mentions.

JUDGING: By nationally known judges. Not responsible for loss or damage.

ENTRY FEE: $1 each. Entrant pays postage (include SASE).

DEADLINES: Entry, March. Awards, May.

312

New Worlds Unlimited Poetry Contest

Sal St. John Buttaci, Susan Gerstle, Editors
P.O. Box 556-F
Saddle Brook, New Jersey 07662
U.S.A.

Spring

International; entry open to all; annual; established 1974. Sponsored by New Worlds Unlimited. Publish *Anthology of Poetry* (annual).

POETRY CONTEST: Various Categories, titled, unpublished; typed, double-spaced, on 8 1/2x11-inch paper or clearly hand-printed, 1 per page; 1 per category. Categories: Funny (20-line limit); Today (modern verse, 24-line limit); Yesterday (traditional including sonnet, 20-line limit); Nature (Haiku to 3 lines, nature poems to 6); Love (24-line limit).

AWARDS: $10, $5 each Best Funny, Today, Yesterday, Nature. $20, $10, $5 Books, Awards Certificates (Love). Winners published in New Worlds Unlimited.

ENTRY FEE: $1 each (Funny, Today, Yesterday). $1 for 2 (Nature). $2 (Love).

DEADLINES: Entry, April. Published, Fall.

313

Oregon State Poetry Association (OSPA) Poetry Contests

Anita M. Hamm, President
15505 S.E. Arista Drive
Milwaukie, Oregon 97222 U.S.A.
Tel: (503) 659-1067

Spring, Fall

National; **entry open to U.S.;** biannual; established 1950. Purpose: to promote poetry; educate public to appreciate the art. Sponsored by OSPA, member NFSPS. Formerly called "Verseweavers," 1936-1950. Supported by private individuals. Held at different Oregon college campus (fall, spring) each year with luncheon, speaker. Have workshops, films, readings, book sale tables. Tickets: $3.75 (luncheon). Publish *OSPA Newsletter* (quarterly). Second contact: Audrey Barry, 1722 S.W. Vista Avenue, Portland, Oregon 97201.

POETRY CONTEST: Various Categories, unpublished; 1 per category, titled; 2 copies, typed single or double-spaced on standard typing paper. Categories: Humorous Quatrain (4-lines), Shakespearean Sonnet, Paragraph Poems (1 paragraph), Any Form (about 30 lines). No previous contest winners.

AWARDS: $15 First Prize (all categories). Other awards at judges' discretion. May print winners in Newsletter.

JUDGING: By panel from Oregon college faculties. Entrants retain all rights. No entries returned.

ENTRY FEE: None (members), $2 (nonmembers).

DEADLINES: Awards, Spring, Fall.

314

Pennsylvania Poetry Society Poetry Contest

Cecilia Parsons Miller, President
264 Walton Street
Lemoyne, Pennsylvania 17043
U.S.A. Tel: (717) 774-5898

February

International; **entry restricted to amateurs, professionals;** annual; established 1949. Alternates with Affiliated National Federation of State Poetry Societies Annual Poetry Contest. Sponsored by Pennsylvania Poetry Society. Supported by dues, patrons. Publish *Prize Poems* (annual newsletter). Also sponsor Pegasus Award (statewide high school award). Second contact: Jessie Ruhl Miller, Treasurer, 670 West Louther Street, Carlisle, Pennsylvania 17043.

POETRY CONTEST: Various Categories, original, unpublished, not currently considered for publication. Typed on one side 8 1/2x11-inch 20-pound bond, double-spaced, original and one copy, SASE. Limit 1 per category except Grand Prize. Categories: Grand Prize (any form, any subject, 50-line limit, 3 poems maximum); Free Verse (any subject, 20-line limit); Any Form (any subject, 24-line limit); Narrative (on person or event, 28-line limit); Experimental (original form, subject, approach; 24-line limit); Woman (any form, 28-line limit); Other Worlds (any form, 24-line limit); Light Verse (8-line limit). 3 membership-only categories. No previous winners.

AWARDS: $50 Grand Prize. $15, $10, $5 Free Verse and Any Form. $20,

$10 Narrative and Woman. $25, $10 Experimental and Other Worlds. $15, $5 Music or Musician. $25 Light Verse.

JUDGING: By Panel. No entries returned; nonwinners destroyed. May publish winners in annual. Reprint rights granted on request.

ENTRY FEE: Grand Prize, $2. Other categories, $1 each. Members, $1 cover fee.

DEADLINES: Entry, February.

315

Poetry Goes To the Fair World Wide Poetry Competition

Contra Costa County Fair
Lynne L. Prout, Contest Chair
10th and L Streets
Antioch, California 94509 U.S.A.

August

International; entry open to all; annual. Purpose: to bring together poetry and public. Held at and sponsored by Contra Costa County Fair.

POETRY CONTEST: Various Categories, in English, unpublished, any length and form, 3 copies on 8 1/2x11-inch paper. Divisions: Age 17 and Under, Adult. Categories: For Children, Adventure, Environmental, Special Occasions, Philosophical, Sociological, Personal Experience, Historical (U.S., Outside U.S.), Horror, Humor, Inspirational, Political, Theological, Scientific, Songs, Psychological, Miscellaneous.

AWARDS: Adult Best of Show, $50 and Trophy. 17 and Under Best of Show First, Second, Third Place Trophies and Cash ($20, $15, $10). Adult Best of Category, Ribbon and $15; 17 and Under Best Category, Trophy, each category. First, Second, Third Place Ribbons, each category. Displayed at Fair.

JUDGING: Each entry judged on own merit; hence multiple awards at judges' discretion. Entrant retains rights; all entries destroyed at Fair's end.

ENTRY FEE: $.50 each.

DEADLINES: Entry, May. Event, August.

316

Poetry Society of America Awards

Charles A. Wagner, Executive Secretary
15 Gramercy Park
New York, New York 10003 U.S.A.
Tel: (212) 254-9628

Spring

National; **entry open to U.S.;** annual; established 1910. Instrumental in establishing Pulitzer Prize for poetry. Purpose: to foster wide interest in poetry. Sponsored by Poetry Society of America (PSA) Nonprofit cultural organization founded 1910. Supported by publishers, editors, foundations, corporations, patrons. Average statistics: $10,000 annual cash awards. Have seminars, workshops, educational programs, library, advisory service. Publish *PSA Bulletin* (quarterly), major anthologies, 5 centennial memorial editions. Also sponsor 11 ($100-$2000) membership awards.

POETRY CONTEST: Various Categories, unpublished; typed in quadruplicate on 8 1/2x11-inch paper; 1 poem per category (same poem may not be entered in 2 contests with same deadline). Categories: Narrative in English *(Masefield Award,* 300-line maximum); Poem Worthy of Poetry Tradition *(Wagner Award,* any style or length); By U.S. Preparatory or

High School Students *(Lieberman Award,* any length).

BOOK CONTEST: Poetry *(Cane Award),* given in even years and published in odd years. Submit 4 copies.

Small or University Press Poetry *(Williams Award),* original by permanent U.S. resident, published by small press, no translations, not previously published. Submit 4 copies.

Poetry Translation into English *(Witter Bynner Prize).* Published in prior 2 years. Collaborations (2) accepted (1 translator must be U.S. citizen or resident alien; require proof of either status). Submit 4 copies.

POETRY GRANTS: Living American Poet *(Shelley Memorial Award).* Up to $1750. Nomination only, selected by 3-poet jury with reference to genius and need.

Poetry Book Translation in Progress *(Witter Bynner Poetry Translation Grant-in-Aid)* $1000. U.S. citizens or resident aliens. Submit 3 copies of outline of translation in progress, 20-page translation sample, original text. Require proof of citizen or alien status.

AWARDS: Poetry Contest: $500 John Masefield Memorial Award. $250 Charles and Celia B. Wagner Award. $100 Elias Lieberman Award. Book Contest: $500 Melville Cane Award. PSA purchase of copies of winning book ($1250 value) for distribution to members, 10% royalty of retail price for William Carlos Williams Award. $1000 Witter Bynner Poetry Translation Prize. Original poems, samples from published work published in *PSA Bulletin.*

JUDGING: Require reprint rights for one-time use of sample poems. Rights revert to winning authors upon publication in Bulletin.

ENTRY FEE: None.

DEADLINES: Entry, May (Williams); August (Witter Bynner Grant and Contest); December (Masefield, Wagner, Lieberman, Cane).

317

Poetry Society of Virginia (PSV) Poetry Prizes

Margaret Rudd
6925 Columbia Pike, Apt. 635
Annandale, Virginia 22003 U.S.A.
Tel: (703) 941-7270

March

International; entry open to all; annual. Sponsored by PSV. Held at PSV meeting in Charlottesville, Virginia. Also sponsor Virginia College Student Poetry Prize, PSV Member Poetry Prizes. Second contact: Ellen Anderson, 4004 Taylor Drive, Fairfax, Virginia 22032.

POETRY CONTEST: Various Categories, unpublished; typed double-spaced; 2 copies; in English. Categories: Sea (48-line limit), Drama, Any Subject (48-line limit), Shakespearean Sonnet, Cat (48-line limit, any form), Humorous (32-line limit, any form-subject).

AWARDS: $100 Best Any Subject (Edgar Allen Poe Award). $50 each: Best Sea (Brodie Herndon Memorial Prize), Drama (Drama Prize), Sonnet (Anna Allen Ford Memorial Award), Cat (Ki Memorial Award), Humorous (Alice Sherry Memorial Award).

JUDGING: By nonmember poets. All entries read in entirety. No poems returned.

ENTRY FEE: $1 each, nonmembers, free to members.

DEADLINES: Entry, January. Awards, March.

318

Poet's Nook Poetry Contest

Weekly Journal-Tempo
Gary Rogers, Publisher
P.O. Box 4769
Whittier, California 90605 U.S.A.
Tel: (213) 698-5259

Continuous

International; entry open to all; continuous; established 1969. Purpose: to encourage reader participation, creative writing. Sponsored by *Weekly Journal* (newspaper) Tempo Publications.

POETRY CONTEST: Various Categories, original, unpublished; any length; 1 per page, typed single-spaced in duplicate on 8 1/2x11-inch white paper. Categories: Free Verse (32-line limit), Rhymed Verse (32-line limit), Haiku (untitled).

AWARDS: $15 First, $10 Second, $5 Third Place; Honorable Mentions, each category. Winners published in "Poet's Nook" column of newspaper.

ENTRY FEE: $1 each. Entrant pays postage (include SASE).

DEADLINES: Open.

319

Poets of the Vineyard Yearly Poetry Contest

Winnie E. Fitzpatrick, President
P.O. Box 77
Kenwood, California 95452 U.S.A.
Tel: (707) 833-4422

March

International; **entry restricted to adults;** annual; established 1975. Purpose: to bring poetry to everyone through workshops, readings, encouraging young poets in local schools. Sponsored by Poets of the Vineyard, nonprofit organization. Average statistics: 350 entries, 280 entrants, 36 awards. Have monthly workshops in Santa Rosa, California. Second contact: Nicole Dobson, 518 North Street, Healdsburg, California 95448.

POETRY CONTEST: Various Categories, original, unpublished, not under consideration for other contests. Require 2 copies typed on 8 1/2x11-inch white paper. 1 poem per page except Haiku. Categories: Traditional Form-Rhyme-Meter (any theme, 32 lines maximum); Free Verse (any theme, 32 lines maximum); Light-Humorous Verse (any theme or form, 32 lines maximum); Short Verse (any theme or form, 12 lines maximum); Haiku-Senryu (3 per page); Tanka (2 per page); California (California poets only, on California living, history, 32 lines maximum); Theme (any form, 32 lines maximum). No previous winners.

AWARDS: $25 Grand Prize, $20 First, $15 Second, $10 Third Place, each category. First and Second Honorable Mentions (book awards). First and Second Eminent Mentions (certificates; poems unpublished).

JUDGING: By 8 judges, one each category. May publish winners (except Eminent Mentions) in Anthology. Poems remain property of winners. No entries returned. Not responsible for loss or damage.

ENTRY FEE: $1 each. Haiku, Senryu, Tanka, $1 per page.

DEADLINES: Entry, March. Winners announced, May.

320

South Dakota State Poetry Society (SDSPS) Poetry Contest

Barbara Stevens, Treasurer
909 East 34th Street
Sioux Falls, South Dakota 57105
U.S.A. Tel: (605) 338-9156

October

International; entry open to all; annual; established 1976. Purpose: to encourage writing of better poetry. Sponsored and supported by SDSPS. Recognized by NFSPS. Average statistics: 100 entries. Awards banquet held in various South Dakota locations. Have state meetings, workshops. Publish *Pasque Petals* poetry magazine (monthly), *Serendipity Newsletter* (quarterly). Also sponsor Poetry Book Contest, School Poetry Contest. Second contact: Robert G. Vessy, State President, 2313 Western, Yankton, South Dakota 57078.

POETRY CONTEST: Various Categories, original, unpublished; 40-line limit; 1 entry per category; submit original and 1 copy. No previous money-prize winning poems. Categories: Sonnet, Humorous (any form), Midwest (any form), Free Verse, Family (any form), 3 additional categories for members only.

AWARDS: $25 First, $15 Second, $10 Third Prize, each category. 3 Honorable Mentions per category. Winners published in *Pasque Petals.*

JUDGING: By out-of-state judges, usually NFSPS members. No entries returned. Not responsible for loss or damage.

ENTRY FEE: $2 each (covers all categories). Entrant pays postage (include SASE).

DEADLINES: Entry, August. Awards, October.

POETRY (Specific Form-Subject)

Includes ANIMAL, BUSH VERSE, CONTEMPORARY, HAIKU, JESSE STUART TRADITION, LACHIAN LANGUAGE, MODERN LIFE, NARRATIVE, PHYSICAL-MENTAL DISABILITY, SHAKESPEAREAN SONNET, SONG LYRICS, TRADITIONAL. (Also see other POETRY CATEGORIES.)

321

American Song Festival Lyric Competition

Jill Frisbee
P.O. Box 57
Hollywood, California 90028 U.S.A.
Tel: (213) 464-8193

January

International; entry open to all; annual; established 1974. Sponsored by American Song Festival, Inc. and Welk Music Group.

POETRY CONTEST: Song Lyrics, original; unproduced commercially; in English; any number of entries. Submit 1 lyric per page, typed or printed clearly. Categories: Top 40 (Rock-Soul), Country, Easy Listening, Folk, Gospel-Inspirational, Open.

AWARDS: Grand Prize, $1250 plus publishing contract. 6 category winners, $250 each. 12 semifinalists, $100 each. 300 quaterfinalists, $25 each. 1000 Honorable Mentions. All entrants receive 2 handbooks for lyricists, anthology of winning lyrics.

JUDGING: By music industry professional. Based on originality, lyrical content. No entries returned. Authors retain rights. Not responsible for loss or damage.

ENTRY FEE: First category, $8.95 each. Additional categories, $4.95 each.

DEADLINES: Entry, May. Judging, July-January. Awards, January.

322

Animal Kingdom Annual Poetry Competition

Carlisle Poets Workshop
Kay M. Freiberg, Contest Chair
40 Meadowbrook Road
Carlisle, Pennsylvania 17013 U.S.A.
Tel: (717) 249-5758

March

International; **entry open to U.S., Canada;** annual; established 1971. Purpose: to recognize poetry by lovers of animals and the natural world. Theme: The Animal Kingdom. Sponsored by Carlisle Poets Workshop, chapter of Pennsylvania Poetry Society. Recognized by NFSPS. Average statistics: 200 entries, 88 entrants, 12 winners. Have monthly workshops, poetry readings. Second contact: Pennsylvania Poetry Society, Jessie Ruhl Miller, Treasurer, P.O. Box 446, Carlisle, Pennsylvania 17013.

POETRY CONTEST: Animal Kingdom, unpublished; unlimited entry; in English; 32 lines or less. Submit 2 copies each, typed, double or 1 1/2-spaced on 8 1/2x11-inch white paper. Categories: Carlisle Poets Award (serious poetry, any form), Florence Mort Kent Memorial Award (humorous or light verse, any form).

AWARDS: $20 First, $15 Second, $10 Third Place, each category. Honorable Mentions.

JUDGING: Entries screened by contest chairman. Final by 2 judges, based on originality. May include winners in anthology. Not responsible for loss or damage.

ENTRY FEE: $1 each. Entrant pays postage (include SASE).

DEADLINES: Entry, December. Judging, January-February. Awards, March.

323

CPS (Czech, Polish, Slovak) Competition

Lachian Art Lettres
Bohumila or Edwin A. Falkowski
208 West Latimer Avenue
Campbell, California 95008 U.S.A.
Tel: (408) 379-8555

April

International; **entry open to U.S., Canada;** annual; established 1942. Sponsored by Bohumila and Edwin A. Falkowski. Supported by Gusto Publications, New York. Average statistics: 100 awards.

POETRY CONTEST: About Lachian Language People (Czech, Polish, Slovak), published or unpublished; in English; limit 1 per author; 20 lines maximum. Submit 3 copies, typed, single-spaced on 8 1/2x11-inch white bond. Subject to center on lives-contributions of Lachian people.

AWARDS: Cash Prizes, $200, $150, $100, $75, $50, $25; plus 10 subscriptions to *Poet* (intercontinental monthly magazine), 20 copies *Premier Poets* (biennial anthology), 60 copies of *Poet* (special edition). Winners published in *Poet.*

JUDGING: By literary professionals. Rights revert to author after publication. No poems returned.

ENTRY FEE: None.

DEADLINES: Entry, event, April.

324

Hephaestus Poetry Contest

Walter F. Stromer
410 Seventh Avenue South
Mt. Vernon, Iowa 52314 U.S.A.

June

International; **entry restricted to physically or mentally handicapped;** annual; established 1978.

POETRY CONTEST: About Physical or Mental Disability; original; submit 1 or 2 poems, maximum 20-lines each.

AWARDS: $10 First, $7.50 Second, $5 Third Prize.

JUDGING: Sponsors have first rights to all submitted.

ENTRY FEE: None. Entrant pays postage (include SASE).

DEADLINES: Entry, May. Event, June.

325

International Narrative Contest

Poets & Patrons, Inc.
Mary Mathison, Contest Chair
13942 Keller Avenue
Crestwood, Illinois 60445 U.S.A.

October

International; entry open to all; annual; established 1974. Purpose: to encourage creativity among poets, appreciation of poetry. Sponsored by Poets & Patrons, Inc. Average statistics: 200 entries, 25 semifinalists, 4 finalists, 2 awards.

POETRY CONTEST: Narrative, any form-subject; original, unpublished; 1 entry maximum, 40-line limit. Original and 1 copy typed on 8 1/2x11-inch paper.

AWARDS: $25 First, $10 Second Prize. 2 Honorable Mentions.

JUDGING: Preliminary by contest chair. Final by non-Illinois judge. Poets retain all rights. No entries returned.

ENTRY FEE: None. Entrant pays postage (include SASE).

DEADLINES: Entry, August. Judging, September-October. Awards, October.

326

International Shakespearean Sonnet Contest

Poets Club of Chicago (PCC)
Anne Nolan, Contest Chair
Nolan Boiler Co.
8531 South Vincennes Avenue
Chicago, Illinois 60620 U.S.A.
Tel: (312) 994-4700

Fall

International; entry open to all; annual; established over 30 years ago. Purpose: to continue interest in writing, enjoyment of Shakespearean sonnet. Sponsored by PCC.

POETRY CONTEST: Shakespearean Sonnet, original, unpublished; 1 entry maximum, 3 copies, typed double-spaced on 8 1/2x11-inch paper. No previous PCC contest cash winners.

AWARDS: $50 First, $25 Second, $10 Third Prize. 3 Honorable Mentions.

JUDGING: By qualified poetry editors, educators, established poets. Preliminary by 3 PCC-member judges, final by PCC membership. No entries returned. Poet retains all rights.

ENTRY FEE: None. Entrant pays postage (include SASE).

DEADLINES: Entry, August. Judging, September-October. Awards, October.

327

Jesse Stuart Poetry Contest

Seven Magazine
James Neill Northe, Editor
3630 N.W. 22nd
Oklahoma City, Oklahoma 73102
U.S.A. Tel: (405) 232-1066

May

International; entry open to all; annual; established 1969. Purpose: to encourage classical poetry expression; communicate ideals, hope. Sponsored by *Seven Magazine.* Average statistics: entries from 7 countries. Second contact: 115 South Hudson, Oklahoma City, Oklahoma 73102.

POETRY CONTEST: In Jesse Stuart Tradition, unpublished; any length; any form or free verse, communicating Stuart's poetry and-or prose embodying basic factors or emotions simply and directly without being obtuse, crude or depressive. Submit entries in triplicate on 8 1/2x11-inch paper, 3 maximum.

AWARDS: $25 First, $15 Second, $10 Third, $5 Fourth Prize.

JUDGING: By 3 judges.

ENTRY FEE: None.

DEADLINES: Entry, February. Awards, May.

328

Joycean Lively Arts Guild Poetry Contest

Jack Sughrue
Box 459, Martin Road
East Douglas, Massachusetts 01516
U.S.A. Tel: (617) 476-7630

April-May

National; **entry open to U.S.;** annual; established 1979. Named after *Joycean Lively Arts Guild (JLAG) Review.* Purpose: to encourage poets who write contemporary poetry. Sponsored by JLAG, nonprofit organization. Recognized by COSMEP, NESPA, SPRIL. Average statistics: 2400 entries, 604 entrants, 60 finalists, 10 winners. Held in East Douglas, Massachusetts for 1 month. Have poetry readings-workshops, in-school programs, library, studio facilities, printing and promotion services. Publish *JLAG Review* (36-page poetry magazine), chapbooks, broadsides. Also sponsor Annual Blackstone Valley Arts Festival.

POETRY CONTEST: **Contemporary,** published or unpublished; maximum 36-lines each; submit 1 per page in batches of 3 or 4, typed; include permission to reprint, credits, if published.

Massachusetts Contemporary, for Massachusetts residents only. Requirements same as for National Contest.

AWARDS: First, Second, Third Place, each contest. Two Honorable Mentions. Winners receive certificates and copy of magazine with winning poems.

JUDGING: By 4 poet-editors. May print or reprint poems (all other rights retained by authors). Not responsible for loss or damage.

ENTRY FEE: None. Entrant pays postage (include SASE).

DEADLINES: Entry, March. Judging, April. Awards, May. Publication, August.

329

Lyric Collegiate Poetry Contest
The Lyric Poetry Magazine
Leslie R. Mellichamp, Editor
307 Dunton Drive S.W.
Blacksburg, Virginia 24060 U.S.A.

Fall

International; **entry restricted to U.S., Canadian undergraduate students;** annual. Purpose: to stimulate writing of traditional poetry. Sponsored by *The Lyric* poetry magazine. Average statistics: 250 entries, 8 awards. Also sponsor $25-$100 Lyric Awards for poems published in *The Lyric.*

POETRY CONTEST: Traditional, by U.S. and Canadian undergraduate college-university students; in English; unpublished, original; 32-line limit, 5 maximum per entrant.

AWARDS: $200 First, $100 Second, $50 Third Prize; $25 Honorable Mentions. $100 to college library of First Prize (provided library is *The Lyric* subscriber).

JUDGING: Varies. No poems returned.

ENTRY FEE: None.

DEADLINES: Entry, June. Awards announced, Fall issue of *The Lyric.*

330

Pegasus Awards Contest
Pennsylvania Poetry Society
Cecilia Parsons Miller, President
264 Walton Street
Lemoyne, Pennsylvania 17043
U.S.A. Tel: (717) 774-5898

April

State; **entry restricted to Pennsylvania high school students of English or creative writing;** annual; sponsored and supported by Pennsylvania Poetry Society. Second contact: Toni-Francoise Lyons, 3621 North Second Street, Harrisburg, Pennsylvania 17110.

POETRY CONTEST: By Pennsylvania High School. Typed on 8 1/2x11-inch white paper, double-spaced, original and one carbon. Categories: Narrative (any form, 24-line limit), Traditional Form (any subject, 16-line limit), Free Verse-Experimental Form (any subject, 16-line limit), Light Verse (any subject, any form, with wit-humor, 9-line limit).

AWARDS: Narrative, $25. Traditional, Free Verse-Experimental, $10, $5. Light Verse, $5.

JUDGING: No entries returned.

ENTRY FEE: None. Enclose SASE with queries.

DEADLINES: Entry, event, April.

331

South Dakota State Poetry Society (SDSPS) School Poetry Contest
Mrs. Alan Bogue, Contest Chair
Route 3, Box 39
Beresford, South Dakota 57004
U.S.A.

April-May

State; **entry restricted to South Dakota junior, senior high school students;** annual. Sponsored and supported by SDSPS. Recognized by NFSPS. Publish *Pasque Petals* (monthly), *Serendipity Newsletter* (quarterly). Also sponsor open-entry poetry contest. Second contact: Barbara Stevens, 909 East 34th Street, Sioux Falls, South Dakota 57105.

POETRY CONTEST: By South Dakota Student, original, 1 entry per category; 1 copy, typed. Divisions: Grades 7-8, 9-10, 11-12. Categories: Tanka (5 lines), Rhymed Quatrain (1-4 stanzas), Free Verse (20-line limit), Any Form (20-line limit).

AWARDS: Winners printed in *Pasque Petals,* receive copy of issue.

ENTRY FEE: None. Entrant pays postage.

DEADLINES: Entry, March. Awards, April-May.

332

Western World Haiku Society (WWHS) Contest
Lorraine Ellis Harr, Founder
4102 N.E. 130th Place
Portland, Oregon 97230 U.S.A.

January

International; entry open to all; annual; established 1974. Sponsored by WWHS. Publish *Dragonfly* (quarterly), *WWHS Newsletter.*

POETRY CONTEST: Haiku, original, unpublished, not under publication consideration; on 8 1/2x5 1/2-inch paper, 3 maximum per entrant per category. No pseudo-haiku. Categories: Dragonfly or Dragonflies, Season Word, 5-7-5 Form, Zen Quality, Sabi (sadness, inevitability of passing time).

AWARDS: $20 each: Dragonfly Award, Best Haiku on Dragonfly; Kametaro Yagi Award, Best Season Word; Oliver Statler Award, Best 5-7-5 Form; Alan Watts Memorial Award, Best Zen Quality; Gary A. Haldeman Award, Best Sabi. $15 Second, $7.50 Third Prize, each category. Runner-Up Mentions. Honorable Mention Book Awards.

JUDGING: Sponsor may use entries in WWHS publications. Nonwinners destroyed.

ENTRY FEE: $1 per category.

DEADLINES: Entry, July-October. Awards, January.

333

Wilory Farm Poetry Contest
M. B. Williamson, Preliminary Judge
Wilory Farm
Route 1
Quemado, Texas 78877 U.S.A.
Tel: (512) 757-1122, 757-1172

March

International; entry open to all; annual; established 1977. Purpose: to encourage poetry as communication-entertainment for general audiences. Theme: Modern Life. Motto: "Bringing it back alive." Sponsored by Wilory Pecan Farm. Average statistics: 2000 entries, 800 entrants, 8 countries, 250 semifinalists, 120 finalists, 20 winners. Publish *Brief Encounters* (book of winners).

POETRY CONTEST: Modern Life, any type, style; unpublished, original; 30-line limit; clear and satisfying (nothing downbeat, hopeless, obscure); typed double-spaced on 8 1/2x11-inch paper. Multiple and group (poems by one poet) submissions permitted.

AWARDS: $500 First, $250 Second, $100 Third, $20 each Fourth-Tenth, $10 each Eleventh-Twentieth Prizes. Certificates of Merit. Winners published in illustrated *Brief Encounters* (copy to winners).

JUDGING: Preliminary by sponsor, final by 1 judge. All entries read. No entries returned. Author retains all rights.

ENTRY FEE: $3 first, $1 each additional.

DEADLINES: Entry, December. Judging, January. Awards, March.

334

Bronze Swagman Award for Bush Verse
Winton Tourist Promotion Association
Mrs. Molly Hickson, Coordinator
P.O. Box 44
Winton, Queensland 4735,
AUSTRALIA Tel: 110 Winton QID

September

International; entry open to all; annual; established 1972. Winton is small bush town near where "Banjo" Paterson wrote words to ballad "Waltzing Matilda," beginning of bush verse style. Named after Australian Swagmen. Purpose: to foster, encourage writing of traditional bush verse. Sponsored by Winton Tourist Promotion Association. Supported by WTPA and Literature Board of the Australian Council of Arts. Held during 1-week Outback Festival. Publish *Bronze Swagman Award Book of Bush Verse* (annually).

POETRY CONTEST: **Traditional Bush Verse,** original, unpublished in English, 1300-words maximum, unlimited entries, each entry typed on separate paper. No previous winners or works used in other media. No entrant eligible to win more than once in 3 years.

AWARDS: Bronze Swagman Statuette ($500 value); Winton Opal ($100 value). Winner announced at Winton Outback Festival, receives newspaper-radio publicity. All published entrants receive free copy of book.

JUDGING: Winner by 1 judge. 5 judges review remaining entries for publication. No entries returned.

ENTRY FEE: $1 any number of entries.

DEADLINES: Entry, May. Award, September.

POETRY (Changing Themes)

Various changing themes. Includes Short Story. (Also see other POETRY CATEGORIES.)

335

Adventures in Poetry Magazine Poetry Contest
Stella Woodall Poetry Society International (SWPSI)
Stella Woodall, Editor-Publisher
P.O. Box 253
Junction, Texas 76849 U.S.A.
Tel: (915) 446-2004

Quarterly

International; entry open to all; quarterly; established 1968. Purpose: to help poets publish Good Clean Poetry. Theme varies yearly. Sponsored by SWPSI (formerly called SAN ANTONIO POETRY SOCIETY; 1000 members). Supported by Sponsor, membership dues, donations. Recognized by American Biographical Institute, World Congress of Poets, United Poets Laureate International, International Academy of Poets, AAP. Average statistics: 14 countries. Publish *Adventures in Poetry Magazine* (international quarterly). Also sponsor annual Patriotic Poetry Seminar.

POETRY CONTEST: **Changing Themes,** original, unpublished, not awarded, 2 copies each. No slanderous, vulgar, prejudicial poems.

AWARDS: Winners published in *Adventures in Poetry Magazine,* receive poetry book.

JUDGING: Based on excellence, relevance to theme. All rights to author after publication.

ENTRY FEE: None.

DEADLINES: Entry, 3 months before publication. Awards, after publication.

336

All Nations Poetry Contest
Triton College
Erika Boehm, Director
2000 Fifth Avenue
River Grove, Illinois 60171 U.S.A.
Tel: (312) 456-0300, ext. 278

May

International; entry open to all; annual; established 1973. Sponsored by Triton College School of University Transfer Studies. Average statistics: 3200 entries, 58 countries, 30 awards, over 20,000 total entries to date.

POETRY CONTEST: **Changing Themes,** 3 categories, 60-line limit; any form, not published or copyrighted; 1 maximum per entrant per category. Require English translation.

AWARDS: Inscribed Medallions to 10 finalists, each category.

JUDGING: Preliminary by Triton College professors; final by poet. No entries returned, become property of Triton College.

ENTRY FEE: None.

DEADLINES: Entry, March. Judging, April. Awards, May.

337

California Federation of Chaparral (CFCP) Poets Monthly Contests
Chaparral Poet Magazine
Pegasus Buchanan, Editor
1422 Ashland Avenue
Claremont, California 91711 U.S.A.

Monthly

International; **entry open to U.S. and Canada;** Monthly. Sponsored by CFCP, annual membership $7. Also sponsor annual CFCP Poetry Competition.

POETRY CONTEST: **Changing Themes,** unpublished, 24-line limit, typewritten, 1 copy, no carbons, various monthly themes.

AWARDS: Cash Prizes of $25, $15, $10 each month. Winners published in *Chaparral Poet Magazine.*

ENTRY FEE: $1 each.

DEADLINES: Entry by last day of contest month, throughout year.

338

California State Poetry Society (CSPS) Monthly Contests
Sally Herres, Contest Chair
374 East Cypress Street
Covina, California 91723 U.S.A.
Tel: (213) 332-3742

Monthly

International; entry open to all; monthly. Sponsored by CSPS.

POETRY CONTEST: **Changing Themes;** unpublished, original; in English; themes vary monthly; 1-page limit, typed single or double-spaced. No other contest-publisher submissions (December entrants may submit previously published and-or award-winners).

AWARDS: One-half of entry fees to monthly winner.

JUDGING: Anonymous. No entries returned. Author retains rights.

ENTRY FEE: 1-3 poems, $1; 4-6 poems, $2; 7-9 poems, $3; etc. Entrant pays postage (include SASE).

DEADLINES: Entry by last day each month throughout year.

339

St. Hedwig's Day Poetry Contest
1716 North Humboldt Avenue
Milwaukee, Wisconsin 53202 U.S.A.

October

International; entry open to all; annual. Motto: "Helping poets meet the challenge." Publish *Golden Eagle Newsletter.*

POETRY CONTEST: **Changing Themes,** any length; in English or Polish (with English translation); any number of entries.

AWARDS: $50 First, $25 Second Prize. St. Hedwig Cross.

JUDGING: By 3 judges. May publish entry without further recompense.

ENTRY FEE: None.

DEADLINES: Entry, August. Winners announced, October (St. Hedwig's Day).

340

Two-in-One Poetry Contest
Creative With Words Publications
Brigitta Geltrich, Editor and Publisher
24665 Cabrillo Street
Carmel, California 93923 U.S.A.

Summer

International; entry open to all; annual; established 1975. Purpose: to promote creative writing by and for children; provide creative outlet for senior citizens. Theme varies annually. Sponsored by Creative With Words Publications. Average statistics: over 300 entries. Publish semiannual anthologies. Second contact: Spencer Ludgate, 8259 Fountain Avenue No. 5, West Hollywood, California 90046.

POETRY CONTEST: **Changing Themes,** original, unpublished, 16 lines maximum, 3 maximum per entrant. New forms invited.

SHORT STORY CONTEST: **Folklore Tales,** unpublished original or retelling, 2 maximum per entrant.

AWARDS: Monetary. Winners published in semiannual anthologies.

JUDGING: By jury of editors, writers, educators. Rights revert to author after publication. Not responsible for loss or damage.

ENTRY FEE: Adults: $1 each; senior citizens: $.50; children under 18 free. Send SASE with inquiry. No materials returned.

DEADLINES: Entry, August. Awards, September.

RESIDENCE GRANTS

Primarily for RESIDENCE STUDY, RESEARCH, CREATIVE WRITING. Includes Play, Poetry, Prose, Publishing, Script. (Also see SCHOLARSHIPS, FELLOWSHIPS.)

341

Creekwood Writers' Colony Residencies
Alabama School of Fine Arts
Charles Ghigna, Poet-in-Residence
Creative Writing Department
820 North 18th Street
Birmingham, Alabama 35203 U.S.A.

Continuous

International; entry open to all; continuous. Sponsored by Creekwood Writers' Colony. Held at sponsor's antebellum mansion on 100 acres of woodland providing solitude for poets-authors. Have studio, barn, cottage, greenhouse, fishing pond.

WRITING RESIDENCE GRANT: **Creative Writing.** Residents assist with daily chores in return for room and board for 1-3 weeks. Include SASE with inquiries.

DEADLINES:

342

Cummington Community of the Arts Artist in Residence Scholarships

Molly Snyder, Director
Potash Hill Road
Cummington, Massachusetts 01026
U.S.A. Tel: (413) 634-2172

Continuous

International; entry open to all; continuous; established 1923. Formerly called THE MUSIC BOX (1923-1930), PLAYHOUSE IN THE HILLS (1930-1953), CUMMINGTON SCHOOL OF THE ARTS (1953-1968). Purpose: to stimulate individual artistic growth-development while providing atmosphere for communication, interdisciplinary cooperation. Sponsored and supported by Cummington Community of the Arts, 150-acre educational community of filmmakers, photographers, writers, musicians, painters, sculptors, other artists, in Massachusetts Berkshires. Supported by NEA, Massachusetts Council for the Arts. Average statistics: 10-30 artists. Have library, darkrooms, kiln, studios, individual living accommodations, kitchen, dining hall, garden. Tuition: $275 per month, includes room, board, studio space. Publish *Cummington Journal.* Also sponsor workshops, readings, shows at local galleries.

WRITING RESIDENCE SCHOLARSHIPS: **Fiction Writing,** partial tuition abatements per month, based on financial need. Require work samples (about 10 pages poetry, 20-50 pages fiction or drama), resume, work plan, complete financial statement (including past 2 years' income, tax forms, savings, holdings, projected income, expenses), interview.

JUDGING: By Admission Committee. Based on work, interview. All entries reviewed in entirety.

DEADLINES: Application, 2 months before desired residency.

343

Fine Arts Work Center in Provincetown Resident Fellowships

Bill Tchakirides, Director
24 Pearl Street, P.O. Box 565
Provincetown, Massachusetts 02657
U.S.A.

October-May

International; entry open to all; annual; established 1968. Purpose: to help young artists and writers in early, critical period of professional careers with opportunity to live, work in congenial, stimulating environment. Held at and sponsored by nonprofit Fine Arts Work Center in Provincetown (America's premiere art colony on Cape Cod). Supported by NEA, Massachusetts Council on the Arts and Humanities, CCLM. Have 14 studio apartments, gallery, common room, offices, critiques, discussions, readings, exhibitions, visiting artists and writers. Also sponsor 10 artists' fellowships.

WRITING RESIDENT FELLOWSHIP: **Writing,** 10 fellowships to

writers, in $100-$200 monthly stipends, living-studio space, and general equipment. Any age. Require collated, double-spaced writing sample in quadruplicate (1-2 short stories, chapter of novel, or up to 12 poems). No critical writers, journalists.

JUDGING: Based on quality of work. Preference to young writers who have completed formal training and are working on own. Not responsible for loss or damage.

ENTRY FEE: $15. Applicant pays postage (include SASE).

DEADLINES: Entry, January. Notification, May. Residence, October-May.

344

Fulbright-Hays Grants
Institute of International Education (IIE)
Theresa Granza, Manager
809 United Nations Plaza
New York, New York 10017 U.S.A.
Tel: (212) 883-8265

Spring

National; **entry open to U.S.;** annual; established 1946 by legislation authorizing use of foreign currencies accruing to U.S. abroad for educational exchanges (1961 *Fulbright-Hays Mutual Educational and Cultural Exchange Act* authorizes congressional appropriations for these exchanges). Named after Senator J. William Fulbright. Purpose: to increase mutual understanding between U.S. and other nationals through foreign study. Sponsored by IIE, founded to promote peace, understanding through educational, cultural exchanges in all academic fields; U.S. International Communication Agency (USICA). Supported by annual appropriations from U.S. Congress, other governments. Average statistics: 3000 entrants. Have grants to visiting scholars, American scholars-professionals, predoctoral fellowships, teacher exchanges, Hubert H. Humphrey North-South Fellowship Program (study-internships), Faculty Research Abroad Program, Doctoral Dissertation Research Abroad Program, Group Projects Abroad. Fulbright-Hays program booklets available from USICA, 1776 Pennsylvania Avenue N.W., Washington, D.C. 20547. Also Sponsor Fulbright Awards for University Teaching and Advanced Research Abroad.

WRITING RESIDENCE GRANT: Creative Arts Foreign Study, roundtrip transportation, language and orientation course, tuition, books, health-accident insurance, single-person maintenance for 6-12 months study in 1 foreign country (doctoral candidates may receive higher stipends).

ELIGIBILITY: U.S. citizens with majority of high school, college education in U.S., B.A. or equivalent (or 4 years professional experience-study in proposed creative art field). Require host-country language proficiency, certificate of good health, study plan, project proposal, reasons for choosing particular country, what contribution foreign experience will make to professional development, work samples, possible interview.

JUDGING: Professional juries and binational commissions in field of expertise prepare nominations to Fulbright agencies abroad, U.S. Board of Foreign Scholarship.

DEADLINES: Application, November. Judging, November-December. Preliminary notification, January. Awards, April-June.

345

Fulbright Awards for University Teaching and Advanced Research Abroad

Council for International Exchange of Scholars (CIES)
Suite 300
Eleven Dupont Circle
Washington, District of Columbia 20036 U.S.A. Tel: (202) 833-4950

Spring

National; **entry open to U.S.;** annual; established 1946 by legislation authorizing use of foreign currencies accruing to U.S. abroad for educational exchanges (1961 *Fulbright-Hays Mutual Educational and Cultural Exchange Act* authorizes congressional appropriations for these exchanges). Named after Senator J. William Fulbright. Purpose: to increase mutual understanding between U.S. and other nationals through foreign study. Sponsored by CIES, U.S. International Communications Agency (USICA). Supported by annual appropriations from U.S. Congress, other governments. Average statistics: 2500 entrants, 1000 semifinalists, 500 awards. Have other grants for teacher-scholar exchanges, research abroad. Also sponsor Fulbright-Hays Grants.

WRITING RESIDENCE GRANT: **University teaching, Advance Research,** stipend, round-trip transportation, other allowances for 1 academic year or less of university teaching and-or postdoctoral research abroad.

ELIGIBILITY: U.S. Citizens, scholars, creative artists, professionals, institutions. Require host-country language proficiency if needed; university teaching experience; doctorate, if specified by host country (for teaching); doctorate or recognized professional standing (for research); project presentation, other documentation.

JUDGING: 50 discipline-area committees and binational commissions assist CIES in preparing nominations to Fulbright agencies abroad and U.S. Board of Foreign Scholarship. All entries reviewed.

DEADLINES: Application, June (American Republics, Australia, New Zealand), July (Africa, Asia, Europe). Judging, September-December. Notification, January-April. Awards given 12-18 months following notification.

346

Helene Wurlitzer Foundation of New Mexico Residencies

Henry A. Sauerwein, Jr., Executive Director
P.O. Box 545
Taos, New Mexico 87571 U.S.A.
Tel: (505) 758-2413

Continuous

International; entry open to all; continuous. Sponsored by Helene Wurlitzer Foundation of New Mexico. Have 12 studio apartments in Taos, New Mexico. Also accept painting, sculpture, choreography, allied fields.

WRITING RESIDENCE GRANT: **Writing,** furnished studio apartment (including linen, utilities) for 3-12 months. Residents purchase, cook, serve own meals; clean apartments. No families, transportation, living expenses, materials.

DEADLINES: Open.

347

Howard University Press Book Publishing Institute Scholarships

Janell E. Walden, Program Director
2900 Van Ness Street N.W.

Washington, District of Columbia
20008 U.S.A. Tel: (202) 686-6498

Spring

International; entry open to all; annual; established 1980. Purpose: to prepare individuals for entry-level positions in book publishing industry. Sponsored by Howard University Press. Supported by Time, Inc., other publishing companies. Recognized by AAP Education for Publishing Program. Held in Washington, D.C. for 5 1/2 weeks. Have lectures, workshops, tours, discussions. Tuition: $900.

PUBLISHING RESIDENCE SCHOLARSHIP: Book Publishing, scholarships to attend Institute to students demonstrating financial need, high motivation, appreciation for books; for tuition, housing, books, meals, transportation to classroom. Must be college senior or hold bachelors degree, wish to begin career in book publishing. Certificates awarded on successful completion of course. Categories: Editorial, Design-Production, Marketing, Business.

JUDGING: Applicants reviewed by admissions committee.

ENTRY FEE: $25.

DEADLINES: Entry, April. Acceptance, May.

348

Indiana University Writers' Conference Scholarships

Roger Mitchell, Director
464 Ballantine Hall
Indiana University
Bloomington, Indiana 47405 U.S.A.
Tel: (812) 337-1877

June

International; entry open to all; annual; established 1941. Purpose: to provide constructive, professional guidance, criticism for writers and their work. Sponsored by Indiana University. Average statistics: 150 entries. Held at Indiana University in June. Have workshops. Fees: $150 tuition plus 1 week room-board. Also sponsor Founder's Award, Indiana Women's Press Association Award, other cash awards to conference participants.

WRITING RESIDENCE SCHOLARSHIP: Fiction, Poetry, fees and tuition for attending conference to entrants submitting best manuscript to each workshop. Categories: Fiction, Poetry, Science Fiction, Juvenile Fiction, Screen Writing.

JUDGING: By conference screening committee. Not responsible for loss or damage.

ENTRY FEE: $15 (refundable). Entrant pays postage (include SASE).

DEADLINES: Entry, April. Acceptance, May. Conference, June.

349

Interlochen Arts Academy Playwright Project

Anne Marie Gillis, Chair, Theatre Arts
Interlochen, Michigan 49643 U.S.A.
Tel: (616) 276-9221

May

International; entry open to all; annual; established 1976. Purpose: to support, encourage talented playwrights; fully develop literary work for theater. Sponsored by Interlochen Arts Academy Theatre Arts Department. Supported by Interlochen Center for the Arts, founded 1962 as 1400-acre international fine arts boarding school (grades 9-12). Average statistics: 100 entries, 10 semifinalists, 5 finalists, 1 winner. Have theater, production facilities.

PLAYWRITING RESIDENCY: **Playwriting,** $200, room-board, transportation for residency during production of play. Submit 1 or more plays, resume.

JUDGING: By committee, all entries read and discussed. Applicant retains all rights. Not responsible for loss or damage.

ENTRY FEE: None. Applicant pays postage (include SASE).

DEADLINES: Entry, November. Notification, February. Award, May.

350

MacDowell Colony Residence Grants
680 Park Avenue
New York, New York 10021 U.S.A.

Continuous

International; entry open to all; continuous; established 1907 by American composer Edward MacDowell. Purpose: to help creative professional artists pursue work under optimal conditions. Sponsored by and held at MacDowell Colony (Peterborough, New Hampshire), nonprofit membership corporation providing working, living accommodations and solitude (no instruction) for writers, visual artists, filmmakers, composers of demonstrated talent. Supported by NEA, private donors. Average statistics: 190 residents (98 writers, 58 visual artists, 34 composers), 39-day average stay, nearly 2000 residents to date. Have 30 isolated studios, 3 residence cottages, graphics workshops, library, main hall, on 450 acres of fields, woods. Also sponsor Edward MacDowell Medal, presented to major artist annually in August. Second contact: MacDowell Colony, High Street, Peterborough, New Hampshire 03458.

WRITING RESIDENCE GRANT: **Writing,** tuition waiver, based on number of accepted applicants (selected from writers, filmmakers, composers, visual artists) and financial need, for room, board, private studio. Require sample manuscripts, publications list, recommendations.

JUDGING: By professionals in each discipline. Based on talent shown in submitted work samples, recommendations.

DEADLINES: Entry, January (for June-August), April (September-November), July (December-February), October (March-May). Request application from New York office.

351

Niagara Frontier Christian Writers' Workshop Scholarships
Don Booth, Director
6853 Webster Road
Orchard Park, New York 14127
U.S.A. Tel: (716) 662-5259

June

International; entry open to all; annual; established 1970. Purpose: to challenge, encourage writers to share faith in Christ through short stories, poetry, devotionals. Sponsored by Niagara Frontier Christian Writers' Workshop. Average statistics: 45 attendance. Held for 1 day at Houghton College, Buffalo campus (910 Union Road, West Seneca, New York 14224; 716-674-6363). Have manuscript criticisms, marketing suggestions. Tickets: $17 registration. Also sponsor Nonfiction Writing Residence Scholarships.

WRITING RESIDENCE SCHOLARSHIP: **Christian Fiction,** to attend Christian Writers' Workshop. Submit up to 2000 words. Categories: Book, Script, Short Story, Poetry.

JUDGING: By workshop leaders. Entries reviewed in entirety.

DEADLINES: Application, May. Notification, June.

352

Northwood Institute Creativity Fellowships

Alden B. Dow Creativity Center
Judith O'Dell, Director
3225 Cook Road
P.O. Box 1406
Midland, Michigan 48640 U.S.A.
Tel: (517) 631-1600, ext. 208

Summer

International; **entry restricted to English-speaking persons;** annual; established 1979. Named after Alden B. Dow, AIA. Purpose: to encourage creative thought; provide time, work facilities for creative persons to concentrate on ideas without financial worries; establish internationally recognized center for creativity technology. Sponsored by Northwood Institute, Alden B. Dow. Average statistics: 6 awards. Held at Northwood Institute, Midland, Michigan.

WRITING RESIDENCE FELLOWSHIP: **Creative Project,** for study, creation, innovation, appreciation. 3-month study at Northwood institute; includes room, board, professional counsel. Considered applicants flown to personal interview. Applicants welcomed from all disciplines, areas of interest covering spectrum of written communications (e.g., language development, prose, poetry, publishing, distribution of literature). Require description of proposed project, resume, budget projection. College credit arranged upon request. Special certificates, recognition upon successful completion.

JUDGING: By Board of Directors, Advisory Panel, Northwood Institute Alden B. Dow Creativity Center. All entries viewed in entirety. Project ideas remain property of applicant. Not responsible for loss or damage.

ENTRY FEE: None. Entrant pays postage (include SASE).

DEADLINES: Entry, December. Judging, December-March. Winners announced, April. Award, June-August.

353

Playwrights' Center Residence Grants

Kevin Berigan, Public Relations Director
2301 East Franklin Avenue
Minneapolis, Minnesota 55406
U.S.A. Tel: (612) 332-7481

March, November

National (Playwrights-in-Residence) **entry open to U.S.;** Regional (Midwest Playwrights' Program) **entry restricted to Midwest playwrights;** annual; established 1971 (Playwrights-in-Residence, PR), 1976 (Midwest Playwrights' Program, MPP). Formerly called MIDWEST PROFESSIONAL PLAYWRIGHTS' LABORATORY to 1980 (sponsored by University of Wisconsin). Purpose: to bring together playwrights for work with Midwest actors, directors, dramaturgs. Sponsored and supported by Playwrights' Center, Jerome Foundation, Minnesota State Arts Board, various agencies. Recognized by TCG. Average statistics: (PR) 120 entries, 60 entrants, 25 semifinalists, 17 finalists, 6 winners; (MPP) 250-300 entrants, 25 semifinalists, 10 winners; 60 workshops, 30 staged readings, 100 cold readings. Held in Minneapolis, Minnesota (PR), different locations (MPP). Have workshops, performance areas, writers' studios, rehearsal rooms, national touring program of open play readings. Publish monthly newsletter. Also sponsor Play Production Program. Second contact: Thomas G. Dunn, Artistic Director (PR), Dale Wasserman, Artistic Director (MPP).

PLAY RESIDENCE GRANT: Playwriting *(Playwrights-in-Residence)* 6 $3000 stipends per year plus developmental, professional services. Submit 1-2 plays, resume, letter of intent. Require residence in Minnesota during award year.

Midwest Playwriting *(Midwest Playwrights' Program),* 10 $500 stipends per year, travel and expenses for 2-week seminar (including professional staged readings), to residents of Dakotas, Illinois, Indiana, Iowa, Kansas, Michigan, Minnesota, Missouri, Nebraska, Ohio, Wisconsin. Submit 1 play, unpublished, unproduced. Require short biography.

JUDGING: By 5 readers. Not responsible for loss or damage.

DEADLINES: Application, March (PR), November (MPP). Acceptance, March (MPP). Event, August (MPP).

354

United States and Japan Exchange Fellowship Program

Japan United States Friendship Commission
Francis B. Tenny, Executive Director
1875 Connecticut Avenue N.W.
Suite 709
Washington, District of Columbia
20009 U.S.A. Tel: (202) 673-5295

April, October

National; **entry restricted to Mid-career U.S. and Japanese artists;** semiannual; established 1975. Purpose: to aid education and culture at highest level; enhance reciprocal people-to-people understanding; support close friendship and mutuality of interests between U.S. and Japan. Sponsored by Japan United States Friendship Commission, NEA (U.S.), Agency for cultural Affairs (Japan). Have fellowships in dance, design, folk arts, music composition, theater, visual arts, crafts. Also sponsor Journalism Fellowships, Book Translation Awards, American Performing Arts Tours in Japan, Japanese Cultural Preformances in U.S. Second contact: Nippon Press Center Building, 2-1 Uchisaiwai-cho, 2 chome, Chiyoda-ku, Tokyo tel., 508-2380

WRITING RESIDENCE FELLOWSHIP: Literature Work-Study in Japan. 5 fellowships of $1600-monthly stipends plus round-trip transportation for 6-9 months to creative and practicing artists well established in field, to observe Japanese traditional and contemporary artistic developments. (Overseas travel fares for spouse; children to 18 also provided.) Require completed training; not recent resident or working in Japan at time of application. Funds also available for additional expenses. Written report required at conclusion. No historians, scholars, art critics, students. Proficiency in Japanese not required.

JUDGING: Reviewed by private citizens, experts in respective fields. American selection committee chooses semifinalists. Final by Japanese awards committee.

DEADLINES: Entry, March, September. Fellowships, October, April.

355

Virginia Center for the Creative Arts (VCCA) Residence Fellowships

Sweet Briar College
William Smart, Director
Box VCCA

Sweet Briar, Virginia 24595 U.S.A.
Tel: (804) 946-7236

Continuous

International; **entry restricted to professional writers;** continuous; established 1971. Purpose: to provide dedicated, talented, professional writers with uninterrupted time, adequate space to concentrate on their art. Sponsored by VCCA. Supported by NEA, Virginia Commission for the Arts, foundations. Average statistics: 100 entrants, 5 countries, 10 writer residencies. Have studios, pool, 450 acres of pasture and woodlands, library, recreation facilities, cultural events. Held at Mt. San Angelo Estate adjacent to Sweet Briar College for 6 weeks. Residency costs: $10 per day. Also sponsor residencies for visual artists, composers.

WRITING RESIDENCE FELLOWSHIP: **Fiction Writing,** up to $40 per day for 6 weeks room-board, studio space. Have concerts, plays, films, dance recitals, art exhibits, lectures. Require manuscript samples, 2 professional recommendations, curriculum vita, project description.

JUDGING: By 5-member professional writer panel. Entries reviewed in entirety. Based on achievement, promise, financial need.

ENTRY FEE: None. Entrant pays postage (include SASE).

DEADLINES: Entry, open. Notification in 6 weeks.

356

Wallace E. Stegner Fellowships in Creative Writing

Dolly Kringel, Secretary to Director
Creative Writing Center, English Department
Stanford University
Stanford, California 94305 U.S.A.
Tel: (415) 497-2637

May-June

International; **entry open to all (prefer under age 30);** annual; established 1946. Purpose: to give talented young writers year's residence at Stanford University with professional writing supervision. Sponsored and supported by Stanford University Department of English Creative Writing Center. Average statistics: 400 entrants, 24-30 semifinalists, 12-14 finalists, 6 awards. Held at Creative Writing Center, Stanford, for one year. Tuition: $1500 (writing graduate course). Also sponsor Mirrielees Fellowship for Stanford University M.A. degree candidate in creative writing.

WRITING RESIDENCE FELLOWSHIP: **Fiction, Poetry Writing,** 4 $5000 fellowships plus tuition in fiction, 2 in poetry, for 1-year residence, instruction, criticism to young professional writers with proposed, in-progress projects. Fellows enroll in advanced fiction, poetry-writing seminar (other degree credit courses optional). May be admitted as regular graduate, undergraduate students. Require project prospectus, outline; 2 sample chapters, 50 pages; 2-3 short stories; or 12 poems.

JUDGING: By minimum 6 judges. All entries reviewed 3 times. No entries returned. Not responsible for loss or damage.

ENTRY FEE: None. Entrant pays postage (include SASE).

DEADLINES: Application, January. Notification, May-June.

357

Wesleyan Writers Conference Scholarships and Fellowships

John W. Paton, Executive Secretary
Wesleyan University
Middletown, Connecticut 06547
U.S.A. Tel: (203) 347-9411, ext. 602

June

International; entry open to all; annual; established 1956. Formerly called SUFFIELD WRITER-READER CONFERENCE. Purpose: to provide intensive workshop for writers. Sponsored by and held at Wesleyan University for 1 week. Supported by Connecticut Commission on the Arts and Humanities, publishers, bookstores. Average statistics: 25-30 awards, limited to 100 attendance. Have writing classes (novel, short story, poetry, for young people, for performance, factual), speakers, writing appraisals. Tuition: $295 room-board; $250 day student; $90 1 seminar only; $25 registration. Also sponsor Nonfiction Writing Residence Scholarship.

WRITING RESIDENCE FELLOWSHIP: **Fiction, Poetry,** 2 full fellowships (1 poetry, 1 fiction) to young writer for 1 week tuition, room-board, stipend, for status as student-staff member. Submit 5-7 poems, 1-2 short stories, or 1-2 novel chapters, recently or soon to be published. Editor, agent supporting letters welcome. Applicants automatically considered for scholarships.

WRITING RESIDENCE SCHOLARSHIP: **Fiction,** 20 full or partial scholarships to writers, college students, literature-writing teachers, working journalists, for 1 week tuition, room-board. Require experience, aspirations; welcome supporting letters. One $295 full scholarship to woman writer (Connecticut Federation of Women's Clubs) preference to Connecticut resident. One full scholarship (Xerox Corporation) to individual writing for young people. Several scholarships (Adelphic Literary Society); preference to college or recently graduated students. Submit 5-7 poems, 1-2 short stories, or 1-2 novel chapters.

JUDGING: By writing professionals on Advisory Board. All entries read in entirety. Not responsible for loss or damage.

DEADLINES: Application, May. Notification, June.

358

William Flanagan Center for Creative Persons Residencies

Edward F. Albee Foundation
14 Harrison Street
New York, New York 10013 U.S.A.

June-October

International; entry open to all; annual; established 1978. Sponsored by Edward F. Albee Foundation. Held at William Flanagan Memorial Creative Persons Center on Long Island (South Fairview Avenue, Montauk, New York 11954).

WRITING RESIDENCE GRANT: **Writing,** for room-board for at least 1 month to writers, painters, sculptors. Require intention letter, recommendation, sample manuscript.

DEADLINES: Application, January-April. Notification, June-October.

359

Women's Voices Creative Writing Workshop Scholarships

Kresge College, University of California, Santa Cruz (UCSC)
Marcy Alncraig, Coordinator
1312 Addison Street

Berkeley, California 94702 U.S.A.
Tel: (415) 849-2126

June-July

International; **entry restricted to minority women;** annual; established 1977. Purpose: to further literary expression of women's experience. Sponsored and supported by Women's Studies Program, Humanities Division, UCSC Literature Board. Recognized by Feminist Writers Guild. Held at UCSC for 2 weeks; 42 attendance. Have class sessions, guest speakers. Fees: $170 tuition, $300 room-board. Publish anthology. Second contact: Carol Spindel, 1739 Ward Street, Berkeley, California 94703.

WRITING RESIDENCE SCHOLARSHIP: **Prose, Poetry,** 2 full and several partial scholarships to workshop for low-income, minority writers. Submit 5 pages of prose, poetry.

DEADLINES: Application, May. Notification, June. Workshop, June-July.

SCHOLARSHIPS, FELLOWSHIPS

Primarily for STUDY and RESEARCH. Includes Novel, Play, Poetry, Short Story. (Also see RESIDENCE GRANTS.)

360

Actors Theatre of Louisville Literary Management Internship

Elizabeth King, Literary Manager
316 West Main Street
Louisville, Kentucky 40202 U.S.A.
Tel: (502) 584-1265

September-May

National; **entry open to U.S.;** annual. Purpose: to offer on-the-job training, experience as literary manager. Sponsored and supported by Actors Theatre of Louisville. Held in Louisville, Kentucky. Also sponsor Great American Play Contest, Festival of New American Plays, Playwright-in-Residence program.

PLAY INTERNSHIP: **Playwriting Literary Management.** Full-time position (no salary-tuition), possible college credit for reviewing new plays (about 4000); researching, organizing, coordinating Festival of New American Plays and Great American Play Contest. Require application letter, resume, photograph, 2 recommendation letters, possible personal interview. May apply for all or part of season (preference for entire season).

DEADLINES: Application, April. Internship, September-May.

361

Appalachian Writers' Workshop Tuition Scholarships

Mike Mullens, Coordinator
Hindman Settlement School
Hindman, Kentucky 41822 U.S.A.
Tel: (606) 785-5475

August

International; entry open to all; annual; established 1978. Sponsored by Hindman Settlement School, founded 1902 for promotion, preservation of culture and history of Appalachia. Held in Hindman, Kentucky. Have readings, workshops, conferences, field trips. Fees: $70 tuition, $70 room-board. Also sponsor Appalachian Family Folk Week, Appalachian Visual Arts Week.

WRITING SCHOLARSHIP: Ap-

palachia Novel, Short Story, Poetry, covers tuition for needy individuals who submit manuscript for evaluation. Submit short story, chapter or synopsis of novel, poems.

DEADLINES: Not specified. Conference, August.

362

Boston University Creative Writing Fellowships

Boston University Creative Writing Program
Leslie Epstein, Director
236 Bay State Road
Boston, Massachusetts 02215 U.S.A.
Tel: (617) 353-2510

April

International; **entry restricted to graduate students;** annual; established 1979. Purpose: to support poet or fiction writer entering 1-year M.A. program. Sponsored and supported by Boston University Creative Writing Program. Average statistics: 150 entrants; 2 awards. Held as part of Boston University Creative Writing Program.

WRITING FELLOWSHIP: Fiction, Poetry, 2 $4000 fellowships plus tuition to poet or fiction writer entering 1-year Boston Creative Writing M.A. program.

JUDGING: By members of Creative Writing Program and English Department, Boston University.

DEADLINES: Application, January. Notification, April.

363

Centrum Poetry Symposium and Fiction Seminar Scholarships

Jim Heynen, Coordinator
P.O. Box 1158
Port Townsend, Washington 98368
U.S.A. Tel: (206) 385-3102

July

International; entry open to all; annual; established 1973. Purpose: to provide professional and preprofessional training. Sponsored by Centrum, nonprofit organization dedicated to presenting year-round cultural, educational activities. Recognized by Washington State Arts Commission. Average statistics: 32 entries. Held at Fort Worden State Park for 12 weeks. Have poetry symposium, fiction seminar (children's literature, general fiction), writing composition workshop, festivals, and public performances. Fees: $130-$200 (poetry), $185 (fiction), $135 (room-board). Also sponsor workshop fee-waiver assistantships for extremely needy.

WRITING SCHOLARSHIP: Fiction, Poetry *(Norm Goodwin and Ona Siporin Scholarships)*, 2 tuition scholarships to Centrum workshop. Submit 3-7 pages for Fiction Workshop, 3-5 poems for Advanced Poetry.

JUDGING: By 3 judges. Not responsible for loss or damage.

ENTRY FEE: $25 deposit (refundable).

DEADLINES: Application, May. Notification, June.

364

Lucy Martin Donnelly Fellowship

Bryn Mawr College
Office of the President
Bryn Mawr, Pennsylvania 19010
U.S.A.

Periodic

International; **entry restricted (nomination by college)** periodic.

Fellowship to Women for Belle Lettres (including Writing, Playwriting) U.S.-British Commonwealth citizens, without regard to financial circumstances. Request visits to college for workshops, readings, talks. Sponsored by Bryn Mawr College.

365

Santa Cruz Writers' Conference Scholarships

University of California, Santa Cruz (UCSC)
Santa Cruz, California 95064 U.S.A.

June

International; entry open to all; annual. Purpose: to focus on writing as craft, expression, exploration, art. Sponsored by and held at UCSC for 2 weeks. Have workshops; lecture series; option for housing. Tuition: $305 plus $20 nonrefundable application fee. Also sponsor Nonfiction Writing Residence Scholarship.

WRITING SCHOLARSHIP: **Fiction, Short Story, Poetry,** scholarships to Writers' Conference. Submit recent unpublished manuscript; typed, double-spaced; 7000-word limit (short story), 5000-word minimum and outline (novel), 4-12 poems. 1 entry per category. Require letter indicating experience, financial need.

ENTRY FEE: Entrant pays postage (include SASE).

DEADLINES: Application, May. Notification, June.

366

Stanford Writing Scholarship

University of Melbourne
P.G. Morgan, Assistant Registrar (Arts)
Faculty of Arts
Parkville, Victoria 3052, AUSTRALIA
Tel: 345-1844

Fall

National; **entry restricted to young Australians;** annual. $4000 **Writing Scholarship** for 1-year study at Stanford University Writing Center (Palo Alto, California, U.S.A.). Sponsored by University of Melbourne. Held during Academic year.

367

Mexican Center for Writers Fellowships

Centro Mexicano de Escritores, A.C.
Felipe Garcia Beraza, Secretary
San Francisco, No. 12
Mexico 12, D.F., MEXICO
Tel: 543-79-31

April

National; **entry restricted to Mexican writers;** annual. 25,000 and 35,000 pesos 1-year **Fellowships for Creative Writing.** Sponsored by Mexican Center for Writers (Francisco Monterde, Director), established 1951 as nonprofit writer's liaison organization. Awards announced, April.

368

Robert Burns Fellowship in Literature

University of Otago
Registrar
P.O. Box 56
Dunedin, NEW ZEALAND
Tel: 771640

September

National; **entry restricted to New Zealand resident writers;** annual; established 1959. Travel Expenses, $8000 (N.Z.) **Fellowship to Literature Writer** for 1 academic year. Purpose: to encourage-promote imaginative New Zealand literature. Sponsored and held at University of Otago. Award, September for academic year.

SCRIPT (Film, Television, Radio)

Includes Script Production, Book, Book-Publication Design and FOR CHILDREN, HIGHWAY SAFETY, HUMANITARIAN. (Also see PLAY and BOOK CATEGORIES.)

369

Chicago
Communications Collaborative
410 South Michigan Avenue
Suite 433
Chicago, Illinois 60605 U.S.A.
Tel: (312) 633-9566

Summer

International; entry open to all; annual; established 1978. Purpose: to recognize finest communications nationally and internationally through Chicago shows. Sponsored by Communications Collaborative, organization of Chicago communication associations. Recognize by Art Directors Club of Chicago, Artists Guild of Chicago, American Society of Magazine Photographers, Graphic Arts Council. Have visual media categories. Publish *Chicago Annual* (yearbook of winners).

SCRIPT CONTEST: **Film, Television, Slide,** produced or unproduced; written after March previous year. Require 5 copies, original printed or typed.

BOOK CONTEST: **Any Type,** published or unpublished. Requirements same as for Script.

BOOK-PUBLICATION DESIGN CONTEST: **Design, Typography,** published. Book categories: Hardcover, Jacket, Paperback, Typography, Entire Book. Publication categories: Consumer, Trade (Black & White, Two-Color, Four-Color Cover; same for Body); Company (Black & White, Two-Color Cover; same for Body); Newspaper-Magazine (Black & White, Two-Color); House Organ.

AWARDS: Best of Category, Best of Show at judges' discretion. Winners exhibited for 1 month.

JUDGING: By media experts, based on 5-point scale.

ENTRY FEE: Single $15, Campaign $35. Not-for-Profit Public Service Single $7, Campaign $17. Acceptance: Single $50, Campaign $150. Not-for-Profit Public Service Single $25, Campaign $75. Entrant pays postage. No entries returned.

DEADLINES: Entry, August. Event, Summer.

370

Datsun Focus College and University Student Film and Writing Competition
FOCUS
Tina Forleiter, Director
1140 Avenue of the Americas
New York, New York 10036 U.S.A.
Tel: (212) 575-0270

April

National; **entry restricted to U.S. college-university students;** annual; established 1976. Considered among most pretigious college script competitions. Named after Films of College and University Students (FOCUS). Purpose: to recognize excellence, assist winning students into film industry. Sponsored and supported by Nissan Motor Corporation in U.S. (Datsun), EMI Films, *National Lampoon,* Magnasync-Moviola. Average statistics: 500 entries; 45 finalists; 15 winners. Award ceremony held at FILMEX in Hollywood. Second contact:

Dr. Gene S. Weiss, Communication Arts and Theatre Department, University of Maryland, College Park, Maryland 20742.

SCRIPT CONTEST: **Original Feature Screenplay,** any subject, produced or unproduced; completed within previous 2 years; feature length, 90-140 pages; 2 copies; 8 1/2x11-inch 18-25 pound bond type paper, bound (2-3 holes) with metal binding posts. Require 1-page treatment (5 copies).

ELIGIBILITY: Written noncommercially by U.S. college, university, art institute, professional film school student.

AWARDS: First Place, $2000 Scholarship, Datsun car and Internship by *National Lampoon* (motion picture division). Second Place, $1250 Scholarship. Third Place, $750. Honorable Mention, $500. School of first place winner receives $1000 in sound equipment. Winners flown to Los Angeles for 4 days, hotel and transportation paid.

JUDGING: Treatments reviewed in Los Angeles; finalists' scripts read in entirety by panel of eminent film industry judges. Sponsor holds rights to winning scripts for 2 years after awards. Not responsible for loss or damage.

Entry Fee: $15. Sponsor pays return postage.

DEADLINES: Entry, February. Judging, February-March. Event, April.

371

Highway Safety Editorial Awards Contest

National Foundation for Highway Safety
William H. Veale, President
P.O. 3043 Westville Station
New Haven, Connecticut 06151
U.S.A. Tel: (203) 387-2977

Spring

International; entry open to all; annual. Purpose: to reach thousands of drivers, influence them to be courteous at the wheel, saving lives, preventing injuries. Theme: Driving Carries a Moral Responsibility. Sponsored by National Foundation for Highway Safety, founded 1951.

SCRIPT CONTEST: **Highway Safety Television or Radio Program.**

ELIGIBILITY: May depict any phase of theme (including drinking and driving, speedsters, tailgaters, bright lighters, thoughtless and careless operation of car). Require 3 clip sheets, typed copies of television or radio editorials or programs. Any number of entries.

AWARDS: $100 U.S. Savings Bond for Best Feature or Editorial, Best Cartoon. Bronze Plaques, Special Printed Awards. Foundation may reproduce entries without profit in interest of highway safety, certifying the source.

ENTRY FEE: None.

DEADLINES: Entry by January. Awards, Spring.

372

Houston International Film Festival (Festival of the Americas) Script Contest

Cinema America Inc.
J. Hunter Todd, President-Founder
P.O. Box 56566
Houston, Texas 77027 U.S.A.
Tel: (712) 757-0028

April

International; entry open to all; annual; established 1968. Formerly called ATLANTA INTERNATIONAL FILM FESTIVAL to 1974, VIRGIN ISLANDS INTERNATIONAL FILM FESTIVAL to 1977, GREATER MIAMI INTERNATIONAL FILM FESTIVAL to 1978. Purpose: to honor excellence in film and TV. Sponsored and supported by Cinema America, Houston Film Society. Recognized by IFFPA, IAIFD, Paris. Average statistics (overall festival): 2100 entries, 900 entrants, 30 countries, 600 semifinalists, 150 winners, 50 exhibitions, 15,000 attendance. Held at Stouffers Hotel, Greenway Plaza, Houston, Texas, for 6 days. Tickets: $4 each premiere, $50 series. Second contact: Rikki Kipple, Assistant Director, 2100 Travis, Central Square, Suite 626, Houston, Texas 77002.

SCRIPT CONTEST: Feature, Short Screenplay, any type, produced or unproduced; completed in previous 2 years, in shooting script form. Categories: Feature, Short or Experimental.

AWARDS: Grand Prize, each category, includes assistance in option and production. Short Award includes raw stock and cameras.

JUDGING: International Blue Ribbon Committee of 100 selects top 3, each category. Final by International Grand Awards Jury of 7. May change categories.

ENTRY FEE: $75. Sponsor pays return postage.

DEADLINES: Entry, March. Event, April.

373

Humanitas Prize
Human Family Institute
Judy Conway Greening, Executive Director
P.O. Box 861
Pacific Palisades, California 90272
U.S.A. Tel: (213) 454-8769

July

National; **entry open to U.S.;** annual; established 1977. Considered largest money prize for entertainment industry writers. Purpose: to encourage, recognize, sustain U.S. writers of teleplays communicating human values; bring insights of Judeo-Christian vision of human condition to bear on contemporary life. Theme: Values That Most Enrich the Human Person. Sponsored by Human Family Institute, which seeks to promote greater appreciation of human dignity.

SCRIPT CONTEST: Humanitarian Television Broadcast. Written, produced, aired (on ABC, CBS, NBC) 7P.M.-11P.M., first televised May previous to May current year. Require 2 copies, 1-page typed storyline summary. Categories: 90-Minutes, 60 Minutes, 30 Minutes.

AWARDS: $25,000 (90-Minutes), $15,000 Prize (60 Minutes), $10,000 Prize (30 Minutes). Also give nonmonetary prizes to producers, directors, story editors, production companies, networks of these entries, and to news-documentary program.

JUDGING: All entries read by Executive Committee, Trustees. No entries returned.

ENTRY FEE: None.

DEADLINES: Entry, April. Awards, July.

374

National Radio Theatre (NRT) of Chicago Production of New Radio Scripts
All-Media Dramatic Workshop
Yuri Rasovsky, Producer-Director
612 North Michigan Avenue
Chicago, Illinois 60611 U.S.A.
Tel: (312) 751-1625

Continuous

International; entry open to all; continuous; established 1973. Nonprofit, one of 3 major U.S. radio theater companies. Purpose: to put good radio drama on air. Sponsored by NRT of Chicago (All-Media Dramatic Workshop), nonprofit organization. Supported by grants, donations. Recognized by NEA, Markle Foundation, Illinois Arts Council. Publish *NRT Audiobill.*

SCRIPT PRODUCTION: Radio Any Subject, unproduced, unpublished, any style, about 1 hour in length. No adaptations.

AWARDS: $25 per minute playing time ($1500 maximum). Sponsor requires unlimited free broadcast rights for 3 years after premiere.

ENTRY FEE: None. Entrant pays postage.

DEADLINES: Entry, April. Produced throughout year.

375

Sherwood Oaks Experimental College Screenwriting Contest

Gary Shusett, Director
1445 North Las Palmas
Hollywood, California 90028 U.S.A.
Tel: (213) 462-0669

September

International; entry open to all; annual; established 1975. Sponsored by Sherwood Oaks Experimental College, founded 1971 as nonprofit film-video school. Have script library, workshops, annual summer Screenwriting Conference (July), screenwriters cooperative (6-15 students), professional script-reading service. Also sponsor scholarships, filmmaking competition, acting competition.

SCRIPT CONTEST: Feature Film, 80-150 pages. Submit typed, bound script, optional 3-5-page treatment. No Writers Guild members. Categories: Comedy, Drama.

AWARDS: $3000 each, Best Comedy, Best Drama. Aaron Spelling Writing Award. Finalists' scripts seen by established writers, directors, producers.

JUDGING: Preliminary by professional script readers (5 finalists). Final by industry professionals, Entrants retain all rights. Not responsible for loss or damage.

ENTRY FEE: $15, each. Entrant pays postage (include SASE).

DEADLINES: Entry, September. Scripts returned in 12 weeks.

376

AWGIE Awards

Australian Writers Guild (AWG)
Angela Wales, General Secretary
83 York Street, Suite 505
Sydney 2000 NSW, AUSTRALIA
Tel: (02) 29-1402

June-August

National; **entry restricted to Australian AWG members;** annual; established 1968. AWGIE Awards to **Australian Film, Radio, Television Scripts, Stage Plays, including For Children, Comedy.** Purpose: to encourage, award excellence in scriptwriting. Supported by AMPOL Petroleum Ltd. Average statistics (including Nonfiction): 80 entries, 65 entrants. Publish *Viewpoint* (monthly newsletter). Awards, June-August.

377

Canadian Motion Picture Distributors Association (CMPDA) Script Development Program

Joan London
22 St. Clair Avenue, Suite 1703
Toronto, Ontario M4T 2S4 CANADA

Continuous

National; **entry open to Canada;** continuous; established 1978. Purpose: to provide writers access to Canadian motion picture industry; allow member companies review of commercial script properties. Sponsored by CMPDA.

SCRIPT PRODUCTION: **Feature Film,** typewritten. Require waiver of claims against similar-identical idea, plot, situation, story, treatment, theme, scheme.

AWARDS: Accepted scripts forwarded to production heads of U.S., Canadian CMPDA-member companies for possible purchase, development.

JUDGING: Preliminary by sponsor; final by member companies. Based on commercial potential. No scripts returned.

ENTRY FEE: None. Entrant pays postage.

DEADLINES: Open.

SHORT STORY

Short Fiction including Book, Novella and FLORIDA, NEW TOWN LIFE, SEA, STUDENT-TEENAGE. (Also see other SHORT STORY and BOOK CATEGORIES.)

378

Aga Khan Fiction Prize

Paris Review
541 East 72nd Street
New York, New York 10021 U.S.A.

Fall

International; entry open to all; annual. Sponsored by *The Paris Review.* Second contact: Paris Review, Flushing Office, 45-39 171 Place, Flushing, New York 11358.

SHORT STORY CONTEST: **Any Subject,** unpublished, 1000-10,000 words; in English or English translation (include copy of original text).

AWARDS: First Prize, $500 and publication in Fall issue.

JUDGING: By *The Paris Review* editors. Not responsible for loss or damage.

ENTRY FEE: None. Entrant pays postage (include SASE).

DEADLINES: Entry, May-June. Winner announced, Fall.

379

Crosscurrents' Annual Fiction Awards

Linda Brown Michelson, Editor
2200 Glastonbury Road
Westlake Village, California 91361 U.S.A.

November

National; **entry open to U.S.;** annual; established 1981. Purpose: to award excellence in short story writing. Sponsored by *Crosscurrents* magazine (quarterly, established 1980).

SHORT STORY CONTEST: **Any Subject,** original, unpublished; 1000-6000 words; 1 entry; typed double-spaced on 8 1/2x11-inch white paper (photocopies acceptable). No juvenile, erotica, Western, or religious material.

AWARDS: $200 First, $100 Second, $75 Third Prize. Winners published in *Crosscurrents* Winter issue.

JUDGING: Based on craft, substance. Sponsor owns first-time publishing rights to winners. No entries returned. Not responsible for loss or damage.

ENTRY FEE: Not Specified.

DEADLINES: Entry, July-September. Winners announced, November.

380

Gulfshore Life Annual Fiction Contest

Merri Renfro, Editor
3620 Tamiami Trail North
Naples, Florida 33940 U.S.A.
Tel: (813) 262-6425

May

International; entry open to all; annual; established 1978. Purpose: to promote interest in fiction writing. Sponsored and supported by *Gulfshore Life*. Average statistics: 300 entries. Publish *Gulfshore Life* (monthly).

SHORT STORY CONTEST: **Florida Locale.** Must have Florida setting; other requirements not specified.

AWARDS: $100 First Place and publication in May issue. $50 Second Place. $25 Third Place.

JUDGING: By staff of *Gulfshore Life* and 1 international author.

ENTRY FEE: Not specified.

DEADLINES: Entry, March. Winners announced, May issue.

381

Harian Creative Press-Adirondack-Metroland Writers & Educators Conference Fiction Awards

Dr. Harry Barba, Writing Director
47 Hyde Blvd.
Ballston Spa, New York 12020
U.S.A. Tel: (518) 885-7397

Fall

International; entry open to all; annual; established 1967. Purpose: to encourage, teach, publish, promote socially functional writing, education, art, culture. Theme: The Workshop under the Sky. Motto: "One world is better than none." Sponsored and supported by Harian Creative Press, Adirondack-Metroland Writers & Educators Conference. Recognized by MLA, CEA, NEA, AWP, COSMEP. Average statistics: 1500 entries, 1200 entrants, 15 semifinalists, 8 finalists, 15-20 attendance. Held in Saratoga County and Metroland, New York. Have workshops, lectures, panels, consultations, readings. Also sponsor Poetry Contest.

SHORT STORY-NOVELLA CONTEST: **Any Subject,** unpublished, 3000-20,000 words, strong characterization, plot, written in functionally suitable style with social context; typed double-spaced. Quality stories that communicate moral texture. No obscenity, violence, scrambled writing. Finalists submit photos, evidence of other published works.

AWARDS: $300 First, $100 Second, 2 $50 Third Prizes. Will critique entries, consider for publication.

JUDGING: By Harry and Marian Barba and consultants. May withhold awards. All entries read in entirety. Sponsor owns first publication rights. Not responsible for loss or damage.

ENTRY FEE: $5 per story, $25 per novella. Entrant pays postage (include SASE).

DEADLINES: Entry, not specified. Awards, Fall. Materials returned in 6-8 weeks.

382

John H. McGinnis Award
Southwest Review
Margaret L. Hartley, Editor
Southern Methodist University
Dallas, Texas 75275 U.S.A.
Tel: (214) 692-2263

February

International; **entry restricted (published in Southwest Review);** biennial; established 1960. $500 **Award to Short Story** published in *Southwest Review* during 2 years previous. Judging by staff. Awards, February.

383

Redbook's Young Writers' Contest
Redbook Magazine
Mimi Jones
230 Park Avenue
New York, New York 10017 U.S.A.
Tel: (212) 983-8798

Spring

International; **entry restricted to age 18-28;** annual; established 1976. Purpose: to encourage young short story writers. Sponsored by *Redbook Magazine.* Also sponsor Redbook Photography Contest for Women. Second contact: Jacqueline Johnson, Associate Fiction Editor.

SHORT STORY CONTEST: Any Subject, original, unpublished; 1 entry; 20-page limit, 25 lines per page; 1 copy, typed double-spaced on one side of 8 1/2x11-inch paper.

ELIGIBILITY: Women, men, 18-28, who have not published fiction in magazine with over 25,000 circulation. No employees, relatives, of Charter Publishing company, subsidiaries, or affiliates.

AWARDS: $500 First Prize plus $1000 for publication in *Redbook.* $300 Second Prize. 3 $100 Third Prizes.

JUDGING: By editors. May purchase, publish all entries. Not responsible for loss or damage.

ENTRY FEE: None. Entrant pays postage (include SASE).

DEADLINES: Entry, May. Awards, not specified.

384

Seventeen's Annual Fiction Contest
Seventeen Magazine
Karin Mills, Public Relations Director
850 Third Avenue
New York, New York 10022 U.S.A.
Tel: (212) 759-8100

Spring

National; **entry restricted to U.S. teenagers;** annual; established 1976. Sponsored and supported by *Seventeen Magazine,* Triangle Communications. Average statistics: 2000 entries. Also sponsor photography, art, dress design contests.

SHORT STORY CONTEST: Teenage Any Subject, original, unpublished; 3000 words maximum; typed double-spaced on one side only. Unlimited entry. Must be U.S. teenager aged 13-20 on July 1. Require notarized birthdate certification. No Triangle Communications employees or families.

AWARDS: $500 First, $300 Second,

$200 Third Prize. 6 $50 Honorable Mentions.

JUDGING: By *Seventeen* editors in New York. Based on literary worth, originality, naturalness of dialog, convincing characterization, suitability for publication in *Seventeen.* Winning entries become and remain sole property of Triangle Communications. Not responsible for loss or damage.

ENTRY FEE: None.

DEADLINES: Entry, June. Winners announced, Spring.

385

Today's Secretary Annual Fiction Contest
Today's Secretary Magazine, Gregg Division of McGraw-Hill Book Company
Diane M. Kaylor, Fiction Editor
1221 Avenue of the Americas
New York, New York 10020 U.S.A.

May

International; **entry restricted to students;** annual; established 1978. Purpose: showcase for student fiction. Sponsored by *Today's Secretary* magazine, Gregg Division of McGraw-Hill Book Company. Average statistics: 50 entrants, 2 countries, 8 semifinalists, 3 finalists. Publish *Today's Secretary* (monthly).

SHORT STORY CONTEST: **Student Any Subject,** original, unpublished, 800-1000 words; 1 entry, typed.

AWARDS: First, Second, Third Place and Honorable Mention winners receive Achievement Certificates, are considered for publication (authors credited).

JUDGING: By editorial staff. Based on originality of expression, content, writing skills, general readability. All entries read. Sponsor owns all rights to published entries. Not responsible for loss or damage. No entries returned.

ENTRY FEE: None. Entrant pays postage.

DEADLINES: Entry, November. Judging, December-February. Winners announced, May issue.

386

Sid Chaplin Literary Award
Aycliffe Development Corporation
Leslie R. Cole, Press & Public Relations Officer
Churchill House
Newton Aycliffe, County Durham, DL5 4LE, ENGLAND Tel: (0325) 312521

November

International; entry open to all; annual; established 1977. Named after Sid Chaplin, colliery blacksmith turned writer, born in Aycliffe, first New Town in northern England. Purpose: to increase awareness of new towns; encourage factual or fictional stories with new town backgrounds. Sponsored by Aycliffe Development Corporation, Glenrothes New Town Development Corporation, *The Guardian.* Average statistics: 160 entrants. Held in Aycliffe. Also sponsor cash awards to Glenrothes New Town writers.

SHORT STORY CONTEST: **New Town Life** (real or fictional), in English; 2000 words maximum; typed or clearly written on 1 side paper.

AWARDS: 100 pounds Sid Chaplin Literary Award, Best Story. 25 pounds, Best by writer aged 18 or under. Merit Certificates to Runners-Up. Winners may be published in *The Guardian.*

JUDGING: Not responsible for loss or damage.

ENTRY FEE: Not specified.

DEADLINES: Entry, August. Event, November.

387

International Week of Sea & Naval Film Sea Stories Contest
Enrique Perez-Cuadrado de Guzman, Director
Plaza Castellini 5 & 7
Cartagena, SPAIN

November

International; entry open to all; annual. Purpose: to celebrate Sea & Naval Film Festival. Sponsored by International Week of Sea & Naval Film Festival Commission.

SHORT STORY CONTEST: **About Sea, Lake, River, in Spanish,** original, unpublished; typed on 1 side, double-spaced, 3-5 pages, unlimited entries. Require 3 copies, each entry.

AWARDS: 10,000 pesetas First, 5000 pts. Second Place. Commemorative Festival Medals to First, Second, Third.

JUDGING: Decisions final. Entries destroyed if not reclaimed 1 month after contest.

ENTRY FEE: None. Entrant pays postage (include SASE).

DEADLINES: Entry, October. Awards, November.

388

New Zealand Women Writers' Society Awards
E. G. Stahl, Secretary
75 Hall Crescent
Epuni, Lower Hutt, NEW ZEALAND
Tel: Wellington 671-678

October

National; **entry open to New Zealand;** biennial; established 1959 (Mansfield), 1964 (Young Writers), 1969 (Secondary School), 1981 (Historical Novel). $500 Katherine Mansfield Memorial Award for **Short Story;** Bank of New Zealand (BNZ) Young Writers' Awards, $250 to age 24 and under, $150 to **Secondary School Pupils for Short Stories.** $2000 First, $1000 Second to age 18 and over for **Historical Novels.** Purpose: to encourage young writers. Sponsored and supported by BNZ. Judging by BNZ-appointed writers. Second contact: Laurie Mantell, P.O. Box 42-092, Homedale, Lower Hutt, New Zealand. Awards, October.

SHORT STORY, POETRY

Short Fiction and Poetry, including JUVENILE, PRISON, RELIGION, SATIRE. (Also see POETRY, SHORT STORY.)

389

American Penal Press Contest
Southern Illinois University
W. Manion Rice, Director
School of Journalism
Carbondale, Illinois 62901 U.S.A.

December

National; **entry restricted to inmate staffs of U.S. penal institution newspapers-magazines;** annual; established 1965. Sponsored by School of Journalism, Southern Illinois University at Carbondale. Also sponsor newspaper-magazine art, cartoon, photo contests, and periodic Charles

C. Clayton Award for outstanding contribution to prison journalism (not open to entry).

SHORT STORY CONTEST: Fiction in Penal Newspaper-Magazine, printed October previous to October contest year; 3 entries per category, pasted, taped, or stapled to 8 1/2x11-inch paper (not larger).

POETRY CONTEST: Any Type in Penal Newspaper-Magazine. Requirements, restrictions same as for Short Story.

AWARDS: First, Second, Third Place Certificates, Honorable Mentions, each division.

JUDGING: Based on general excellence, appropriateness to prison media. May withhold awards.

ENTRY FEE: None.

DEADLINES: Entry, November. Winners announced, December.

390

Arkansas Writers' Conference (AWC) Literary Awards

Anna Nash Yarbrough, Director
510 East Street
Benton, Arkansas 72015 U.S.A.
Tel: (501) 778-2833

June

International; entry open to all; annual; established 1944. Purpose: to help writers become better. Sponsored by AWC; Arkansas Pioneer Branch, NLAPW. Average statistics: 200 attendance. Held at annual 2-day AWC Conference in Arkansas. Tickets: $1.50 per day. Have lectures, workshops. Also sponsor Nonfiction Essay and Article Contests.

SHORT STORY CONTEST: Various Categories, unpublished; typed. Categories: Adult Fiction (1500 words, entrant must attend); with Juvenile Words (1000-word limit), Short Story (up to 1500 words; up to 2500 words), For Children 6-10 Years (up to 1000 words).

POETRY CONTEST: Various Categories, unpublished; typed. Categories: Shakespearean Sonnet (any subject); Light Verse (14-line limit); Villanelle (iambic meter, any subject); General (any subject, 30 lines, entrant must attend); Arkansas Subject, Place, or Person (30 lines, entrant must attend); Free Verse (30 lines); Ercil (iambic, specific subject); Sonnet; Grayette (iambic, 12 lines, 2 stanzas); For Children (20 lines); Lyric by Arkansas Resident (any subject, 28 lines; theme, 30 lines).

AWARDS: $100 Alice Leigh Gift; $75, $50, $25 Gifts.

JUDGING: No poems returned. Include SASE for prose. Not responsible for loss or damage. All materials without SASE destroyed.

ENTRY FEE: $3 registration fee (nonreturnable).

DEADLINES: Entry, May. Awards, June.

391

Black Warrior Review Literary Awards

Michael Pettit, Editor
P.O. Box 2936
University, Alabama 35486 U.S.A.
Tel: (205) 348-5526

May

International; entry open to all; annual; established 1978. Sponsored by *Black Warrior Review.* Supported by Society for the Fine Arts, University of Alabama. Publish *Black Warrior Review* (semiannual).

SHORT STORY CONTEST: Any

Subject, original, unpublished, typed, 7500-words maximum, 1 per entrant.

POETRY CONTEST: Any Type, original, unpublished, typed, any length, 1 per entrant.

AWARDS: $400 each (fiction and poetry) published in Fall, Spring issue.

JUDGING: Require first refusal rights on all submissions.

ENTRY FEE: None. Entrant pays postage (include SASE).

DEADLINES: Entry, October (Fall), February (Spring). Winners announced, May.

392

Conference on Christianity and Literature (CCL) Student Writing Contest

Editor of Christianity and Literature
Calvin College
Grand Rapids, Michigan 49506
U.S.A. Tel: (616) 949-4000, ext. 264

Spring

International; **entry restricted to U.S., Canadian undergraduates;** annual; established 1974. Purpose: to encourage student writing on relation of religion to literature-life experience. Sponsored by CCL, founded 1956 as international organization for understanding relationship between Christianity and creation, study, teaching of literature. Supported by William B. Eerdmans Publishing Co. Average statistics: 180 entries. Publish *Christianity and Literature* (quarterly journal). Also sponsor CCL Book of the Year Award. Second contact: Roy Battenhouse, English Department, Indiana University, Bloomington, Indiana 47401.

SHORT STORY CONTEST: Religion and Literature.

POETRY CONTEST: Religion and Literature.

AWARDS: First, Second, Third Prizes, each category. Prizes are books.

ENTRY FEE: None. Entrant pays postage.

DEADLINES: Entry, March. Judging, April. Awards, May.

393

Explorer Writing Awards

Explorer Magazine
Raymond Flory, Editor-Publisher
538 West Grove Street
Mishawaka, Indiana 46544 U.S.A.

Spring, Fall

International; entry open to all; semiannual; established 1960. Sponsored and supported by *Explorer Magazine.*

SHORT STORY CONTEST: Any Subject, original, unpublished; 1000-words maximum.

POETRY CONTEST: Any Type, original, unpublished; 16 lines maximum.

AWARDS: First Prize, $10 and Plaque. $5 Second, $4 Third, $3 Fourth Prizes.

JUDGING: By subscribers.

ENTRY FEE: Not specified. Entrant pays postage (include SASE).

DEADLINES: Entry, not specified. Awards, Spring, Fall.

394

Hospitalized Veterans Writing Project (HVWP)

Veterans Voices Magazine
5920 Nall, Room 117
Mission, Kansas 66202 U.S.A.

March, June, October

National; **entry restricted to U.S. hospitalized-outpatient veterans;** triannual; established 1946. Purpose: to encourage creative writing, art, photography, recreation-rehabilitation to hospitalized-outpatient veterans. Sponsored and supported by HVWP, nonprofit volunteer service organization. Average statistics: 47 entries; 20 entrants. Publish *Veterans' Voices,* triannual magazine established 1951 for creative writing, art (Margaret Sally Keach, founder-publisher; Margaret Clark, editor). Also sponsor $50 Joseph Posik Award (by nomination only), $15 Logan Art Award, poster contest, HVWP Scholarship for English or Journalism graduate work at Veterans Administration hospital. Second contact: Hospitalized Veterans Writing Project, 4801 Linwood Blvd., Kansas City, Missouri 64128.

SHORT STORY CONTEST: **Any Subject,** original, unpublished; 1-4 pages typed double-spaced; 3 entries maximum. Require original, 3 copies, service serial number; entries mailed by hospital staff member.

POETRY CONTEST: **Any type,** original, unpublished; 24 lines maximum, typed double-spaced; 3 entries maximum. Requirements same as for Short Story.

AWARDS: $45 Good Prose Prize. $30 Major Katherine Stull Valor Award for story or poem detailing special courage-determination experience. $30 Good Poetry Prize. $25 Gladys Feld Helzberg Poetry Award. $25 Gordon Thompson Humor Award. $25 Margaret H. Tyler Humor-Prose Award. $25 Della VanOsdol Award for Best Story. $15 Juanita Harvey Award for Poetry-Prose. $15 Beginners' Prose Award. 5 $5 Sally-Sue Hughes Perpetual Prizes for Poetry. Prizes for John Abercrombie Humor Award; Ruth Cheney Streeter Prose Award; Ned Edwards Award for Best Story by or about Marine.

JUDGING: No entries returned.

ENTRY FEE: None.

DEADLINES: Entry, Awards, March, June, October.

395

Illinois Wesleyan University (IWU) Writers' Conference Awards

Kate Romani, Coordinator
IWU Writers' Conference
Illinois Wesleyan University
Bloomington, Illinois 61701 U.S.A.
Tel: (309) 556-3065

August

International; **entry restricted to Conference participants;** annual; established 1977. Cash awards to **Conference Fiction, Poetry, Satire, Juvenile,** unpublished, 20-page maximum (or 10 poems). Purpose: to offer writers opportunity to work with professionals, have manuscripts critiqued. Sponsored and supported by IWU, United Methodist Church, Central Illinois Branch, National League of American Pen Women. Average statistics: 40 entries, 60 attendance, 5 awards. Held at Illinois Wesleyan University for 1 week in August. Have workshops, seminars, critiques, conferences. Second contact: Bettie Wilson Story, Conference Director, IWU, Bloomington, Illinois 61701. Entry, June. Conference, August.

396

"Joint" Conference Poetry and Fiction Contest

King Publications
Kathryn E. King, Editor-Publisher
P.O. Box 19332
Washington, District of Columbia
20036 U.S.A. Tel: (202) 234-1681

September-October

International; **entry restricted to correctional institution inmates in U.S., Canada;** annual; established 1978. Began as fiction, 1980 added poetry. Purpose: to encourage writing fiction and poetry among correctional institution inmates. Sponsored and supported by King Publications. Average statistics: 200 entries, 180 entrants, 5 awards.

SHORT STORY CONTEST: Any Subject, original, unpublished; 2000-5000 words, 3 entries maximum, photocopies or carbons acceptable.

POETRY CONTEST: Any Type, original, unpublished, 15 lines minimum, 3 entries maximum, photocopies or carbons acceptable.

ELIGIBILITY: Author must be incarcerated (in federal, state prison or local jail) at time of submission; need not be imprisoned when prizes awarded.

AWARDS: $100 First Prize, $50 Second, each category. Winners published in copyrighted magazine.

JUDGING: 1 judge per category. All entries read. Rights revert to author after magazine publication.

ENTRY FEE: None. Entries returned if accompanied by SASE.

DEADLINES: Entry, August. Awards, September-October.

397

Julian Ocean Literature and Poetry Awards

Triple "P" Publications International
Eugene F.P.C. de Mesne, Editorial Manager
Box 8776 Kennedy Station
Boston, Massachusetts 02114 U.S.A.
Tel: (617) 437-1856

March

International; entry open to all; annual; established 1980. Named after Julian Ocean, author-publisher-poet. Purpose: to further cause of art and the artist. Theme: Full Spectrum of Literature and Poetry, No Taboos or Restrictions. Sponsored by Triple "P" Publications International. Supported by de Mesne, Inc. Recognized by National Writers Club, COSMEP, International Biographical Association. Average statistics: 2800 entries, 938 entrants, 10 semifinalists, 5 finalists, 2 awards. Publish books, *Persuasion Magazine, Kiosk Newsletter.*

SHORT STORY CONTEST: Any Subject. Typed, double-spaced, on 8 1/2x11-inch paper, 3000-3500 words, unlimited entries.

POETRY CONTEST: Any Type, typed, double-spaced, on 8 1/2x11-inch paper, 25-line maximum, unlimited entries.

AWARDS: $20, Short Story. $10, Poetry. Certificates to winners.

JUDGING: 5 judges review each entry. Based on professionalism, high literary standards. Not responsible for loss or damage.

ENTRY FEE: $1 each. Entrant pays postage (include SASE each entry).

DEADLINES: Entry, December. Judging, January. Awards, March. Materials returned, following January.

398

Kansas Quarterly-Kansas Arts Commission Awards

The Editors
Denison Hall
Kansas State University
Manhattan, Kansas 66506 U.S.A.
Tel: (913) 532-6716

Winter

International; **entry restricted to short stories, poetry, published by Kansas Quarterly;** annual; established 1972. $25-$250 to *Kansas Quarterly* **Short Stories, Poetry.** Sponsored and supported by *Kansas Quarterly*-Kansas Arts Commission. Publish *Kansas Quarterly.* Also sponsor Seaton Awards of $1100 to Kansas writers. Awards, Winter.

399

NIMROD Literary Prizes
Arts and Humanities Council of Tulsa
Cathi Stockton, Contest Director
2210 South Main
Tulsa, Oklahoma 74114 U.S.A.
Tel: (918) 583-8716

November

International; entry open to all; annual; established 1979. Contest affiliated with University of Tulsa to 1979. Purpose: to promote *NIMROD* (international literary journal); establish market for new literary works. Sponsored and supported by NIMROD, Arts and Humanities Council of Tulsa. Average statistics: 400 entries, 350 entrants, 10 countries, 40 finalists, 4 awards. Have collaborative and fiction writing workshops.

SHORT STORY CONTEST: **Any Subject,** original, unpublished; 7500 words maximum, typed double-spaced, 1 maximum per author per genre. Not accepted for publication; no dual submissions.

POETRY CONTEST: **Any Type,** original, unpublished; any length, 1 maximum per author per genre (1 poem or sequence of related poems), typed. Restrictions same as for Short Story.

AWARDS: Katherine Anne Porter Prize for Fiction: $500 First, $250 Second Prize. Pablo Neruda Prize for Poetry: $500 First, $250 Second Prize. Winners brought to Tulsa for reading and awards. Winners published in *NIMROD.*

JUDGING: Preliminary by staff, editors, readers. Final by 1 judge each category. *NIMROD* has first refusal rights.

ENTRY FEE: Purchase of 1 copy of *NIMROD* at $2.50. Entrant pays postage (no return without SASE).

DEADLINES: Entry, February. Judging, April-May. Winners announced, June. Awards, November.

400

Ozark Writers and Artists Guild Writing Contest
Maggie Smith, Director
Box 411
Siloam Springs, Arkansas 72761
U.S.A. Tel: (501) 524-3591

July

International; entry open to all; annual; established 1935. Purpose: to provide workshop of writers and artists for idea-exchange in friendly atmosphere. Sponsored by Siloam Springs Writers and Northwest Arkansas Branch of American Pen Women. Supported by Siloam Springs banks, savings and loans, individuals. Recognized by Poets' Roundtable of Arkansas. Held at John Brown University for 1 day. Tickets: $6 (luncheon). Have seminar, speakers, poetry for popular-vote award.

SHORT STORY CONTEST: **Any Subject,** unpublished; on 8 1/2x11-inch paper, 5000 words maximum, 1 per entrant. Must not have won over $10.

POETRY CONTEST: **Various Categories.** Categories: Lyric, Free Verse, Any Type (24-line maximum); Sonnet; Juvenile Verse (1 page); Bible (1 page); Ballad (50 lines maximum); Limerick; Haiku; Tanka; Doriece (honoring mother-daughter relationship); Dorsimbra (3 verses; iambic pentameter); Illustrated Poetry (9x11 maximum size, both art and poetry by same entrant). Requirements same as for Short Story.

AWARDS: $25 First, $15 Second, $10 Third Prize. 2 Honorable Mentions to Short Story, most Poetry categories. Limerick, Haiku, Tanka, Doriece: 5 prizes, $5 each category. Touring exhibition of winners.

JUDGING: All entries read in entirety by judge in appropriate field. No entries returned. Not responsible for loss or damage.

ENTRY FEE: $4 1-4 entries. $1 each additional.

DEADLINES: Entry, June. Awards, July.

401

Pacific Northwest Writers Conference (PNWC) High School Writing Contest
Gladys Johnson, Executive Secretary
1811 N.E. 199th
Seattle, Washington 98155 U.S.A.
Tel: (206) 364-1293

February

Regional; **entry restricted to Northwest U.S.-Canada high school students;** annual. Sponsored by PNWC. Held at PNWC Mid-Winter Awards Banquet in Seattle, Washington. Have workshops. Tickets: $11. Also sponsor open-entry Creative Writing Contests for novels, short stories, poetry, plays, nonfiction books, articles.

SHORT STORY CONTEST: By High School, Any Subject, 3000 words maximum; 1 entry; 1 photocopy (no originals); typed double-spaced on 8 1/2x11-inch white paper.

POETRY CONTEST: By High School, Any Type, 3 poems-pages maximum. Other requirements same as for Short Story.

ELIGIBILITY: High school students in Alaska, British Columbia, Idaho, Montana, Oregon, Washington.

AWARDS: $75 First, $50 Second, $30 Third Prize, each contest. Honorable Mentions. Books to library of school sending most entries.

JUDGING: By published writers. Entries critiqued by professional poets, writers. Not responsible for loss or damage.

ENTRY FEE: $2 per entry. Entrant pays postage (include SASE).

DEADLINES: Entry, January. Awards, February.

402

PEN Writing Award for Prisoners
PEN American Center
Karen Kennerly, Executive Secretary
47 Fifth Avenue
New York, New York 10003 U.S.A.
Tel: (212) 255-1977

May

National; **entry restricted to U.S. prisoners;** annual; established 1974. Sponsored by 1800-member PEN American Center (founded 1922), division of 10,000-member, 80-country International PEN (Poets, Playwrights, Essayists, Editors, Novelists), founded 1921 as independent, nonprofit world association of writers. Supported by NEA. Average statistics: 1500 entries. Also sponsor PEN Literature Awards, PEN Translation Awards, PEN Fund for Writers; Lucille J. Mednick Memorial Award ($500, annual) for distinguished service to literary community and commitment to serve the young, unrecognized, unpopular (by nomination only).

SHORT STORY CONTEST: Any Subject, unpublished; 5000 words maximum, 1 per entrant.

POETRY CONTEST: Any Type, unpublished; 100 lines maximum, 1 per entrant.

ELIGIBILITY: Unpublished (prison publications excepted), double-spaced, typed or handwritten, on 8 1/2x11-inch paper; by U.S. prisoners incarcerated September previous to March current year.

AWARDS: $100 First, $50 Second, $25 Third Prize, each category.

JUDGING: By 5 judges.

ENTRY FEE: None.

DEADLINES: Entry, March. Winners announced, May.

403

Spectrum Magazine Writing Contest

Associated Students: UC Santa Barbara (UCSB)
Joan L. Chappell, Managing Editor
Box 14800
University of California at Santa Barbara
Santa Barbara, California 93107 U.S.A.

Spring

International; **entry restricted to students, nonprofessional;** annual; established 1957. Changed from quarterly to annual in 1979. Purpose: to publish student, nonprofessional work. Sponsored by UCSB English Department, Associated Students, Alumni Association. Supported by UCSB sales of *Spectrum Magazine.* Average statistics: 700 entries, 250 entrants, 50 awards. Have readings. Publish *Spectrum Magazine* (annual). Second contact: Ellen Girardeau, 6504 Seville, Apt. 7, Goleta, California 93017.

SHORT STORY CONTEST: Any Subject, published, unpublished, reasonable length, translations acceptable, unlimited entries. No simultaneous submissions.

POETRY CONTEST: Any Type. Requirements, restrictions same as for Short Story.

AWARDS: Winners published in magazine.

JUDGING: By 8-10 student judges. Copyright reverts to author after publication. Not responsible for loss or damage.

ENTRY FEE: None. Entrant pays postage (include SASE).

DEADLINES: Entry, February. Judging, February-March. Winners notified, April. Publication, May.

404

Writer's Digest Creative Writing Competition

Henry E. Dorfman, Director
9933 Alliance Road
Cincinnati, Ohio 45242 U.S.A.
Tel: (513) 984-0717

October

International; entry open to all; annual. Sponsored by *Writer's Digest,* F&W Publishing Corporation. Publish *Writer's Digest* (monthly). Also sponsor Article Contest.

SHORT STORY CONTEST: Any Subject, 2000-word limit, original, unpublished, not accepted for publication elsewhere; 1 entry (photocopies acceptable), typed double-spaced on one side 8 1/2x11-inch white paper.

No F&W employees.

POETRY CONTEST: Any Type, 16-line limit. Other requirements, restrictions same as for Short Story.

AWARDS: Grand Prize Best Overall Entry (including Article Contest), $500, Silver Cup, and name engraved on sponsor's plaque. First Place, electric typewriter and commemorative plaque. Second-Third Places, Commemorative plaques. Fourth-100th Places, Certificates of Achievement. Grand Prize and top 3 winners, each contest, published in winners booklet.

JUDGING: Based on saleability. Sponsor retains one-time publication rights to Grand-Third Prize winners. No entries returned.

ENTRY FEE: None. Entrant pays postage.

DEADLINES: Entry, June. Winners notified, October; announced, November issue.

405

Writers' Forum Writing Contests
Pasadena City College
Jane Hallinger
1570 Colorado Blvd.
Pasadena, California 91108 U.S.A.
Tel: (213) 578-7261

May

Regional; **entry open to Southern California;** annual; established 1952. Sponsored by Writers' Forum, Pasadena City College. Held at Pasadena City College for 1 1/2 days. Tickets: $10. Also sponsor Nonfiction Essay Contest.

SHORT STORY CONTEST: Fiction, not previously published in major magazine. Categories: Adults, College, High School Students.

POETRY CONTEST: Any Type. Requirements, categories, same as for Short Story Contest.

AWARDS: Cash Prizes.

JUDGING: Entrant retains all rights. Not responsible for loss or damage.

ENTRY FEE: None.

DEADLINES: Awards, May.

SHORT STORY, PLAY, POETRY

Short Story, Poetry, Play, Script, including BY CHILDREN, YOUTH. (Also see other PLAY, POETRY, SHORT STORY CATEGORIES.)

406

Irvine Writers' Conference Awards
University of California Extension, Irvine
Laura Ferejohn
P.O. Box AZ
Irvine, California 92716 U.S.A.
Tel: (714) 833-5192

August

International; **entry restricted to Conference participants;** annual; established 1981. $100, $50, and Honorable Mention Certificates to **Conference Short Stories, Stage Plays or Film-Television Scripts** (unpublished; entrant enrolled in workshop). Purpose: to give writers recognition, opportunity to share experiences. Sponsored by U.C. Irvine Extension and Stephen Cannell. Average statistics (including Nonfiction): 50-75 entries, 6 awards, 100 attendance. Held at U.C. Irvine for 4 consecutive Saturdays. Entry, June. Awards, August.

407

McKendree Writers' Association Writing Contest
Evelyn Best, Director
105 Florence Street
Lebanon, Illinois 62254 U.S.A.

May

International; entry open to all; annual. Sponsored by McKendree Writers' Association. Held at McKendree College, Lebanon, Illinois. Have annual conference.

SHORT STORY CONTEST: **Any Subject,** original, unpublished; typed on one side, double-spaced, unsigned, 3000-word maximum, unlimited entries.

POETRY CONTEST: **Various Categories,** 3 poems maximum (totaling 40 lines maximum). Requirements same as for Short Story. Categories: Serious Verse, Light Verse.

PLAY CONTEST: **One-Act.** Requirements same as for Short Story.

AWARDS: $25 First, $15 Second, $10 Third Place, each category. Winners published in MWA publication.

JUDGING: May withhold awards. No entries returned.

ENTRY FEE: $1 each category.

DEADLINES: Entry, March. Winners announced, May.

408

Parents Without Partners (PWP) International Youth Exhibit Awards
Ann Parks, Director
7910 Woodmont Avenue
Washington, District of Columbia 20014 U.S.A. Tel: (301) 654-8850

January

International; **entry restricted to children-youth of PWP members;** annual. Local Chapter, Regional, Zone, and International Awards to **Short Stories, Poetry, Plays by Children.** Sponsored by PWP. Have art, sculpture, crafts, science, music divisions. Also sponsor 30 scholarships of $500 each to PWP-member children.

409

Scholastic Writing Awards
Scholastic Inc.
50 West 44th Street
New York, New York 10036 U.S.A.

May

International; **entry restricted to U.S., Canadian students under age 20;** annual; established 1926. Considered largest student writing program in U.S. Purpose: to recognize creative writing in junior high school students in U.S., U.S. territories, Canada. Sponsored by Scholastic Inc. Supported by Scholastic, Smith-Corona, International Paper Company, National Broadcasting, Paper Mate. Recognized by National Association of Secondary School Principals. Average statistics: 200,000 entries in writing, art, and photography divisions. Also have original song category. Also sponsor art and photography awards, annual Lucky Book Club Four Leaf Clover Awards to Scholastic Book Service published authors of age 7-8 children's books (established 1971).

SHORT STORY CONTEST: **Any Subject.** Divisions: Senior Grades 10-12 (1300-3000-word narrative with unified tone, about 1 or more characters living through single significant action-experience; 600-1300-word tightly constructed story concentrating on 1 central idea-conflict-situation; 600-1500-word satire, parody or humorous anecdote); Junior Grades 7-9 (600-1800-word narrative about true-to-life or imagined characters and their experiences).

POETRY CONTEST: Any Type, any form-verse, rhymed or free. 1 entry maximum (may be poem or group of poems). Divisions: Senior Grades 10-12 (50-200 lines); Junior Grades 7-9 (35-100 lines).

SCRIPT-PLAY CONTEST: Dramatic. Divisions: Junior-Senior Grades 7-12 (30 minutes maximum performing time). Original radio, television, film script or one-act stage play. No adaptations of stories, novels, plays.

ELIGIBILITY: U.S., Canadian students under age 20, grades 7-12, regularly and currently enrolled in public or nonpublic schools (including U.S. territories, U.S.-sponsored schools abroad). Original work, typed double-spaced on plain 8 1/2x11-inch paper. Entries may be submitted by students (with teacher verification) or by teachers. Limit 3 entries per student. Teachers may submit 10 entries maximum in each competitive class. No plagiarism, joint authorship; no entries copyrighted, printed in copyrighted publications, entered in award competitions (NCTE Awards excepted), or currently submitted for publication (uncopyrighted school newspapers or magazines excepted).

AWARDS: National Honor Awards: 3 $100 First, 3 $50 Second, 3 $25 Third, 10 $15 Fourth Place Awards, each class in Senior and Junior-Senior Divisions. 3 $50 First, 3 $25 Second, 3 $15 Third, 10 $10 Fourth Place Awards, each class in Junior. Up to 30 Honorable Mentions, Merit Certificates, each classification. 3 Typewriters to teachers for most outstanding group of entries, any division or classification. $250 Kenneth M. Gould Memorial Award to Senior for outstanding ability in varied forms, creative writing. Smith-Corona Short Story Awards, 7 Typewriters (5 in Senior, 2 in Junior). Paper Mate Poetry Awards, products valued at $100 to 3 outstanding poetry entries, each division. $500 Smith-Corona Scholarship to Senior for outstanding short story. $500 Paper Mate Scholarship to Senior for outstanding poetry. $500 National Broadcasting Company Scholarship to Senior for outstanding dramatic script. 2 $250 National League of American Pen Women Scholarships to Seniors showing outstanding creative writing ability. Winners may be published in *Literary Cavalcade*, other Scholastic magazines.

JUDGING: By authors, educators, editors. Based on originality, quality of expression, writing skill. National winners property of sponsor for possible publication (may edit for reading level, space requirements). No entries returned.

ENTRY FEE: None.

DEADLINES: Entry, February. Awards, May.

410

Youth Magazine Creative Arts Awards

132 West 31st Street
New York, New York 10001 U.S.A.

Summer

National; **entry restricted to U.S. youth age 13-19;** annual. Sponsored by *Youth Magazine*. Also have art, sculpture contests. Second Contact: *Youth Magazine*, Room 1203, 1505 Race Street, Philadelphia, Pennsylvania 19102; tel: (215) 568-3950.

SHORT STORY CONTEST: By Youth, fiction including humor, satire, true-to-life stories. Limit 5 entries.

POETRY CONTEST: By Youth. Limit 5 entries.

PLAY CONTEST: By Youth. Limit 5 entries.

AWARDS: Winners published in special awards issue of *Youth Magazine.*

JUDGING: Only nonwinners returned.

ENTRY FEE: None.

DEADLINES: Entry, May. Awards, Summer.

411

Edmonton Journal Literary Awards
Promotion Department
Box 2421
Edmonton, Alberta T5J 2S6
CANADA

Summer

Regional; **entry restricted to Edmonton Journal area novice writers;** annual; established 1962. Sponsored and supported by *Edmonton Journal.*

SHORT STORY CONTEST: Any Subject, 3000 words maximum, limit 1 per entrant.

POETRY CONTEST: Any Type, 72-line limit, limit 3 per entrant.

PLAY CONTEST: One-Act, 20-45 minutes, limit 1 per entrant.

ELIGIBILITY: Unpublished, original; current work by permanent year-round residents of *Edmonton Journal's* trading zone (northern Alberta, Peace River Block, Yukon and Northwest Territories; southern boundary is east-west line through and including Red Deer; western boundary is Rocky Mountains; eastern boundary is Saskatchewan border). No previous working writers; *Edmonton Journal* employees and immediate families; elementary, junior, senior high school students.

AWARDS: Short Story, Play $500 each. Poetry, $350.

JUDGING: Sponsor may divide, withhold awards; publish winners. Not responsible for loss or damage. No poetry returned.

ENTRY FEE: Not specified.

DEADLINES: Entry, April. Awards, Summer.

WRITING-ARTICLE

General Fiction Writing-Articles, including CYSTIC-FIBROSIS, FANTASY, HARNESS RACING, PACIFIC TRAVEL.

412

Cystic Fibrosis Foundation (CFF) Communications Awards Competition
6000 Executive Blvd., Suite 309
Rockville, Maryland 20852 U.S.A.
Tel: (301) 881-9130

February

National; **entry open to U.S.;** annual; established 1975. Formerly called LEROY WOLFE COMMUNICATIONS AWARDS. Purpose: to recognize news and feature reports on cystic fibrosis, the disease and its consequences. Theme: Cystic Fibrosis. Sponsored and supported by CFF. Held at Spring Board of Trustees Meeting, Washington, D.C.

WRITING CONTEST: Cystic Fibrosis, Children's Lung Disease, published for U.S. general public in previous calendar year. Require tearsheet and typewritten copy. No CFF personnel.

AWARDS: $1000 to top winners each category.

JUDGING: By professional communicators. Based on accuracy, quality, impact, ability to stimulate greater public knowledge and concern.

ENTRY FEE: None.

DEADLINES: Entry, February. Event, Spring.

413

International Conference on the Fantastic in the Arts

Thomas Burnett Swann Fund
Dr. Robert A. Collins, Coordinator
College of Humanities
Florida Atlantic University
Boca Raton, Florida 33431 U.S.A.
Tel: (305) 395-5100, ext. 5238

March

International; entry open to all; annual; established 1979. Purpose: to recognize, emphasize, explore tradition of the fantastic in Western literature; promote writers in the field. Sponsored by Thomas Burnett Swann Fund. Recognized by Modern Language Association. Average statistics: 7 countries, 500 attendance. Held at Florida Atlantic university for 4 days. Have shows, exhibits, readings, lectures. Publish *Sentient Cosmos* (newsletter), *The Scope of the Fantastic* (annual essay collection). Also sponsor Annual Workshop on Teaching Science Fiction.

WRITING PRESENTATION: Fantasy, 30-minute maximum readings. Require query, 100-word abstract, biographical information. Categories: Poetry, Short Story, Fiction.

AWARDS: Noncompetitive. Sponsor insures solicited material only.

ENTRY FEE: $30 registration.

DEADLINES: Materials, December. Acceptance, January. Event, March.

414

John Hervey Awards for Excellence in the Reporting of Harness Racing

United States Trotting Association (USTA)
Philip Pikelny, Publicity Director
750 Michigan Avenue
Columbus, Ohio 43215 U.S.A.
Tel: (614) 224-2291

March

National; **entry restricted to U.S. freelance writers;** annual; established 1977. Named after John Hervey, author, sports journalist. Purpose: to encourage writing harness racing articles in U.S. newspapers, magazines. Sponsored by USTA, United States Harness Writers Association (USHWA). Supported by USTA. Average statistics: 40 entries, 14 semifinalists, 6 awards.

ARTICLE CONTEST: Harness Racing, published December previous to November current year; photostats acceptable; 1 entry per division. No USTA, race track publicity department employees. Divisions: Newspaper, Magazine. Categories: Short Story, General Writing.

AWARDS: $500 First, $250 Second, $100 Third Place each division.

JUDGING: Entries from members, at-large members, nonmembers judged separately by local USHWA chapters, independent panel, university journalism educators. Grand Prize winner selected from 15 excellence winners. Not responsible for loss or damage.

ENTRY FEE: None.

DEADLINES: Entry, November-December. Winners announced, January. Awards, Spring.

415

Mississippi Valley Writers' Conference (MVWC) Awards
Writers' Studio
David R. Collins, Director
3403 45th Street
Moline, Illinois 61265 U.S.A.
Tel: (309) 762-8985

June

International; **entry restricted to Conference participants;** annual; established 1974. 11 $25 Awards to **Conference Writing,** unpublished. Sponsored by MVWC. Average statistics: 60 entrants, 20 awards. Held at Augustana College, Rock Island, Illinois for 4 days. Judging by workshop leaders. Second contact: Bess Pierce, MVWC, Augustana College, Rock Island, Illinois 61201. Awards, June.

416

Museroom
Center for Internationalising the Study of English (CIE)
Mike Hazard, Director
628 Grand Avenue, #307
St. Paul, Minnesota 55105 U.S.A.
Tel: (612) 222-2096

Periodic

International; entry open to all; periodic; established 1974. Formerly called WALT WHITMAN INTERNATIONAL MEDIA COMPETITION to 1976. Purpose: to promote, encourage literature and media. Sponsored by CIE.

WRITING CONTEST: **Various types and themes.**

AWARDS: Not specified.

ENTRY FEE: Not specified.

DEADLINES: Not specified.

417

National Council of Teachers of English (NCTE) Achievement Awards in Writing
Leona Blum, Director
1111 Kenyon Road
Urbana, Illinois 61801 U.S.A.
Tel: (217) 328-3870

February

National; **entry restricted to U.S. high school juniors (nomination by school teachers-students);** annual; established 1956. Achievement Awards, Commendation Certificates, College Admission and Financial Assistance Recommendations for **High School Juniors' Writing Skills.** Purpose: to encourage writing in schools, honor outstanding English students. Sponsored and supported by NCTE, nonprofit educational association; Maurice R. Robinson Fund. Average statistics: 6000 entrants, over 850 finalists. Entry, February.

418

New Jersey Harness Writers Award
Edward C. Mueller, President
101 Marian Street
Toms River, New Jersey 08753
U.S.A. Tel: (201) 341-2081

March

State; **entry open to New Jersey residents or employees;** annual. Sponsored by Horse & Racetrack Bureau of New Jersey. Held at New Jersey Harness Writers annual dinner. Second contact: P.O. Box 372, Toms River, New Jersey 08753.

ARTICLE CONTEST: **Harness Racing,** any literary form; published in circulated media during previous calendar year (NJHW members), written or published during previous year (nonmembers). Submit published in original-duplicate; unpublished as typewritten, double-spaced. Categories: Members, Nonmembers. Sponsor may publish unpublished entries.

AWARDS: $100 to Best Entry.

ENTRY FEE: None.

DEADLINES: Entry, January. Winner announced, March.

419

Pacific Travel Story Contest
Pacific Area Travel Association (PATA)
Graham Hornel, Director, Public Relations
228 Grant Avenue
San Francisco, California 94108
U.S.A. Tel: (415) 986-4646

February

International; entry open to all; annual; established 1958. Sponsored by PATA, nonprofit association founded 1951 to stimulate travel to, among Pacific Basin countries-island groups. Held at PATA annual conference. Also sponsor Pacific Film Contest, Publicity Photo Contest, Travel Poster Contest, Promotional Travel Brochure Contest (all open to PATA members only).

ARTICLE CONTEST: **Pacific Travel Newspaper, Magazine,** published December of previous to November of contest year; 1 per category, 2 unmounted copies, tearsheets or clippings showing publication date and name. Require English translation of foreign language entries (except French, German). Categories: Best Story Any Language, In French, In German, In English, Self-Illustrated Story (any language), Newspaper Story (any language), Magazine Story (any language). No travel trade publications.

AWARDS: Excellence Certificates, inclusion on PATA Media Familiarization programs lists, hosted trips to PATA destinations, Best Each Category. Grand Prize winner presented on stage at conference.

JUDGING: Based on motivational impact, "friendly Pacific" image, informational value, writing skill.

ENTRY FEE: None.

DEADLINES: Entry, November. Awards, February.

420

Playboy Magazine Annual Awards
Patricia Papangelis, Administrative Editor
919 North Michigan Avenue
Chicago, Illinois 60611 U.S.A.
Tel: (312) 751-8000

International; **entry restricted to writing published by Playboy Magazine;** annual; established 1956. Cash Awards, Medallion to **Playboy Magazine Writing, Illustration, Photography, Cartoons.** Purpose: to recognize and award *Playboy's* most significant contributors during year. Sponsored and judged by *Playboy Magazine.*

ALPHABETICAL EVENT/SPONSOR/AWARD INDEX

Alphabetical index to each EVENT, SPONSOR, and AWARD (followed by identifying CODE NUMBER of the event).

A

B

C

D

E

F

G

H

I

J

K

L

M

N

O

P

Q

R

S

T

U

V

W

Y

SUBJECT/CATEGORY INDEX

Index to AREAS OF SPECIAL INTEREST (followed by identifying CODE NUMBER of each event).

HAVE WE MISSED A CONTEST/EVENT?

Please let us know so that we may correct our future editions. Thank you.

FESTIVAL PUBLICATIONS
P.O. Box 10180
Glendale, California 91209 U.S.A